FRIENDS

BOYNTON BEACH CITY LIBRARY

In Memory Of

EDWARD F. HARMENING

Presented By
Boynton Beach City Manager & Staff
Frank & Virginia Farace
William G. Graham
William R. Hough & Co.
Mayor, Commission, Staff,
and Residents of Manalapan
Tommy J. & Lee Payne
J. Michael & Mary H. Pitman
Margaret Johnson
Tim Johnson & Family
Mr. & Mrs. Joel Johnson & Family
Mr. & Mrs. James E. Jordan & Family
Ed & Helen Kilby
August & Virginia Leagre
Mr. Francis S. McLaughlin
Curtis D. & Michelle Meade
J. F. & W. M. Merritt
Henrietta Solomon
Southern Bell T.O.P.'s Office
Harry B. Stein
Dorian Trauger
Margaret S. & Mark W. Wade
Ed & Joan Wilkins
Bob, Patti, & Christian Winzeler
Carl & June Zimmerman

ANOTHER MAN'S SOMBRERO

A CONSERVATIVE BROADCASTER'S UNDERCOVER JOURNEY ACROSS THE MEXICAN BORDER

DARRELL ANKARLO

THOMAS NELSON

Since 1798

NASHVILLE   DALLAS   MEXICO CITY   RIO DE JANEIRO   BEIJING

Published in Nashville, Tennessee, by Thomas Nelson. Thomas Nelson is a registered trademark of Thomas Nelson, Inc.

Thomas Nelson, Inc., titles may be purchased in bulk for educational, business, fund-raising, or sales promotional use. For information, please e-mail SpecialMarkets@ThomasNelson.com.

Page Design by Casey Hooper

Drop House photos provided by Maricopa County Sheriff's Department. All other photos provided by the Ankarlo team. Used with permission.

Library of Congress Cataloging-in-Publication Data

Ankarlo, Darrell, 1959–
  Another man's sombrero : a conservative broadcaster's undercover journey across the Mexican border / Darrell Ankarlo.
    p. cm.
  Includes bibliographical references and index.
  1. Illegal aliens—United States. 2. Mexicans—United States. 3. Alien labor, Mexican—United States.
4. United States—Emigration and immigration—Social aspects. 5. Mexico—Emigration and immigration—Social aspects. 6. Ankarlo, Darrell, 1959– I. Title.
  E184.M5A69 2008
  342.08'30973—dc22

                                                                          2008012139

Printed in the United States of America

08 09 10 11 QW 5 4 3 2

To Laurie—who has tried hard to teach me
that the glass is always at least half full

CONTENTS

SECCION DOS: TO KILL A COUNTRY (AKA SOVEREIGNTY TERRORISTS)

INTRODUCTION

You're a racist! Take a look at those three loaded, angry, and, as we said growing up in St. Louis, "fighting" words. When someone fires them point blank, the victim immediately moves to a defensive posture, stuttering and stammering as he bounces into the ropes and then down for the count because he doesn't want *that* phrase attached to him.

At our core, most people really do just want to "get along" as Mr. King (Rodney, not MLK) once said on the side of a Los Angeles roadway (although, it was Rev. King who first preached it to America). We hate to be labeled as something we are not and usually go overboard to distance ourselves from the label. Take a look at what I just did—I went out of my way to clearly identify the two Kings because I didn't want anyone to think I might be attempting to disrespect a legend. How sad that in today's American culture we have become so sensitive to every single word uttered. Sadder still are the people who usurp select words and phrases to intentionally create their own agendas or industries. I call them "Race Industrialists," and they work overtime to define us so they can put a few bucks in their pockets.

In Chandler, Arizona, authorities searched for well over a year to find a thirty-something, short, balding, stocky male who became infamous for breaking into homes while the families were present and raping or sexually assaulting defenseless teenage girls. In each case the victim used the description I just used and added that he spoke with a Spanish accent and was Hispanic. After police issued bulletins so the community could help apprehend the criminal, a Phoenix-area Spanish-language talk station reprimanded the police and local media for discriminating against Mexicans and Hispanics by using the word *Hispanic*. Needless to say, a new tactic in the arsenal to legitimize invasion is now being used.

One of the people at that radio outlet called my show to do what they all do when confronted by honest Americans who talk about the issue—act belligerent and toss around the "racist" word. A few days later, during a Veteran's Day parade, I ran into some of her group—one lady in particular. She was about five-foot-three and petite, with dark hair and darker eyes. A very pretty lady. When she realized who I was she turned ugly and began shouting, "Ankarlo—I'm a Latina. I'm a Latina. What do you have to say to me?!" She had the strut of an attack dog and was pounding her fingers into her chest. "You hate Latinas. Why do you hate Latinas? You know you do."

Thump. Thump. Thump went the fingers into her chest—I thought for a moment that she might harm herself before I stopped her. "Lady," I said, "I don't hate you; I don't even know you. What makes you think I don't like Latinas?"

"I've heard your radio program—you hate all Mexican people."

Now, obviously, there's not a lot that can be said to someone in this state of mind that will make a whole lot of sense. But I thought, *What the heck, I'll try.* "I have said a thousand times that I love your people, culture, language—the entire package."

She gave me one of those Pennsylvania deer-in-the-headlights looks. "Well, why don't you say that on your radio show?"

"I do, but you want to hear only what you want to hear." She was swept away by her parade friends, so the conversation ended as abruptly as it began. If I had had a few more seconds with her I would have put this question back at her: Why do you hate your fellow Latin people? Your permissive attitude locks them in drop houses, empowers them to break multiple laws, and keeps them in shadows.

Illegal immigrants come here for a better life but settle for poverty. Look at the top five state poverty levels from the Center for Immigration Studies. These percentages are for illegal immigrants with U.S. born children (anchor babies) living in or at poverty levels: Colorado 75 percent, Arizona 73 percent, Texas 68 percent, California 62 percent, and Florida 57 percent.[1] Welfare use for illegal alien-headed households: New York 49 percent, California 48 percent, Texas 44 percent, Georgia 42 percent, and Colorado 41 percent.[2] The illegal suffers daily and the U.S. citizen pays for it; and when citizens try to point out the obvious, the race machine goes into full throttle.

In a meeting with an Arizona Latino activist I was told, "Today's illegal immigrant is yesterday's nigger." The very outspoken man was attempting to say that people who complain about illegal immigration in America are really—here it comes—*racists,* and that when we put the term *illegal immigrant* into the public arena we lump all Americans of Mexican and South American descent, legal and illegal, together. While there is always the potential that some segments of the population will equate all "brown skinned" people with illegal immigration, the greater issue is the attempt by Race Industrialists in the Latino community to attach the "n" word to the illegal issue so people will run from it and be frightened from conversations about it. This not only does a disservice to U.S. citizens, but it also helps to further segment the immigrants of the country due to the contentiousness of the debate.

Sure, we have idiots in our midst who are haters and elitists, but most of us run when we see them coming; this nation has struggled to move from its troubled past. With this said, I assert that this country cannot afford to allow fellow citizens to endure such negative attacks when their greatest offense is to stand up for this nation's sovereignty and well-being. If people remain silent on this most important issue it could prove disastrous.

Look at the power word in the sentence: You're a *racist*. In its purest sense, it means that I believe one group of people is superior to all others based on their color and that I have animosity toward all who aren't "good enough" to come from my batch. How obscene! I'm better than you because my wrinkly, smelly, aging, and once pimple-ridden covering takes the top prize? It is simply one of the most idiotic concepts that man has ever created in an effort to distinguish himself as top dog.

When I was a kid growing up in southern Illinois I used to watch the old Civil War movies where the Yankees and Confederates battled over slavery (and states' rights, of course), and I believed a bunch of Yanks had come to save the day for the poor and mistreated slaves. As a result, I always rooted for their deliverance. I promised way back then that I would never be a party to slavery and would fight it if it ever raised its head again. Well, in a roundabout way, illegal immigrants are the newest slaves (though they choose to come) of the modern-day plantation owner. It's easy to see that big business represents the large and sprawling plantations, but the smaller player in the slave trade is *any* U.S. citizen who hires an illegal alien for any purpose. Though Latino activists and lobbyists, who are connected to the issue because they must support their livelihoods, ridicule people like me for our anti-illegal immigration positions, I can speak from a clear conscience when I say that I am actually fighting to help these people. I want them to stay home and build better home nations instead of becoming indentured here. And, to my fellow Americans who hire these people, you are nothing more than hypocrites—which may be why this issue is so hard to win, because we have too many closeted participants.

If you plan to fight against the out-of-control illegal immigration issue killing this country, then expect to hear the word *racist* often. We Americans must stand together so we stop arguing about the word and, instead, fight about the real issue. On a personal level, I've learned to wear it like my own personal badge of honor, not that I *am* a—shhh, let me whisper it—*racist*. But because I know that when the other side can't defeat my argument, they resort to childhood-playground name calling. So, I'm pleased when they do use the word when speaking about my position on illegal immigration because they have tipped me off to the fact that they are shallow thinkers and that I am going to be quite effective in dismantling their pathetic declarations.

In Phoenix, a furniture store owner called the local sheriff because so many illegals were congregating in the parking lot that customers were afraid to pull in and shop. A few years earlier, the illegal immigrants would have scampered for the darkness, but this community became so emboldened that they gathered weekly with fellow law-breakers and ill-informed U.S. citizens to openly protest in an effort to emotionally blackmail the owners into letting them loiter on the property.

They showed up with big signs and babies in carriages and handed out circus-looking fliers that said, "Don't Support Racism!" Don't support racism?! I call this *racial extortion*. A business owner (whose workforce is more than 50 percent minority) is now considered a racist because he wants his customers to have easy access to his front door, without cat calls, whistles, or taunting!

The real racists connected to this story, xenophobes too, are the ones holding their protest signs in one hand and their stolen IDs in the other. Someone at the top of the political food chain in Phoenix—a city described by Mayor Phil Gordon as "America's Ground Zero on Illegal Immigration"—is truly afraid of the fallout from the Latino lobbyists. His administration has issued guidelines saying that illegals will not be arrested. Even if the protesters are blaring their music beyond legal limits, they are to be left alone.

Since the 1990s I have used radio and television shows, public platforms, websites, blogs, magazine columns, and now a book to speak about this issue because I know history has already foretold what awaits us. My take: until my country is no longer in existence, I have an obligation to speak out and fight hard to save her. Maybe enough fellow Americans will join the effort to stop what seems to be a done deal—the loss of the greatest country in the history of the world.

A word of warning as you continue reading: if you are looking for a screaming, venom-spewing tome, this isn't it. My goal is to tell stories that will give you a grasp of this problem from a variety of perspectives, outline the ultimate damage being done, and look for a few solutions. My hope is that we may remove the hot-headed emotions and replace them with a quality plan of action. What would happen if my few ideas were met by similar thoughts from people across the country? Could the answer be just one mind away?

Think about it. What compels a person to drag his kids away

from the familiarity of home, past gun-toting border agents, on a life-threatening journey through miles of sun-drenched desert sands—with little food or water—just so they can spend the rest of their lives looking over their shoulders at every turn when they finally arrive at their destination?

I wanted to know the mind of the immigrant (illegal and legal), so I took a team of five people into Mexico to wander some of its cities and towns. I talked to rich and poor—mostly poor—to get their take. I interviewed "coyotes" (the people who smuggle illegals over the border), had fully automatic weapons pointed at me by Mexican Federales, and climbed under the thing that passes for a border fence while sneaking back into the United States—without papers.

This trip would never have happened without the individual efforts of each person on my five-man team:

Rob Hunter, my radio producer, is the man who actually came up with the idea to do a radio show from the Arizona desert, an idea that turned into an undercover mission in Mexico. (Now that I think of it, I wonder if he was just trying to get rid of me once and for all!)

Adam Ankarlo, my second son and a former Fallujah, Iraq, sniper with the U.S. Marine Corp, handled all safety/intelligence/security for the trip. The whole team felt safer because this true American had our backs. Thanks, Son, and Semper Fi.

Gary Smith is a fifty-something mastermind of technology. His job was to give me the tools to get the interviews, find our way through, and broadcast from places that we were told would be impossible. His twenty-five years as a river guide and survivalist trainer came in handy in quite a few desert situations.

Rounding out the wild bunch was Alonzo Cruz. He is a Spanish-speaking U.S. citizen of Mexican heritage who crossed the U.S./Mexico border as a teen. (He was legal; his pals weren't.) He went as my translator but ended up opening doors to so many stories that I couldn't have done without him. Alonzo, you are my brother.

If you want perspectives, life stories, and some solutions to a problem that is changing big and small cities alike—a problem than can bring this great country to its knees—then read on.

Gary, Rob, Darrell, Adam, and Alonzo moments before we left for our adventure into the great unknown that is the world of human smuggling.

SECCION UNO
ESTADOS UNIDOS MEXICANOS

To get a firsthand idea about immigration in our country, I felt I needed to see what caused so many people to run from theirs—thus a well-designed trip to Mexico! It should be noted that not all aliens breaking the law to get into the U.S.A. come from Mexico; the numbers typically stay in the upper 80th percentile while people from more than fifty other nations complete the full numbers of those who make the run for the border. But one must realize the enormousness of the burden Mexican immigrators place on the backs of average American families when they creep toward our promised land for their better life. To find how far reaching the problem is for both sides of the issue I decided to see for myself in Estados Unidos Mexicanos.

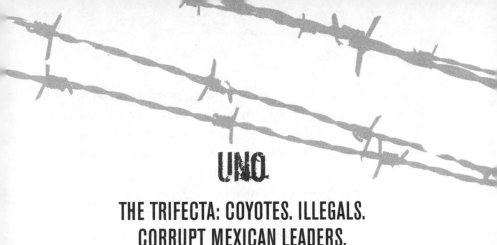

UNO

THE TRIFECTA: COYOTES. ILLEGALS. CORRUPT MEXICAN LEADERS.

Twelve-year-old Gabriel watched as his mother struggled and staggered just to move a few more inches. When they started their walking journey four days and sixty miles earlier, the thirty-one-year-old Latina beauty had deep smooth skin, and her silky black hair was held up by a soft pink-and-red scarf she made from scraps. Earlier still, as Maria paid the deposit for their trip, she tried to show her son as much enthusiasm as she could, her stories peppered with words like Disneyland, baseball, and video games. Her cousin, who had made the trip a year earlier, had already arranged a job for her cleaning houses and routinely sent her magazines of what life was like in America. Maria was as giddy as a school girl because her new life was just a few days away.

Now, the dreams were too distant to remember. It had taken the better part of six hours for them to travel less than a mile. Maria's skin was clammy, she was out of spit and sweat, her chest was heaving, and her heart was racing. She had stopped walking a long time ago; her leg movement was more of a halting pseudo-glide because she didn't have the strength to lift her feet so much as an inch off of the earth. She had given her son the last of the water more than two hours earlier, and dehydration along with heat exhaustion were working in tandem to stop her—forever. She would have given up much sooner but she owed it to Gabriel. Then, with the next shuffle her left foot twisted and her body collapsed to the powdery mixture of sand and dirt.

Running to the only thing he had left in the world, the boy planted his bottom firmly in the sand and scooted his small frame next to Maria's. Taking the once sweat-soaked scarf from his mother's neck, where she had placed it hours earlier in an attempt to cool herself, Gabriel dabbed it over her forehead and cheeks and softly pleaded, "La madre, no da para arriba; vamos a hacerlo. Usted va a ser aceptable." As he begged her not to give up, he began to cry, but not a single tear welled in his eyes, for he too was feeling the result of the lack of water. "Te quiero madre," he said, waiting for his mother to say she loved him too. It was their ritual in good times and bad to say those three words at least three times a day. "Te quiero madre." Gabriel looked into his mother's beautiful Latin eyes for a connection, but this time the beauty had been replaced by dim, bulging, dry blobs. "Madre?" The child paused, and shook his mother again, "Madre!!" There was no movement, no sound, and no heartbeat.

There, surrounded by nothing but cacti and desert animals sat a child who needed to instantaneously turn into a man and fend for himself if he was ever going to see another day come and go, let alone see the treasures his mother had promised. He hugged his mother as tightly as he could and tried to squeeze out at least a single tear of his own to mourn the loss of his parent and any possible hope.

Stranded. Alone. Lost. Broken. Gabriel, like thousands before him, knew firsthand what it was like to be abandoned in the desert by an anxious time-conscious coyote. By noon the following day the Border

On the Nogales, Mexico side of America's giant border wall is a make-shift shrine created by the locals. Each cross represents an illegal entrant to the U.S. who died during the journey.

Patrol found his once lovely mother's body and—following the small footprints—only twenty or thirty steps away they stumbled over his. The two men with badges cried for both.

Maria and Gabriel's sad story is just one of thousands replayed in the deserts of the American Southwest every year. Hearing the story stirred something in my soul like never before—something that demanded that I see the humanity up-close and hear the stories first-hand. I needed to grasp the motivation that causes a person to leave all he knows and trade it for fear, sorrow, illegal acts, and loathing by many. I had to know for myself.

My radio station management was concerned that my team might go in and never come out, so I chose border cities like El Sasabe and

Nogales, Mexico, for security purposes—though it should be noted that once inside the country, we routinely roamed to less secure areas and, sometimes, directly into the path of danger. Gary confided on day one of the excursion that he had been selected, in part, because some in our company's leadership believed I would go just about anywhere to get a story and they wanted him to minimize the risk. By the halfway mark Gary recognized that some exposure was essential if we were to get the real story, and he and the rest of the team were willing to travel wherever the days and trails would take us.

One person I ran into numerous times was the coyote, a man whose legend is well-known in the Southwest as the one who leads illegal immigrants over hills, through rivers, and across borders. But by the time I finished my quest I came to recognize most coyotes to be entrepreneurial teenage thugs who need a whipping from their parents more than anything else.

Philippe is an excellent example of a typical coyote. I met him

The first thing you notice when leaving the comfort and wealth of America are the rundown houses and crisscrossing power lines. It seemed like each person must have strung his own electricity because the lines are everywhere.

as my team struggled to make our way through a seedy side of Nogales—he stood out because of his youthful, quiet, and unassuming demeanor. I was quite certain that I was being introduced to the wrong person due to that almost wallflower disposition, but as soon as I started delving into his life and personality the stories started flowing. When Philippe turned thirteen his older cousin gave him a simple task: "Go down to the village store and let the shopkeeper know another group heads out on Friday." When he returned with word that six more had been added to the group, his cousin tossed him a crisp one-hundred-dollar bill. It was more money than he ever knew existed and, with that, Philippe chose his vocation. Within a few years he would be a coyote earning six figures. His clients have included children, grandparents, a blind man, and a pregnant woman ready to deliver within weeks. He sees himself as a Mexican Robin Hood who wants to beat the evil America because "they make too much money"— though he admits his goal is to "make as much as I can."

Philippe quit high school and doesn't think twice about it. "I make more money than anyone else I know, so who needs school?" He doesn't mind the negative nickname he and other coyotes have been given: Polleros, "chicken herders." He agrees with the name given to his crossers: Pollos, "chickens," "because that's what they are." And he likes his job—a lot. "Before my cousin introduced me to this job I had nothing. My parents had nothing. Next year I will have my own home and it will be completely paid for."

At one point Philippe sounded more like a Wall Street forecaster than a dropout when he talked about his clients and the growing industry he had discovered. "I can put together a group of people in no time. I just go to a bus station or restaurant and start asking around, and people flock to me." Officials in Mexico say the average number of attempts at passage is six times before the illegal immigrant throws in the towel, because they know America starts to prosecute at the half-dozen mark.[1] "I tell my people to keep the faith; I will get you there. But I do want them to make it on the first attempt because I only get part of my money upfront and I want it all! It doesn't pay as well if I have to keep trying."

Though Philippe is doing very well, he confides that many do not. "Some just don't know what they are doing. To make the money they smuggle drugs, and if they get caught they end up giving their money back to police and politicians to stay out of jail." When pressed about whether he moves drugs, he would only say that he didn't think smoking marijuana should be a crime. He must not be the only one, because spot checks of detained groups by the Tucson sector of the Border Patrol found that more than 90 percent had narcotics.

To keep his travelers moving at a fast pace, Philippe admitted to demanding that each person take ephedra tablets—strong stimulants—sometimes as many as five or six at a time, even though the supplement has been proven to cause heart damage and is now banned in America. But where I traveled in the desert, I found empty packages at every turn. The speed tablets also can dehydrate, cause strokes, elevate blood pressure, and make the user anxious. But the coyote doesn't care. "My job is to get them from start to finish in as little time as I can. Their health is not my concern."

The coyote is the central figure in the life of more than a million illegal immigrants a year, and he has at least ten thousand brothers who aid and abet him every step of the way. Though it is mostly a man's job, the average coyote is still in his teens, and plenty of women behind the scenes help coordinate drop points, routes, money, and other job-related responsibilities. If it sounds like a well-run business, it is. From 2000 to 2006 the transport of human beings into the U.S. from Mexico was more than a $10 billion industry—annually. That figure does not represent the ancillary trip-related products, nor does it include the routine demands for more money once the alien has made it to the drop house.[2]

On a global scale the United Nations set the human smuggling of trade nations other than Mexico at $10 billion a year.[3] This annual revenue is on par with Fortune 500 companies like Google, U.S. Airways, Viacom, and Amazon.com. And, as is the case whenever major money is involved, the temptation to skim, cheat, break laws, and live a corrupt life routinely wins out.

I had been scouring the area hoping to find someone who would take me to meet some of the day-to-day players in the smuggling machine when we lucked into a cab driver who had the details. At first I found it strange that so many drivers knew the ins and outs of the illegal immigration industry, but after a certain number of trips it just made sense: many of these guys played bit parts in the smuggling drama as snitches, runners, moles, and liaisons with would-be travelers or well-connected tour guides.

Rumors of corrupt police and military on this side of the border are as old as the border itself, but a few of them re-emerged as my cabbie backed up stories I had only heard in bits and pieces. I asked him to explain the *bajaderos*, another name for the baddest of the bad guys—the one who waits for a coyote to be on his last leg with his human contraband so he can drive in with big guns and big backup to kidnap the illegals. If the coyote puts up a fight, he dies—right then and there, with no time spared for negotiations.

Once the bajaderos, or jackers as they are also known, sell back the stolen people to anxiously overwhelmed friends and relatives, the local Mexican police insert themselves into the process. The cops shake down the jackers for thousands of dollars and then return to them a few hundred dollars along with their guns so the cycle has a chance to work again in subsequent days. Meanwhile, citizens in Mexico who get caught with a gun go away for up to five years, while the bajaderos get zero time and the immediate return of all weapons.

The government, police, and military have it figured out—keep weapons away from the common folk to guarantee continued income from corruption and a limited chance that revolution may break out.

"Tips," otherwise known as bribes, are a common practice if you want to get any kind of information or decent customer service in Mexico. One of the many people to whom I gave money backed up another story about the heavily used border passage cities: the chiefs of the state police in some of those areas are believed to make as much as $30,000 in extra income—per month—to do the exact opposite of the oath they took for the Mexican people. In cities like Naco, El Sasabe, and Nogales, military personnel are known to expect no less than a 10 percent apiece cut of any action going down in their domain. Smugglers build the bribe money into the cost of doing business so it doesn't cut into their bottom line. No wonder investigators, law enforcement, and wayward

The daylight hours were disappearing as I grabbed a quick photo op in front of the border wall in Nogales. Though we lack manpower, technology, and proper fencing along the majority of our border–this larger border town does feel the presence of the U.S. Border Patrol.

Phoenix reporters who get within striking distance can never fully get inside the story—too many people have been "tipped" to keep us out.

I couldn't keep track of all the stories my driver poured out from the front seat, but I had heard enough to know that so many people on the take meant permission had to be granted at extremely high levels of government. The Sopranos would have been proud of all the high ranking people "on the take."

The transition seemed like an obvious one, so I took the shot and asked the cabbie to take us to an area where I could meet and interview a jacker. I was pretty certain he had processed the words from English to Spanish, because his eyes looked like they were going to pop out of their sockets and bounce off the rearview mirror he was using to stare me down. My request was not going to happen—not with him. Before we knew it, my team and I were interviewing new taxi candidates at another street corner.

I sent my translator, Alonzo, to work his magic. He came back with not one, but three drivers in tow, so I was sure I could work something out, especially since two or three more followed to see what the congregating was all about.

"Look people," I said. "I am going to find a jacker or a coyote. It will be done today." I was very firm. I wasn't going to come back without an interview.

"We're not going to take you. It's not going to happen." Each of them took turns with their rejections, sure I would stop being so ignorant.

"No, you've got to take me in." With that, I pulled out a wad of money and moved it from one hand to the other. I didn't want us to get jumped in the middle of the street; I just wanted a passing glance to cause one of them to accept the payoff. After all, everyone else in Mexico seems to.

From the group of five one said, "I'll make you a deal. I'll take you to an area where this happens. I will not take you in because I could easily be killed. You could easily be killed. But I will take you up to that point." That was good enough for me. Flashing the cash again I ensured he would stay with the car if we got out, and he agreed.

"You won't just leave us there and abandon us, because it's a very long stretch of dirt road?" I asked.

"No, I'll stay with you."

That was good enough for me. My teammates looked a little stunned at what I was putting together, but none balked. So, we piled in the front and back seats of the roving used-parts store and thanked the driver in his mid-forties. His slicked, balding hair follicles glistened with sweat while his facial stubble made him look like so many others we had seen at every turn.

The car shook and shimmied to get up the dirt road, and then the cabbie surprised us all by offering to take us to the top of an approaching hill. We had already learned the ridge was notorious for transient activity, but somehow my humorous badgering had persuaded him to go where he had refused to go when the trip began. By now, he resembled a tour guide more than a cab driver as his left hand steered and his right hand pointed at four teenagers walking about seventy-five yards from us. "You may want to watch those boys—they are carrying drugs. That might be a good story."

I checked the young men in question and decided they had to be "mules." A mule is typically a teenager who is hired by the banditos and drug dealers to take drugs, social security cards, fake IDs, and other illegal contraband across the border several times a day. The mules know exactly how to get in and out of both countries in small teams of two to four. The cab rocked back and forth as we hit potholes and lost traction with the back tires. It was like driving straight up the side of a volcano. I hoped he would hurry, though there wasn't a chance; I was amazed the car hadn't already fallen into pieces. I looked for confirmation. "They look like mules to me, how about you? "

"Sí, I recognize them."

Just as the grumbling car engine broke the plane of the hilltop, the boys glanced back, and as we advanced closer they bolted. We slid to a stop and I jumped out of the backseat, but they were too far ahead. I saw movement out of the corner of my eye and didn't like the feeling that struck me. *This could be an elaborate set-up, and there is not one person who will intervene to help us up here.*

My son and security guard, Adam, moved next to me. "We've got company at nine o'clock."

"I see them," I said, uncertain who might be waiting for us in the overgrown brush. Then it struck me. *These are illegals getting ready to cross,* I thought. I was only sure of one thing—I wanted to talk to them! Our producer, Rob, and Alonzo walked next to me, and Adam moved ahead to get a better understanding of where we were, who *they* were, and how to get out of there if we had to.

As we moved into their space five young men jumped up from their crouching position in the bushes, and we threw our hands in the air to show we were not carrying weapons. The leader of the group saw Rob's video camera and used his hand to make the universal "cut it off" signal as he drew his hand across his neck. We complied but kept the audio recording.

When we were twenty or thirty paces away, two ditched down below us while the others walked in our direction—leaving extra distance between each of them in case they needed to escape.

"Where are you from?" I asked as I stepped as close as I could to pick up every syllable and nuance.

"Sonora," said one of them.

"How long did it take you to get here?" The question was leaving my lips when my brain caught up with my eyes to make sense of what I was seeing. Below us was one of the most heavily fortified U.S. Border Patrol and National Guard set-ups anywhere. Un-beknownst to any of us, we had climbed to the lookout area for the crossers. I was both excited and frightened because I knew I was going to get some good information, but invading this area could come at a price.

"I live here," said the one who seemed to be the leader.

"So are you all getting ready to cross, or you helping these guys do it?"

"That's what I do."

He said it so dispassionately that it took me a moment to process. "Wait a minute. You're a coyote?!"

"Sí."

"Excellent." I laughed at myself for picking that word. He was what I was fishing for, but I didn't expect to just stumble into such an interview.

"How long have you been doing this?" A drizzle started to fall and my audio recorders were getting wet, but I didn't care.

"Four years."

"How many people have you crossed?"

"A lot." He and his two buddies stood and talked to me, but their eyes darted in every other possible direction. One fidgeted with something in his pocket and the other held a two-way cell phone/walkie talkie. The two who had been on the lower ledge inched closer to hear the conversation.

"What does that mean? What does 'a lot' mean, my friend? Is it a hundred? A thousand?"

"Oh, thousands, probably more." Though each set of words was being filtered through Alonzo's translating abilities, I clearly picked up on the cock of the head and the change in his tone. He was proud of his number.

"Do you work for yourself or somebody else?" The last two young men were now gathered with us, and the kid with the cell phone had slipped to the back of the group and was whispering an ongoing commentary of some sort as the coyote leader and I spoke. I watched as Adam came around behind me and then moved off to the side; he was paying special attention to this one.

"For another person. I work for someone else."

"What is your charge for bringing people over?"

"They pay me four hundred bucks per person." I knew the prices had doubled and tripled since 9/11, and this boy was reaping the benefits. No doubt he had to share some of that wealth, but even a piece of four hundred times thousands is a lot of money for a teenager from Mexico. Heck, it's a lot of money for most American adults.

"How much do your bosses get?"

I was clearly making him uncomfortable; he was visibly nervous, moving from side to side. "I don't know exactly how much they get, because they got to pay for cars and the expense of the business."

"So the total amount is probably fifteen hundred to two thousand dollars a person?" I asked.

"I'm not sure. Maybe not that much."

"Maybe one thousand dollars? Come on, you have to know."

He turned and whispered something to the kid with the cell and then looked back at me. "No, the only thing that I charge for is just to get them to a certain point, then another coyote will get them, then another one will get them, then another one will get them, and they just keep on paying as you go."

His answer now made sense to me. The system in Mexico is for four to six coyotes to lead people on different legs of the journey. I could understand how these guys didn't know each other. For security purposes it made sense for them not to.

"Are you afraid of the jackers coming in here and taking some of your people?" The kid with the cell was mimicking my actions; when I pointed my microphone at the person speaking it was to get a clear recording. I wondered why he was using his phone the same way.

"Yeah, of course. The jackers are the worst out here. They take your work from you."

"That's what I hear. How do they know how to find people like you?"

"Oh, they know how to find you—that's for sure! A lot of them used to be coyotes, so they know how it runs around here."

"What if the bajaderos approached while you have a group of passers? What happens?"

"That's a tough one. Sometimes we might fight with them, sometimes we might pay them a bribe to go away, but usually, if we're not prepared with back-up, we can only watch them steal our people. I don't want to die doing this." It seemed like a well-reasoned response from someone who makes his living leaving people behind in the desert. The words had a tone that suggested the kid uttering them was already planning his future—perhaps in another line or work.

I glanced over the side of the cliff; it was the perfect place to keep track of any walkers, drivers, or movement on the border. "You're perched up here to watch the border agents—is that what you are doing?"

"Sí."

"What are you waiting for?"

"I'm just waiting for them to leave the area because they just caught some people over there right now."

"The border agents know you're up here. They know you work out of this area. Have you wondered why you keep getting away with this?"

The teen leader laughed and the others joined in. "Because they're dumb; they don't know how we work."

⎯⎯⎯※⎯⎯⎯

Annually, more than a million people pour through our 1,951-mile southern border, but it only takes a few minutes with the stats to see the vast majority use the 261-miles-wide Tucson to San Diego sectors. That works out to approximately 2,800 people per day, or about 120 an hour. According to the U.S. Bureau of Citizenship and Immigration Services, no less than 60 percent of the illegal aliens enter by sneaking across the border, with the other 40 percent coming through legally and then refusing to go home. Unless our federal, state, and local governments get serious about the silent invasion, punks like these guys will continue to parade their groups onto our soil—in broad daylight. I was plagued with how simple it was.

"They know you are up here and they have to know when you are going back and forth; come on! There's only so much they can do from that side," I responded to the young coyote.

"Yeah, but there's only so many places for us to cross, yet we do it every day. Someone on your side sure is dumb," he repeated. He waved his arm in an all-encompassing manner. "We're all coyotes up here, but a couple of these guys are guides too. They'll let us know where the Border Patrol is and then through walkie-talkie we are able to tell the people where to go—left or right."

I had had enough of the boy with the phone and shocked him by putting my microphone directly in his face. "So, you, how old are you?"

He was reluctant to answer at first, but then he mumbled, "Seventeen."

"And what are you doing with that phone? You keep pointing at me and talking to someone. What's that all about?"

"Nothing. I'm just talking to my spotters." I wasn't buying that answer; someone on the other end was interested in the gringos on the hill.

I pointed at an old Ford Explorer kicking up dust in the distance. "You wouldn't be talking to them, would ya?"

"No." He pushed my mic away and turned his head. The truck was closing in fast, but I still had questions.

I looked back at the talkative leader. "How many do you have working in this area right now?"

"About one hundred."

"Right this minute! Wow. And how many border agents are down here right now?"

The Coyote Kid shrugged his shoulders and then, in an effort to show his omnipotence he said, "Not enough, obviously. We are crossing about three hundred people."

"A day? From here?" I asked.

He chuckled. "Three hundred a day right here at this spot? How about three hundred in less than three hours?!"

"No way!! So who's the main coyote? Is it you?" I just couldn't fathom a kid moving these kinds of numbers a few football fields away from a waiting U.S. Border Patrol.

"No, I wasn't lying. The big dog doesn't work here. We're all the same out here. We all do the same work."

I looked down at the big wall with accompanying fence and the mix of highly trained U.S. personnel, and then back at the punk. "How long do they think it's going to take before those border agents leave and you move your people through?"

"An hour, half hour. Soon," he said.

I wondered why we even act like we are trying. This many people don't help that many people break the law without a whole lot of cooperation.

I was forming my next question when the blue truck hit the gas and swerved in our direction. Though he was still at least a mile down the road it caught my attention just long enough for me to take my eyes off the coyotes. When I looked back they were gone—in a flash. I yelled after them, "Where are you guys going? Where're you going?"

The video camera was back on, so I provided some play-by-play for my radio and Internet audiences. "They are now running. Let me just explain. They're now running faster than fast. I mean, those guys have gone three hundred yards in seconds. Holy cow."

Adam was on top of Rob, Alonzo, and me before we could make another move. He grabbed me and demanded, "Move. Now. Move. Move. Move! You are not safe here." He rushed us to the waiting taxi and ordered me to the side of the vehicle, hoping to put two thousand pounds of metal between us and any possible gunfire. "Okay, we've been set up here. They've been stalling us and we need to be on the lookout for somebody to come around and flank us here."

Below us, a dark vehicle with blackened windows was on a collision course with the Ford. In one, we later learned, were drug traffickers and jackers. In the other was the leader of the coyotes I had been interviewing. Either the *banditos* were moving in to take some of the illegals or the boy with the cell phone had been used to detain us because the criminals believed our media company would pay handsomely for our return.

Adam ran to the side of the hill to see how close the vehicles were and rushed back. "Hey, you've got to get moving. Get in the cab and get down. You've got to get moving." At four hundred dollars a crack, there was little likelihood the coyotes, or their bosses, were willing to let their people go without a fight, and if the Americans got caught up in the middle of it all, that wasn't their problem.

I heard Adam's footsteps quickly shuffling around the taxi and looked up just in time to catch a glimpse of our national guardsmen perched in their tower as they watched events unfold from the U.S. side. For a moment I felt helpless because they would not be able to intervene in Mexico's matter and, if they could, they wouldn't be able to get to us in time.

Meanwhile, a couple miles down the road, and within binocular sites, were the Mexican border patrol agents sitting with their feet propped up, eating lunch and listening to the radio. I had no doubt that if something terrible had happened to us that day a few extra bribe dollars would have made the entire affair disappear. Now I had yet another reason to be angry about the complacent Mexican government and their corrupt representatives who for a few dollars will do what they have always done—nothing.

On air describing the vivid details of the incident with the coyotes and the run in between the jackers and drug dealers.

DOS

AMERICAN BORDER PATROL STORIES FROM AGENTS WHO LIVE THEM

I'll take you back into Mexico shortly, but first, let's go back across the border. To adequately understand what our U.S. Border Patrol is up against I joined some of its agents as they traveled the U.S. side of the border. At first, everything I heard was filtered, re-filtered, and passed through Public Information Officers (PIOs) for the Tucson Sector Border Patrol and National Guard, but after several hours together honest emotions and stories came out. In a sentence: they get little support while struggling with numbers that grow by the day and repeat by the hour.

Agents are constantly threatened; drug lords who get hassled routinely put bounties on their heads. One of the ongoing concerns agents in the field shared with me was the length of time they are stationed in the same place. Instead of moving frequently, they remain stationed on the same patch of land for long stretches, which opens the doors to corruption for some and easy identification by drug and human smugglers for others. One will get the agent in trouble; the

This is the Ankarlo Team outside a U.S. Army National Guard station. The Guard has helped create the infrastructure that allows the Border Patrol to do its job. Sadly, many of the guardsmen are being reassigned away from our first line of defense—the U.S. border.

other will get him dead. Leaders have heard the complaints but have been slow to act, which in my mind represents disrespect for people who put their lives on the line. If we can't fix the easy things, how can anyone expect an overall solution?

The heart of each Border Patrol Sector is the Communications Center. Tucson, where more than 40 percent of the illegal immigrants and an even greater amount of drugs enter the country, has one of the most sophisticated centers in the U.S. Sharing the facilities are training, drug impound, and immigrant intake areas, and each is pushed to the max. My guide, a highly skilled agent I will call JR, was focused on guaranteeing me access and answers as I wandered from section to section.

The Communications Center is manned twenty-four/seven as

several agents listen to scanners and walkie-talkies and watch a bank of television monitors from cameras mounted on walls, buildings, towers, and in a few other locations I promised not to disclose. I counted twelve active screens in the area where I stood.

"Darrell, what you're seeing are the daytime cameras, color during the day, but also low-light or night-vision during the evening hours," JR explained.

"Are they mostly in high traffic areas?" I asked.

"Yes. And, actually, they're watching the whole border area, so they see as people attempt to jump the fence or something as simple as just moving around the fence and other areas. But, keep in mind, though, the fence in Nogales, being an urban environment, is not meant to keep people out; it's only meant to slow people down. It'll buy you some time to get agents to the location to apprehend. You can see them jumping every day, and they're taking their chances. The camera operators watch and record and call additional agents in if it is warranted."

Still, I couldn't help but think that if our country's leaders really were serious about this issue they would inundate the border region with technology much like New York City has done near Grand Central Station: more than 3,000 cameras, 116 license plates readers, pivoting road blocks, state-of-the-art computer and tracking centers, and more than $8 million a year designated to manning the center with highly skilled technology and law enforcement experts. I thought, *If NYC can do that for a few blocks, why can't the government do what it takes to stop the flow before they get out of the Tucson Sector?*

JR pulled my attention back to the matters at hand, and while he was explaining the process I glanced over the shoulder of the agent operating the remote cameras as she zeroed in on three men scaling the wall separating Nogales, Mexico, from Arizona. She zoomed and flipped settings, and the bodies went from heat sensitive blobs of color to actual footage of an attempt to break into our country. The agent panned the camera enough to get a solid geographical bearing and radioed ahead. JR was already moving my team out of the center and into a holding area, but I was able to search the screens long enough to see agents descending on the would-be trespassers. *If only it were this easy across the entire border,* I thought.

A short walking distance through safety doors that could have come from a maximum security prison and we stepped into a huge warehouse-like area about the size of half a football field. In it we saw holding cells that looked like oversized lion or tiger cages because of the way the twenty-foot-high chainlink fencing was connected to the

I spent several hours with the U.S. Border Patrol's Jesus Rodriguez as he took me through most aspects of their monumental task.

heavy duty posts. Each "cage" was shaped differently for a variety of reasons, with seating areas ample enough to handle the number of detainees in them. I counted eighteen in the section where I stood. I turned to my host for answers. "JR, tell me about this area. What's the methodology?"

JR swept his arm from left to right. "Those cells in the back are used for what we call the interior re-penetration program that's run by ICE [Immigration and Customs Enforcement], was run by ICE last year, and what we do is put people there who are going to be flying out on those flights back into Mexico." He was describing one of the U.S. programs that puts illegal immigrants from southern Mexico or countries in that region on planes where they are flown back home.

Just more proof that lies run rampant!! While in Mexico I stopped at their border patrol area and was told that America detains Mexican immigrants for hours without food and sends the people home hungry. I saw cases of food at our border patrol—and detainees had complete access!

Alonzo, Border Agent Rodriguez, and me. We were getting the top-to-bottom tour of the Border Patrol Tucson Sector's main facility.

U.S. tax dollars pay for the trips even while some Mexican airlines are now providing cut-rate fares from the same locations back to airports bordering the U.S. It's a maddening cycle.

I was pleasantly surprised by what I was seeing and went out of my way to let JR know. "When Americans think of detention centers or jails we think of televisions, radios, phone calls, and other privileges. This place seems pretty bare-bones, so I applaud you guys for that, but I'm still uncertain about your system. Cell Number One has a couple of people, Number Two appears to be female, and then over there in Number Four you have a couple hundred."

JR said, "All cells are segregated by sex and age. You've got your females in one cell, males in the other, and, I can't see that far, but those are all juveniles in that area. We are the largest center in America and can hold over two thousand people at a time."

"Explain for my readers why you have both large and small holding tanks of men?"

He pointed to one of the smaller cells. "These individuals have already been processed and are ready for voluntary return back to Mexico. These individuals in the larger holding area are going through that process as we speak. It can be anywhere from two hours, at the most up to six to seven hours, just depends on the volume of people in there. We check them for fingerprints; if they don't have any major crimes, we release them to the Mexican government."

My sarcasm came out in the form of a raised eyebrow and a quick reality check. "JR, buddy, that's a free pass."

"Yeah, pretty much. That's a free pass. We put a note in that they've broken in and everything, but, yeah, it's a free pass."

"My friend, we're spending billions on our side, and yesterday I asked one of the border agents I met in the field about the Mexican Border Patrol. You know what he did?"

"What?"

"He just smiled. I could tell what kind of a joke he thought those guys are."

"Not really a joke—they are just pretty much non-existent on the northern border. They do have a bit of a border patrol on their southern border, because they are being attacked by Guatemala, Venezuela, El Salvador, et cetera."

JR was shuffling my team toward the evidence room where hundreds of thousands of pounds of seized marijuana and cocaine come to reside until trials and destruction. As we passed the biggest of the holding cells the reporter in me came out as I noticed a few of the two hundred or so men paying special attention to my recording equipment and crew. I gave a nod at them as if to say, would you like to answer some questions? One of the men shrugged his shoulders and timidly said, "Sí."

I pushed my microphone against the fencing, and within seconds twenty or thirty guys rushed toward my spot, with the remainder now up off their benches and surrounding them. It reminded me of one of those bad prison movies where a whole yard of prisoners revolt when the TV cameras show up. The conditions at this facility aren't the Club Med that we give to most U.S. prisoners but this place was spacious, clean, and everyone that I saw was treated well—including the few times when I was able to move out of the agents' eyesight. I'll admit that I was a little surprised at how vocal this group chose to be. Here they were in U.S. custody but still very cocky and self-assured enough to openly answer my questions.

"How many of you have been through this station before?" I asked. Every hand enthusiastically rose in the air just like children who know the answer and want the teacher to call on them. They seemed almost proud.

"How many of you have been here more than three times?" At least three quarters of the group kept their hands raised. I would like to say that I was shocked, but these days very little on the illegal immigration issue is remarkable.

"How many of you plan to return to the U.S. once you get out of here?" A few bursts of laughter started in the back and within seconds permeated the crowd as every hand shot back into the air.

"Your system is a joke and it is not fair," said one of the more vocal men.

Shoving him out of the way, another illegal alien moved within inches of my face, "We aren't doing anything wrong. We just want to work. What is so wrong with that?!"

Some of the hundreds of illegal immigrants waiting to be processed at the Tucson Border Patrol station. As I interviewed them, most agreed, "America's laws are unfair" and almost all vowed to try again.

Before I knew it, several of the men pushed toward me, voices and energies escalating. At the request of the agents I stepped away from the fence as they demanded that the detainees settle down. The men shouted a few more slogans I've come to hear frequently while living on the border. Things like: "We are all Americans," "We owned your country first," and "Too many in your country are racist." However, they quickly complied with a second request from the border agents. With that my questioning was finished, but not before getting the answers I expected—the detainees have no respect for the laws of the U.S. When respect for the law is absent, weeds of chaos and contention take root, a root that can strangle an entire society.

Several steps away and through two sets of security doors we finally made it to the much heralded drug evidence room. Because of the many stories told to me by border agents, it was one that I had to see for myself. JR did his part in building up my anticipation but toned things down after the heavily bolted door swung open and we saw the room was nearly empty.

I counted about twenty fifty-pound blocks of marijuana; though this is substantial, it was a pittance compared to the more than 600,000 pounds this room had held during the most recent six-month period. I ran the math through my mind: 600,000 at eight hundred dollars per pound came to a half billion dollars—in six months—all from Mexico. I picked up one of the big blocks and thought about the money and messed-up lives it represented; it was surreal to say

Border Agent Rodriguez with one of the seized fifty pound blocks of marijuana. 600,000 pounds were confiscated in the Tucson Sector in one six month period.

the least. As Rob quipped later, "That's their Exxon, right there." We had recently talked about the huge profits the oil giant was enjoying. Then, in an attempt to brush off the magnitude, I grabbed another and put one under each arm. "JR, brother, I thought you said you guys had actual drugs at this facility." The special agent shot a cocky "just wait a few minutes" glance. Since the reputation of this department is known around the country, JR really didn't need to provide any further answers, but he did, "While you were picking up all the blocks of pot I checked with one of the guards in this area, who explained that earlier in the day the room was filled to the brim, but all of those drugs were removed and destroyed. What you see right now came in after that."

Alonzo took a moment to get photographic evidence for the folks back home!

At a value of almost a billion dollars a year I suppose I could have waited another few hours to watch as more bundles were checked in, but the point had been made—besides, I wanted to see exactly how these illegal immigrants were processed—which is where we headed next.

We doubled back to our starting point and then went through isolated halls to internal chambers with the same caging system that I had viewed earlier, except this time there were men and women on both sides of the fencing.

JR said, "Here it is—the INDENT system that I was talking about earlier. It's actually an integrated automated fingerprint identification system linked into the FBI database." Within moments of a digital fingerprint's going into the system, law enforcement agencies will know if they have a match to the person they have an interest in.

He directed my attention to a medium-sized agent who stood behind a computer screen.

"What he's going to do is roll this detainee's fingerprints, and it will find out whether this person's ever been caught or arrested by the Border Patrol or any other law enforcement agency in the U.S. And, as you can see right there, he's rolling his fingerprints as we speak."

I didn't see any ink, which is what I have always associated with fingerprinting. "He's doing it over an infrared-type device, huh?"

"It will take a digital photo of those fingerprints. The agent will also take a photo picture of his face and it'll be run through the system."

"How long does this investigative process take?"

"Oh, it can take anywhere from a minute up to three or four minutes; just depends."

I was hoping that we might get a match while I stood at the station, so I lagged a little.

JR provided some hope. "It'll query all the information they've inputted on this individual and we'll be able to tell whether he's ever been caught even for something as minor as a DUI or as major as a homicide."

I interrupted, "But wait a minute, when you talk about minor and major, let's not forget that he is already here in America. If it's a minor crime, you're going to send him back to Mexico. But how 'big' does it need to be to detain him?"

JR dropped his voice to a whisper so the man waiting for his verdict wouldn't overhear our conversation. "Well, it depends on all of his history. Has he been caught by the Border Patrol numerous times? Is he a known smuggler or guide? Is he a low driver? No idea—bet it's not good though! Has he had various convictions for misdemeanor crimes? You know, it depends. No one person is going to be the same. If we can offer him a voluntary return, then that's what it's going to try to be, but it's up to his discretion whether he wants to voluntarily return and go back to Mexico or whether he wants to see the immigration judge, based on his own decision."

Alonzo jumped in, "How about going back twenty years, before this program was integrated into your system. Have you inputted the prints of those people too, or are they still in paper form?"

"It took a long time to do that on paper. But, yes, they have been inputted."

I looked at the computer. Although my angle kept me from seeing the actual information, I could see it was speeding up. "It looks like the transaction is almost done, JR."

My new agent friend was close enough to read the screen and he detailed what he was seeing. "It's querying the federal database right now and it'll search for any 'lookouts.' This means that the person may have a lookout from another agency, may have a lookout from another Border Patrol station that he is a smuggler or a guide, you know, anything of that nature—a low driver. Or, he needs questioned by Intel for whatever reason it may be."

I moved closer to the screen in time to read the words "No hits found" and asked JR if the alien standing next to me was clear of any charges. "No. You're seeing the information for the guy who was here a minute ago. The second query is coming through now."

"We've got, I don't know, probably forty guys sitting on the floor and hundreds more behind the fence, and they are all watching our every move," I said.

"And we'll check them all and the hundreds after them and the ones after them too. This is what we do." Just then, JR stepped directly in front of the computer monitor. "He just got a hit count of one, right here."

We had a live one, an alien with a former run-in, and I wanted to know what the charge would be. JR told me that a deeper search was set to commence. He again played the role of teacher. "We're waiting for the IAFIS database; that's federal."

"FBI?" I asked.

"It's the FBI database. And, here we have it; this one has been arrested by another law enforcement agency. So, we'll have to wait a few more minutes to see what's up."

Meanwhile, one of the other searches clicked in. This one had no hits. I leaned over and whispered to JR, "So, that guy who was just standing here, I can go give him the good news? He's got a free pass back to Mexico, right?"

"Yes. In fact, as you look around, you can tell here, there are a lot more people that are voluntarily going back to Mexico. They've already been processed, so he'll just join that group."

Border Agent JR was referring to a cell full of guys who were standing directly behind me in a well-mannered single file line, all with their hands held behind their backs.

Inside a Border Patrol office along with items routinely discovered by agents: make-shift burlap shoes for the hot desert sand, caffeine drinks to keep the people amped up and moving, walkie talkies for the coyotes to signal back and forth when agents were spotted, and bricks to throw at the vehicles and heads of U.S. Border Agents!

"They've been processed and if they say, 'I want to go home,' you're not going to put them through a deportation program or anything—"

"They want to go home and, based on whether their records checked, we're allowing them to do that."

I'll admit, I felt sorry for all of these men with the low hanging heads and frumpy, dirty clothes. But that emotion was trumped by my outrage at two failed governments and their equally ridiculous leaders. "And, so, they're going to pop right back out that door, going to walk right across the street to freedom, or worst case scenario, the Mexican government will pick them up—"

"And then they're free. They cannot detain them after that. Once they go back across the border, the Mexican government cannot detain them anymore. They are free to try again."

And stats point out they will indeed try again—many more times.

Night was falling on Nogales, Arizona, and there was still a lot to see, so JR escorted my team out of the building via secure back doors and watched as we piled into one of the patrol vehicles. We had already studied the area during the daylight hours, but just as the desert dramatically changes at sundown, so do the border jumping areas.

We drove along the fence line where one would expect the two-story hunks of metal and beams to deter even the most motivated. There,

This sewage tunnel in Nogales, Mexico runs right into the U.S. Determined immigrants will cross this 1/2 mile tunnel, often standing and crawling in raw sewage for hours at a time, just to cross into the U.S.

at the wall's bottom, stood several young men and women dressed darkly and carrying flashlights. I asked if these were the U.S. connections for immigrants preparing to illegally enter the country. JR nodded his head to affirm my suspicions.

I expected the people to run and scatter at the site of the patrol vehicle that had now slowed to a crawl, but their reaction was exactly the opposite. Not only did they remain, but they were joined by other people who appeared from side streets and alleys. I counted at least fifteen.

"Why don't they run?" I asked.

"Because these people are usually U.S. citizens, and unless we actually see them helping illegal immigrants cross, they have every right to be in this area." I glanced around at the small single-family homes and shacks that lined the street and realized another glaring hole in the system: there is no way our Border Patrol with their current numbers can keep an eye on all of these people. As the agents drive to the next street, the U.S. citizens move quickly to aid any crossers and to provide shelter until they can be transported out of the region.

Every street duplicated the same scene. No doubt the cameras and patrolling agents stop some, but this isn't the only method of entry. JR drove us up

It started as a routine interview but when agent Rodriguez went to check on something in his patrol vehicle Adam and I climbed into this sewage tunnel to discover what, or whom, might be waiting there.

to the top of a few well cultivated hills, and at the top of each was a National Guard compound outfitted with long-distance telescopes, night vision goggles, communications systems, and a series of lights— powerful lights. At the flip of a switch, the dark hillside lit up like Cape Canaveral when a rocket blasts off at night. Suddenly, it was high noon.

One of the National Guardsmen, fresh from a tour in Iraq, pointed to the roads, barriers, and countryside. He explained that his fellow Guardsmen had removed all brush and debris and had leveled the area, because the area where we stood had once been a notorious crossing point. The illegal aliens would hide behind trees and in gullies and make the trip across en masse. Now, two or three people a night still might make the effort but they are routinely caught—especially with the addition of the railroad ties that cut off the flow of trucks and Jeeps driving directly through. Clearly, this was a success story. But, the rare win these few hills reflected was offset by the monumental losses elsewhere.

One of the final stopping points was a massive sewer system that runs between the U.S. and Mexico. We had seen a smaller version earlier in the day, but it could only accommodate a limited number of crossers; this one was huge. A semitruck could easily fit inside, both in height and width, though it was deep enough to ensure this would not happen. But hundreds of passers could move at will if our U.S. Border Patrol did not cruise the area often.

I climbed down into the tunnel. It smelled of human waste and rotting trash. Joined by Adam, I walked into the hole. The warm, noxious breeze took my breath away, and my nose and eyes immediately started running.

"Out." JR's voice cut the tour short. "You guys need to get out of there now. You are not safe down there, and I can't protect you."

As I answered him my voice echoed down the long concrete tunnel, muffled a bit by the sloppy water that ran below us. We had climbed down an iron maintenance ladder and had situated ourselves so as to avoid the filthy water. "Helloo." "Helloo. Helloo," went the echo. Nothing. I yelled again, "Hola." "Hola. Hola." This echo was met by silence too.

Just then, I heard splashing. It sounded like it was quite a ways off, perhaps as far off as Mexico, but I was certain we weren't alone. I moved several feet further into the pitch black corridor.

Adam stopped me, "We're out of here. Now."

A part of me wanted to argue because I wanted a story, but Adam's voice and JR's demands let me know that I was out of my element. If others were down there with me, they had to be led by a coyote or bandito or a similar thug who would not hesitate to do harm if it came to that.

Reluctantly, I grabbed the ladder and pulled myself up, stopping halfway to the top to shine my light back toward the darkness. Nothing. No movement—no sound. I later learned that, just like the coyotes whom I had met on the hillside earlier in my adventure, people on the U.S. side had elaborate systems in place. I was interrupting them by my unplanned and unscheduled visit. No doubt several people were stuck in the tunnel longer than they had hoped but, as soon as we were out of the area, signals would let them know the coast was clear and their journey could continue.

I asked myself, as my nose still burned from the fumes, would I be willing to stand for hours in waist-deep urine, feces, and God knows what else to try my luck at an illegal existence in a country that doesn't want me? I couldn't answer this one, in part because one never knows what he's willing to do or how much he's willing to gamble until he has to.

My tour ended at a rolling checkpoint on Interstate 19 near Duback, Arizona. The agents at this location stop every vehicle and within a few seconds allow most to pass along to their intended destinations. I walked into the middle of the road and stood next to one of the agents as he quizzed drivers and passengers alike.

"What do you check for when you're stopping these folks? You've got five, ten seconds with them?"

"I check for the expiration date and mostly I focus on the picture, on the ears, on the eyes, on the nose . . ."

"Of the driver's license and passports?"

"I also check the feel. Sometimes if it's a false document you can check it right in the feel." As he was answering me a mid-'90s brown Chevy yielded to the agent's outstretched hand. We both looked at the Latina driver and her two kids. I felt like I was invading her space because my eyes tracked with the agent's—where he glanced, I glanced. He spoke while checking her out, "Hello? U.S. citizen, ma'am?"

"Yes."

"Your kids are U.S. citizens, ma'am?"

"Yes."

"Have a good one."

Those were the only questions this agent would ask the lady and her children, and then she would pass into the night. It didn't seem involved enough for me; I expected much more. "That was fast. What telltale signs were you searching for? You had to be looking for eyes and any kind of movement on their part, right?"

"Of course, nervousness. Maybe their neck—you can see the veins popping out. Stuttering, hands shaking . . ."

"And the weight of the car too?"

"Yes sir. If it bounces—if it doesn't bounce, that gives you something to think about."

I listened as the agent repeated a variation of lines on about twenty vehicles. He didn't like the answers he heard from one of the drivers and had the vehicle pulled to the side of the road where a team of agents and specially trained dogs thoroughly investigated the car and its occupants. Sure enough, they were all illegal.

The Border Patrol would like to make this heavily used stretch of pavement a permanent checkpoint. Local citizens are against it because they believe it will hurt their property values, even though the nearest home is about a mile away—another example of Americans looking out for their personal interests and neglecting the overall well-being of the country.

TRES

A VERY SCARY INTERVIEW

I love, respect, and enjoy the Mexican people and their culture. I have said it ten thousand times if I've said it once, and I have tried to prove it via my humanitarian and charity efforts through the years. I think most Americans love the Mexican people but despise the actions of illegal aliens and their big supporters, and will never accept what they are doing to our country.

Just as there are different mind-sets on the U.S. side, there are just as many on the other side: some illegals want to visit, others want to take back the land they believe still belongs to them, and even more just want to come and work. Sadly, if some of today's subversive forces at work in this country have their way, all will continue to play a role in a battle for the heart of America.

I have had the distinct opportunity to interview many people from that "take back" mentality, and to a person, they always say three things: (1) If I am against their tactics, I am a racist, (2) they first owned much of this country, and (3) why are "people like me" always "picking on the Mexicans"? After all, they say, other people sneak into America too, and I don't cry about it. I address the first two points elsewhere in this book, but let me be clear: when the majority of the millions coming here are from Mexico, and when many of the voices coming from the crowd want to "take America back," I would be less than a citizen if I remained silent.

A common thought is gaining steam in some illegal immigrant circles. It is sung about, written about in books, and taught in our nation's colleges: the República del Norte, or Republic of the North. I first heard about it in the early 1990s, and the more I review the concept, the more frightened I am becoming—not for me *per se*, but for this society we call the American way of life. Earlier I mentioned that all illegal immigrants have the ability to play a role in this manipulation of a country's goodwill. The "take it back" community has already exposed its intentions, but the crowd that says "we come here to work" will be the turning factor. They are recognizing their voices and power. Just look at the millions who marched through our streets in the spring of 2006 and again in 2007 as an example. As they are allowed to insert themselves into the process, their numbers will overwhelm.

Will it lead to bloodshed, a coup, annexation, or another scheme? Those questions may sound unlikely, but the mind-set is growing. Recently, I invited one of the leaders of the República del Norte machine to answer questions on my radio show. Dr. Charles Truxillo has been an adjunct faculty member in Chicana/o Studies at the University of New Mexico-Albuquerque since 1982 and is the author of the book *By the Sword and the Cross: An Ideological History of New Spain*. As a broadcaster, I respect Dr. Truxillo's candid answers, because too often, people with such counter-American concepts speak freely in private but then cloak their words when they take their message to the masses.

ANKARLO: You call it the República del Norte. Explain what that is.

DR. TRUXILLO: I have a thesis that eventually, of course, Mexicanos, Mexicans, will become the majority in what is the American Southwest. Well, for a much longer period of time, this area has been known as El Norte, the North, the Far North.

ANKARLO: By people in Mexico. That's what they call us.

DR. TRUXILLO: Yeah. All the way back to Mesoamerican times. I believe eventually, once the Mexican population is a majority, they probably will move towards self-government, autonomy, and then, eventually, sovereignty. The same way the thirteen colonies did from the British Empire.

ANKARLO: You're talking Arizona, New Mexico, Texas, California—is that it or you want . . . ?

DR. TRUXILLO: No, I assume those areas. But also a substantial part of southern Colorado is heavily inhabited by Hispanics from New Mexico; so are parts of Utah and Nevada. And those were all territories that belonged to Mexico until 1848.

ANKARLO: And so, these people, as they grow in power, eventually they take over PTA positions, they take over city council positions . . .

DR. TRUXILLO: School boards.

ANKARLO: They run for governor, et cetera, et cetera, et cetera. Correct?

DR. TRUXILLO: Right. And they'll reverse the English-only legislation that has been passed in the Southwestern states.

ANKARLO: You say it's really going to be a splintering where these four or five states will become an independent nation.

DR. TRUXILLO: Well, with northern Mexico. There is a similarity in the culture of the Mexicans in the Southwest and also northern Mexico. Southern Mexico is different. It is more of an Indian country, and it's part of those old civilizations, but northern Mexico has this ranching, capitalist tradition that's much more close to the frontier spirit of the American West and it has its own identity.

ANKARLO: So what's going to happen in your mind, then? Will it be Mexico annexing these four or five states and bringing them into the fold, or will it be a division of Mexico which also includes these four or five states?

DR. TRUXILLO: I assume Mexico will fall apart in the future. You know, that government can't hold power much longer, and it really has more control around Mexico City and in the South than in the North, and I think the northern part of Mexico, the American Southwest, will form an independent country. Joel Garreau said that in 1985 in the book *The Nine Nations of North America*. He already predicted that.

ANKARLO: I have followed your writings, I have followed your work, I've followed several other gentlemen with your mind-set, and you scare the heck out of me. You understand that because as a U.S. citizen who, by the way, is not Latino, I look at this and I think, okay, this won't just be a splintering, but this will be a wipeout of these states, and if what you have been tracking does come true, you and I both know people are going to fire shots eventually. Yes or no?

DR. TRUXILLO: I doubt that. I really doubt it.

ANKARLO: What's that mean?

DR. TRUXILLO: The United States is way too strong militarily for anybody to take them on in some kind of a civil war . . .

ANKARLO: So, you believe this will be accomplished with a nonmilitary coup?

DR. TRUXILLO: Yeah. I see that, basically, the United States will probably annex western Canada as Quebec breaks away, and then the United States will reconfigure itself as a more Anglo-Saxon country without this large Latino minority that's unassumable.

ANKARLO: So you guys would be down in the Southern states, and we'll just say, okay, now, in order to go into Arizona you've got to have a passport, because that's a part of Mexico?

DR. TRUXILLO: You know, it might actually be a freer kind of a confederation in reality, because the United States is moving towards a confederation with Canada and Mexico since the [George W.] Bush years, you know?

ANKARLO: Yeah, well, we've talked a lot about that. It's called SPP and, Mexico, America, Canada, all playing that stupid game.

DR. TRUXILLO: And, in which case, then autonomy granted to regions, even self-government, won't seem so radical. Quebec will probably be one of the first ones that'll do that in Canada. And if that's done peacefully, then there won't be so—it won't seem so threatening in the Southwest.

ANKARLO: In some of your writings, I see that you say there are about 60 million northern Mexicanos, and you say that there's almost that same amount in these border states here in America, correct?

DR. TRUXILLO: And, in fact, the Census Bureau says by 2040, Latinos, Mexican-Americans, Hispanics—whatever term you want—will be the majority in the Southwest.

ANKARLO: Yeah, well, I come to Arizona by way of Texas, where the number one majority is Latino, Latina, Mexican, or whatever they want to be called. So, it's already happened in Texas.

DR. TRUXILLO: But, you know, it's also the tides of history. Let's remember that. We have to take the historical approach. The United States took these areas in a war; it aggressively took them over in the Mexican-American War of 1846–1848, and now Mexicans are doing what they've been doing for centuries—they're just continuing to move north and colonize these Western lands. If Mexico had kept them, then Mexico would have been the beneficiary of those great resources—the oil in Texas, the gold in California.

ANKARLO: You left out a lot of history, because there was a tidy sum of money on the table for land purchases, but I want to stay focused on this new country of yours; we've got a good chunk of time before the bottom falls out, don't we?

DR. TRUXILLO: I'd say about forty years.

ANKARLO: You think forty?

DR. TRUXILLO: I think forty.

ANKARLO: No way! I was thinking more like, you know, eighty, ninety, or a hundred. You're thinking—

DR. TRUXILLO: Oh, no. Within forty years Latinos will be a majority, and they'll start, you know, agitating towards sovereignty.

ANKARLO: Yeah. Agitating. I know the word that you use, but I know how I received it, and it's not a positive word. I live here in the Southwest, pay taxes, vote for candidates, and all things patriotic, and about six million of my closest friends do the same thing.

Something tells me these folk staking a claim to our property and livelihoods, they aren't going to be too well received. Our mines [in Arizona] deliver more copper than any other state in the Union, but suddenly they will be used to support this new independent nation or to support the nation of Mexico? No way. Plus, let's go back to Texas for a second. If we take the Texas economy and everything they have, it represents the sixth-largest economy in the world. Between these two states there is a lot of money on the line, and if you honestly think it's going to happen without somebody pulling out a gun and saying, "Wait. You think you're going to take my oil well? This has been in my family for 150 years. I'll shoot you dead first," you're out of your mind.

DR. TRUXILLO: You know, it depends on the situation in the Pacific. If China continues to be a rising power, the United States might hesitate doing any kind of military action towards the secession of this region.

ANKARLO: Because?

DR. TRUXILLO: Because the Chinese definitely are going to be more involved in the Pacific, they're very involved in Latin America, they're very involved with Mexico, and many Latino leaders have already made delegations to China. There's already talk going on. The Chinese look at a new configuration of the planet in which they won't let the United States act out of hand anymore.

ANKARLO: Interesting take. Let me walk through something you wrote: "Secondly, as Mexicanos become a majority in the border states, they will use the American system to further their national evolution. American democracy and capitalism will allow them to capture local governments and economies, moving from self-government to autonomy, then, finally, a sentiment for independence. The process will resemble the development of Quebeque Nationale in Canada or that of the Czechs in the old Habsburg Empire . . ."

DR. TRUXILLO: Yes.

ANKARLO: ". . . Undoubtedly, the United States will lash out viciously, but heightened world opinion will moderate its response." Then, Dr. Truxillo, you said, "Furthermore, the moral contradiction of the United States acting like Israel, denying to others the same rights it claims for itself, will force the United States to concede or eventually face long-term Palestinian-style intifada along its border with Mexico." What an interesting picture you draw, one that is so prejudiced that you scare me out of my pants.

DR. TRUXILLO: It's already happening. You just have to go down to the Tucson area and you see the struggle that is going on with these militias and other people moving down there to guard the border. There is already an unreported battle going along the whole border.

ANKARLO: I've been down there, and I've seen exactly what you just described—but I see it in little factions. I see a little drug lord trying to own his piece, and a coyote trying to run those forty people, and a couple of U.S. Minutemen trying to stop the flow and everything else. So I see that in sporadic outbursts. What you describe when you say it's going to become like an intifada creates images of suicide bombers, car bombs, people blowing each other up, shooting each other when they go into a DMZ zone, etc. You think we're going to get that far out of whack?

DR. TRUXILLO: No, no. Because, you know, that whole situation in

Palestine and Israel is fueled by this heightened, religious funda-
mentalism that isn't really part of the border scene.

ANKARLO: Yeah, but don't you think those of us who love this country
as it stands and have members of our families who have fought
and died in various wars for this country as we know it—we're not
just going to roll over and play dead. You and I both know, as soon
as people wake up—and I think they're slowly doing that—as soon
as they wake up, they're going to go buy the biggest gun they can
and they're going to say, "Over my freakin' dead body. You want
my property? I'm shooting you dead."

DR. TRUXILLO: Well, you know, the truth of the matter is, I don't think
there'll be any kind of requisition of property or anything that
will be that forceful. If anything, the Anglos will become increasingly a minority, but they'll still be the wealthiest part of the population. It will be a bilingual society. It'll look much more like the
United States than you can probably even imagine, but the fact
of the matter is, once Latinos are a majority, they're not going
to acquiesce anymore to English-only legislation and the punitive
type of attitude against immigration over the border. It'll change.
That's all I'm predicting, you know?

ANKARLO: Talk to me about illegal immigrants. We have, according to
some reports, 12 million; according to others, as many as 25 million or 38 million. I've never asked you this before. What's your
take?

DR. TRUXILLO: I think that, basically, they're not illegal because these
are areas the United States took from Mexico in an unjust war. It's
the social law of karma. You do something like that to a country
in history, and then you pay the consequences.

ANKARLO: Oh, wait.

DR. TRUXILLO: Mexicans have always moved north.

ANKARLO: Now, come on. Wait.

DR. TRUXILLO: They've moved north since Mesoamerican times into these regions.

ANKARLO: Wait. Time-out a second.

DR. TRUXILLO: It's just continuing. Two movements: westward, the Anglo-Americans, and northward, the Mexicans.

ANKARLO: Yeah, but wasn't Mexico Aztec? Wasn't Mexico Azteca? Yes or no?

DR. TRUXILLO: Yes, of course.

ANKARLO: And who took it?

DR. TRUXILLO: Spain did.

ANKARLO: Spaniards came in, and they whacked 'em.

DR. TRUXILLO: Right, and then Mexico became independent from Spain and even uses the Aztec symbol as the symbol of its nation now.

ANKARLO: Yeah, but, where I'm going with this is, you give me generations, you give me decades, you give me centuries, and I'll show you a complete readjustment of the entire globe because people went in and said, "You know what? I want that property. Now, I'll buy it from you, and if you don't want to sell it to me, then we're going to put together an army and we're going to take it."

DR. TRUXILLO: And that's the tides of history. You're absolutely right.

And so, now, when these areas are turning Mexican again, why all the uproar? It's just the tides of history.

ANKARLO: I recently read a study that showed that only 3 percent of women and approximately 12 percent of men in America care about world history at all . . .

DR. TRUXILLO: That's exactly true.

ANKARLO: Some would say that with such a limited worldview, Americans deserve what they get. I'm just trying to be a wake-up call. Walk me through this process, then. We went to Mexico. We wanted parts, tried to buy parts. Eventually we took areas via war.

DR. TRUXILLO: Why would you sell half of your national territory to another country? Yeah. You took it by force.

ANKARLO: That's how territories are marked and borders are carved out. What I am seeing, and what you are describing, are foreign citizens coming into the U.S.A. under the guise of needing work, while their true plan is to take back what is theirs. Is this what's going on?

DR. TRUXILLO: No, well, it's a recolonization. Most Mexican immigrants don't even have that historical knowledge. They're just coming north because these are the opportunities.

ANKARLO: Yeah, yeah. But some are coming for that purpose. And the many who don't know history will be used as pawns in the whole "power through numbers" game—

DR. TRUXILLO: It's just the draw of the economy, the world economy.

ANKARLO: Yeah, but I would venture a guess that those who are here, many of them will stop and say, "You know what? Now it's not just me and five of my friends, now it's me and 500 of my friends. Now I can march through the streets of Phoenix 150,000 people strong, and, 'Sí se puede! Sí se puede!'" And U.S. citizens sit back and say, "What the heck is going on?" Meanwhile, a few of us are trying to sound the alarm; we're trying to stop the influx in this re-colonization . . .

DR. TRUXILLO: And—

ANKARLO: The Mexicans say, "Well, you know, it's ours. We have a right to come in." And I'm saying, "Look, I've got to stop you, because, if I don't stop you, you're going to take my country." So, really, this is a war as I've described it, and finally, I've got somebody from the other side saying I am right.

DR. TRUXILLO: Well, it's not a war in the sense of a military action, but it is a struggle between different ethnicities and cultures. The Latin Catholic culture of Mexico now has a very large population and they're spilling over the border into lands that used to be Mexico's. The Anglo-American population, the white population is declining in birthrate; the Mexican people are in a perfect position to regain their property. But most are not sympathetic to my ideas.

ANKARLO: What do you mean?

DR. TRUXILLO: Most Latinos are not sympathetic to secession or autonomy because they're too assimilated right now, but, you know, the process is changing because it's a reactive ideology to the hostility towards Latinos. The more hostility there is, the more of them will be drawn to these ideas.

ANKARLO: Don't put this stuff on us, brother. When millions jump the line and then try to make us look like we're close-minded bigots because we disagree with their actions, we respond by drawing the old line in the sand and say, "Wait a minute. You came here without permission, you continue to use all of our resources without really giving a whole lot back, and you demand rights when you march in the streets." You can understand, if we were doing the exact same thing in Mexico or any other country, if we weren't shot for it, we would definitely feel the pain of the citizenry of that country, wouldn't we?

DR. TRUXILLO: But let's remember the Texas analogy of the Alamo. They were crossing illegally into Mexican territory. They were the first wetbacks over the Sabine River from Louisiana in the south, and they eventually revolted and broke away from Mexico. So that is a historical process in the Southwest. Now it's just happening the reverse way. And the Alamo was a Mexican victory, I might add too.

ANKARLO: Yeah. Let me just tell you, brother. We're in Arizona—you'll get away with that here, but if you said it in Texas, there would be more than a few people who would want to string your sorry butt up. Because for them, they'll say, "We fought to the finish to hold the line until reinforcements would get there," and we remember exactly what happened shortly after the Alamo.

DR. TRUXILLO: Yeah, of course. Mexico lost the war of Texas Independence, but the Texans revolted against Mexican law when they swore allegiance to Mexico, and they were shot.

ANKARLO: The U.S. has no desire to bring in its military or Border Patrol; just look at our lack of resolve to date. But the U.S. citizen is the wild card. We have something like a quarter of a billion guns. We are a proud and strong people . . .

Dr. Truxillo: Well, I would say this: If there was that kind of a reaction to Mexican immigration and there was some kind of large confrontation in which many Mexicanos were shot by militias or Minutemen, and so forth, it would provide the catalyst to make that happen.

Ankarlo: But one of the ways to avoid a violent reaction is to stop the flow of 20 million new illegal immigrants before they get here. This will accomplish a couple things: (1) If the Mexican or Latino population doesn't feel a power surge, they will be less inclined to be confrontational, and (2) that's 20 million fewer "reinforcements" we have to worry about. And while we're looking at numbers and people—we don't see the vast move to the U.S. by any other singular group. Isn't part of this equation an impoverished and corrupt country that has needed the gifts of America for all of these years just to get along? Why in the world would all of these people want to come here just so they can re-create what has already failed on the other side? I would expect they would want to come here, assimilate, and just become a part of the United States of America and let failure go.

Dr. Truxillo: Well, no, I agree with you totally. In fact, I'd say the majority of Mexicanos, Chicanos, Latinos, whatever word you want to use, are assimilating, and, in fact, the things that are attractive about the United States will be part of the new country—capitalism, democracy, the social system that allows you to rise up economically. All those are good things; those are universal values that the whole world admires, but on the other hand, all people have a desire for self-government. The thirteen colonies did when they broke with England. The Palestinians do right now because they're occupied by Israel. It's just a natural inclination to be with their own: their own culture, their own language, and their own identity.

ANKARLO: And so, that's what America has been all these years, and slowly, America has said, "Let's diversify. Let's let everybody come in from all over the world, bring their languages, bring their religions, bring their cultures, bring their governments; let's bring them all into our little melting pot." Without paying attention, when you let enough of a singular group do that, eventually that singular group says, "Oh, I hate to break it to you. We make the rules and the laws now. Step back."

DR. TRUXILLO: Well, when they're so large a group. You know, it'd be different if we were talking about seven or eight million Poles or Italians in various cities, but when you're dealing with so many in the same area, it seems inevitable that there'll be that same kind of self-consciousness. And then, quite frankly, faculty members like myself and Jose Gutierrez and Armando Navarro and other Chicano intellectuals, we're espousing these ideas we're maintaining ideologically and intellectually.

ANKARLO: That's what scares me. It's almost treasonous.

DR. TRUXILLO: How can you say that?

ANKARLO: You support the concept of a group of people coming to a sovereign land with their own language, culture, and identity and then pushing that way of life on the occupants of said country. Dr. Truxillo, the people you describe don't want to become Americans; they just want to use our blessings and our systems. This is what you are saying in this interview, and you also support it in some of the writings that you have out there. Several taxpayer-supported professors, some whom you've just named, are teaching—no, they're supporting—this stuff in our schools.

DR. TRUXILLO: What's wrong if they come here to get an economic advantage? They're not interested in becoming Anglo-Saxon, Protestant, English-speaking people.

ANKARLO: But, wait! Isn't that, like, the perfect definition of an enemy?

DR. TRUXILLO: No. My goodness. I mean, you think of some of the founding fathers of the United States, like Patrick Henry, that thought the United States should adopt German rather than English to break the bonds with England.

ANKARLO: There's no correlation. Again, there is a lot more to our early history than I have time to discuss—if you want to know more, just read my first book; I break it all down for you. Let's stay with my line of questioning.

DR. TRUXILLO: But you can't call these people the enemy. Mexicans are good people, and this is their homeland.

ANKARLO: Stop saying that. Yes, they are good people, but the ones coming here as you have described do sound a lot like an invading country. Think about it—why does a nation establish a military? Because it wants to protect its basic way of life; it strives to stay safe. What do you call it when an organized group moves into a country with tanks and machine guns, takes over, and then tells the citizens they will assimilate to and embrace the way of life of the invaders, speak a new language, watch as at least $30 billion is removed from the economy and sent back to the invading country even as the uninvited guests reject the culture and laws of the land they have moved to? Most would call that a military takeover, a coup, or a wartime victory. Isn't this precisely what is happening to America—minus the tanks and missiles? The enemy usually comes when least expected—the thief-in-the-night concept—and the really good one will use my own system to get me. Just look at computer hackers; they set up a virus, worm, or a Trojan horse, and before I know it, they have my bank information, private e-mail messages, and so much more. I've got a sick feeling this is happening to my country.

DR. TRUXILLO: You know, but your conservative American values are closer to most Mexicans. Most Mexicans are Christians. They're hard workers. They're not in favor of radical feminism or gay studies or any of that stuff. They are, in fact, more like conservative backward-looking people. They might be better to maintain those values.

I will end this chapter the same way I began it: I love the Mexican people and their culture. But I would rather visit them in their own country.

CUATRO

NOT YOUR TYPICAL MEXICAN TOURIST TRAP

It was a warm, sunny Sunday afternoon, and I was just finishing my wanderings through the streets of Nogales, Mexico, a border town about an hour outside of Tucson, Arizona, when I approached a taxi driver with a request to see the poorest neighborhood he could find. *The richest nation in the world is a short walk away, so how bad can it be?* I thought to myself. I found it strange that almost every person walking the streets stared me down, shot me the "evil eye," or did a double take as they spotted me. I don't believe I was the first brown-haired, blue-eyed white guy they had ever seen, but something about my presence was setting them off, especially if the first sign of hospitality is supposed to be a tip of the hat and a friendly hello. I think the words of one passerby summed up the feeling in the air when he growled, "Get the - - - - out of here. We don't like Americans" as our paths crossed in a less-than-safe part of town.

Granted, Americans have strong opinions about illegal immigrants, but most of us don't go out of our way to disrespect them—unless they are amassing hundreds of thousands of their best buds to protest in our streets—but that's a different story. *Maybe this is just the way city life is down here,* I thought. *It has to be better when I get to the outskirts.* Indeed it was better. I take that back. The people were kinder, but *better* is not a word I would use to describe what burned my eyes and assaulted my senses.

The minimum wage is five dollars per *day* in Mexico, based on a *twelve- to fourteen-hour* day. When we toss a Lincoln on the counter to "supersize" our meal, most of us do it without a thought. It's just so easy. With the same amount of money needed to clog my arteries, I could own a human for a full day and work him as hard as I need to, because modern-day slavery is alive and well. And, just as in years gone by, there are millions struggling to get by while the plantation owner and his people flourish. Sadly, most of those slave owners and traders have direct connections to the Land of the Free and Home of the Brave.

One thing that did strike me as odd was that the cabbie wanted twenty bucks for a round-trip fare. Perhaps I would pay that in New York or Chicago, but not here; no way. I passed on the price, sure that the next guy in line would jump at the chance to earn my money— which I had hoped would be less than half of what the first one wanted. This guy wasn't biting either. After my fourth rejection it was clear the drivers were all working from the same playbook and in fact had embraced the most American of labor practices from years gone by: they had unionized!

So, up and down the street I walked and negotiated. I mean, how difficult could it be to come to terms with guys driving beat-up mid-1970s Chevys with double the mileage a trip to the moon would require, while distorted Tejana music blasted from their long-ago-blown speakers. But, not even a flinch. These guys were good! Cars lined both sides of the street, and they all knew theirs was the only game in town. If the American wanted to travel, they had the keys, and they certainly knew their price.

Finally, I relented. As I waited for the drivers to decide which one had the next turn, I felt it again. Eyes. After a few moments I turned to Alonzo, my translator, to ask if he had noticed it too. "Do you see them staring at us?"

"Yeah, man," he said in his coolest of Latino accents. "I've never seen this kind of reaction to Americans before—it must have something to do with our country's tougher position on illegal immigrants." I nodded in agreement as we fought our way down the busy sidewalk with my team clustered in such a way as to fight off an attack from any direction. And, yes, we were all braced for a fight—sure that it would come at any instant.

While our fight-or-flight reflexes were on high alert we watched the cabbies continue their bickering with one another. Finally, a young man of about fourteen or fifteen said that he would take us. "You're a cabdriver?" I asked, clearly insulting him. I wasn't trying to be a jerk; I simply had never seen a kid cabbie before. Even if he could get us around, something about his demeanor told me it wasn't going to be the best of trips. Just then his father stepped in. "Yes, he's a driver, but I have decided to take you. Where do you want to go?" I pointed to the hills on the outskirts.

The pavement, which was rough, cracked, and littered with potholes, soon turned to dirt. A thick, dense trail of dust poured from the back of our car, covering everything and everybody in its wake. When we arrived at the little village the earthen road morphed into deep craters made by tires that must have driven on it in a torrential rain. The cab bucked us up and down and back and forth every time it fell out of sync with the cuts it had been following. I asked the driver to stop.

Darrell, Rob, and Alonzo. An area about 15 minutes out of Nogales, Mexico that used to belong to one land owner until the people tore down the man's fences and gates and squatted on the land. Eventually, the man relented to their constant trespassing and a village sprung up. The people here live in homes made from garbage, with limited electricity. They have no sewers or running water.

Rob and Adam walked behind us as Alonzo and I walked up to the first house. Alonzo has an easygoing charm about him that sets people at ease, so I felt confident we would be able to get a few people in the neighborhood to open up to us. At the top of the hill was a crudely built shack. The exterior was constructed of abandoned plywood and particle board with pieces of broken plastic covering the holes cut out to look like windows.

"I'll ask questions, and you interpret without changing them," I said to Alonzo. He laughed in a way that let me know he thought it was a goofy point I was making but, more important, to let me know that I could trust him.

As I approached the front of the building, I was prepared to knock on the door; too bad it didn't have one. I glanced across the street and down the hill—none of them had doors. Each had a cutout frame, big enough for a person to go through, covered by an old blanket or rug, if it had anything defending the passageway at all. We stepped gingerly toward the house, not sure what to expect from the people inside their dwellings. Just to the left of the front opening was a large barrel drum, which I learned was filled with water after my curiosity got the best of me. "I bet they don't have indoor plumbing," I whispered to Alonzo.

"Hola," I said in a rather meek voice. I think I was a bit embarrassed that I was getting ready to ask very personal questions of folks who lived in squalor, knowing that in several days I would be back to my comfortable condo, complete with two big-screen TVs and every nonessential gadget a guy could want.

"Hola," came the answer as the short and plump lady of the house stepped out to greet me.

"Do you speak English?" I asked.

"No."

"I'm with a radio station in Phoenix, Arizona, KTAR, and I'm trying to learn a few things about the people of Mexico. May I ask you a few questions?" She saw my microphone, and though she was a bit hesitant at first, she soon approved. "Do you work? Do you work in the city? Do you work up in this area?"

She explained where she worked as if I should know the name, but I didn't have a clue where it was. I nodded as though I did, though—I wanted her to feel at ease and ready to answer.

"Do you have a husband? Do you have children? How many people live in this building?" I was extra polite while I launched the questions, knowing how I would feel if a complete stranger barged into my space.

If you really want to see third world conditions up close you can easily find them less than an hour from our southern border.

This woman told me that she and her husband usually walk down the hill to use a sister's bathroom, since they don't have one.

People living in these third-world conditions make an average of $5.00 for a 12 to 14 hour day.

"No children," was her very short answer. "It's just me and my husband."

"If I can ask such a very private question—will you tell me how much money you make?"

"Eight hundred fifty pesos."

"A week? A day? What?"

"A week."

I riffled through my mind to translate pesos to dollars. "Eighty-five dollars a week. Is that for both of you?"

"Just me."

"So your husband probably makes the same. So you make about one hundred and seventy dollars a week together?"

"Yes."

One hundred and seventy dollars a week is poor by anyone's count, especially in the twenty-first century, though for a moment I flashed back to my first full-time job at a radio station; I made one hundred and forty dollars a week for a sixteen-hour day. But then again, that was in the 1970s. I flashed forward about three decades and felt great sadness for her. More questions. "This home—do you own it or rent it?"

"We own it."

"Do you have electricity and running water and things?" The place was barely standing. I had built a better tree house when my kids were little, and so I knew her answer before she even provided it.

"Not here. But we do have water. It's in a big water tank." She stepped outside the threshold of her home and pointed. The same barrel I checked out when I arrived.

"So, you don't have indoor plumbing." I paused in a moment of disbelief. The question that barged into my brain was begging to be asked. But I paused. "So how do you go to the bathroom? How do you wash up?"

The lady must have anticipated that query, because she started answering before my final syllable. "There is no drainage up here, so this is the only water." She was pointing at the barrel. "We take a bucket and then fill it with water, pour it in a big pot, boil it, and then put it in another container, and then shower with that."

"And you go to the bathroom in buckets, I guess?"

"Because we just moved up here, we have to go to my sister-in-law's."

"In order to go to the bathroom?"

We're at the top of the hill. Her sister-in-law, who shares the poverty cycle, is down the hill. So every time this kind, younger woman or her husband needs to use the restroom, they have to traverse their way down the hill, even in the middle of the night or a rain-soaked day. I've heard the term "squatter's paradise." No doubt the one who coined the phrase hasn't been on this piece of property. This was no paradise.

I thanked her for her graciousness and slipped a ten spot in her hand; she needed it more than I did. She bowed up and down in the old-fashioned way to let me know how much it was appreciated. And then I was off to meet another family and hear another story.

At first, the young man sitting in the doorway told us that he lived alone but when I asked to see his living conditions he admitted that he had two teenage roommates who shared the small space. The whole "house" was smaller than most bedrooms in the States.

THREE BOYS ON A MATTRESS

The next rigged-up mess looked as though it had been chiseled out of rock—not the place itself—but the foundation appeared as though it had been blown into the side of the hill. It didn't look as if explosives were used; that would be too costly for even many Americans, but instead as though pickaxes had been used to break the rock foundation down so a person could actually get into the side of the cliff area. There I found a young man who couldn't have been more than a teenager—just sitting on his stoop.

As I climbed over each piece of the broken and chiseled rock, I saw a piece of board that had clearly been snagged out of a trash heap somewhere. It was ragged and stained, and holes from nails and termites permeated the entire dilapidated thing. I was a little surprised to see that the house had a front door—though it was broken and didn't want to swing, another gift from the junk man. The entire village was constructed in the exact same way: if it can be pried, ripped, cut, or broken off something else, it becomes a part of the structure. Indeed, on the top of this house was the foundation from a lawn mower, used to plug the roof from rain, I was told.

The sun was already hitting the afternoon landscape with its usual intensity in Mexico. An interesting mix of tacos, dirt, and garbage hung in the air. It wasn't nasty, but it wasn't completely pleasant either.

The kid saw me coming. In fact, I had noticed that he was watching me as I walked past one of the other houses in the little village. Since he didn't try to hide that fact, I felt it represented an open invitation. Instead of the typical "Hola," I just tried the universal "hey" that is shared by young people around the world. He responded in kind. After engaging in the requisite small talk for a few minutes at his door, I asked if I could see inside his house.

"Well, it's regular. We have a mattress; we have a table, couch . . ."

"Can I just take a look? Yes?"

He gave a tentative approval but also fidgeted enough to let me know something else was in play. Only a few breaths before he had told me he was all alone, but now as his eyes darted toward the interior, I knew he was not. He jumped up and asked me to wait where I was. A moment later he was back. There was movement inside, and to this day I am not sure if the occupants were trying to rapidly clean up for their uninvited guest or hide so I wouldn't see them, though the latter is doubtful, because the entire shack was less than the size of my bathroom.

The young man waved me in. "It is fine; come on in."

I pointed at a piece of wood that occupied a space on a wall, and he excitedly told me that it was his cabinet. "This is where the dishes go."

I was confused and surprised, "So are we in a kitchen right now?"

"No, we don't have a kitchen here." The "place where the dishes go" looked like a broken and glued gun rack, circa 1935. I was afraid to touch it for fear that it would crash to the floor and swiftly disintegrate into sawdust. This piece of furniture was no more than three steps inside the front door—on the left side. Another two paces to the right from where we stood, there was a rusty and broken gate, like you would find on old-fashioned chain-link fences. He admitted that he wasn't sure what he was going to do with it, but he was noticeably proud to have it. I thought he might be saving it for trading purposes.

Have you ever been to a really ancient antique store? My wife, Laurie, takes me to those places whenever she can trick me into getting into the car with her. When she suggests she wants to go see a movie or shop for the newest piece of guy technology, I know it's too late, and once we arrive, she always wants to go to the back compartments of the store—the room where old junk has been piled for decades because no one would buy it. Musty, dusty, with a tinge of rust wafting to your nose. That's what this kid's place smelled like.

"So where do you eat if you don't have a kitchen?"

"Where I work at, that's where I eat."

"So you bring the cooked food back here?"

"Sí."

As I stepped around a corner, another three or four feet, I ran into the other occupants of the home: two more boys—mid teens. They greeted me kindly but reluctantly. Alonzo worked overtime to hear three Spanish conversations, translate for me, and translate back to them. Words were flying everywhere. Then I noticed something completely out of place. Cell phones. These three kids, living without adult supervision in a seventy-five-square-foot trash pile, had the latest flip phones on the market.

"You have cell phones. How much do cell phones cost here?"

"Fifteen hundred for the cell phone."

"Fifteen hundred pesos."

"Yes, fifteen hundred pesos."

"One hundred and fifty dollars for the cell phone. If you don't mind my asking, where did you boys get the money?"

"From work." My host quickly added, "I am given food at my restaurant, and I make enough money to pay for the phone."

"Do you have a television or a car?"

"No television. No car."

"Is there an adult who lives here?"

"Just us three." He pointed at the other two—a brother and a cousin—as they sat on the edge of the bed. After entering the house and taking the required few steps to where these kids were sitting, it became clear, in an awkward way, that we were now standing in their one and only bedroom. It's one thing to talk to people at their door, in their yard, and even in their living room, but there is an intimateness about speaking to people in a bedroom—one where part of the room belongs to an open bucket for a toilet and a corner with a big piece of plastic running from top to bottom.

"So do you guys sleep in the same bed?"

"And on the couch."

"And is that where you shower?" I asked while pointing at the plastic—the only obvious conclusion I could draw.

"Sí. Right here."

"May I look?" He had already motioned to the area, but I wanted to be certain I wasn't overstepping some sort of Martha Stewart etiquette boundary. As I took the few steps to the corner, I asked how the shower worked, since the place had no running water, indoor plumbing—or electricity for that matter. "In order to take a shower, somebody's got to climb on the roof and pour the water down? How's it work?"

The young man explained in such a way as to suggest that I was a little slow for not knowing; it was as if he thought what he and his roommates did to clean themselves was how everyone does it everywhere.

"With the bucket. We will pour the water in the bucket and then with a dish we will pour the water on top of ourselves."

My heart sank as I listened to him, and just before we exited, I took one more snapshot with the camera that is my mind. I wanted to remember it all: the dirt floor; the old, beat-up couch that was taken from the trash somewhere—the worst and most soiled couch you could ever see in a local junkyard. Roll off the couch and you fall directly onto the bed—which someone else probably slept on thirty or forty years earlier. Each teen alternated the sleeping arrangements. If one slept on the couch one night, he could sleep on the bed the next. This was their life. No radio, no TV. No cool posters on the walls. Just three life forms—existing.

I pulled out some money and again I pressed it into the hands of people who needed it. I told them it was payment for the interview, though of course I was only trying to give them a gift without causing anyone to lose face. I have four kids, so my soul wrenched with sorrow for these boys who had no parents, had little in life, and had only a thread of hope of moving to the next level. Would they make the trip to America? Would they resort to selling drugs to get by? Would they become coyotes and lead teams of illegals over my borders? Conditions were right for any and all options—only time will tell.

The bright spot—one that most wouldn't recognize as a bright spot—was the cell phone. They had put together the money to buy a cell phone, which could seem stupid or selfish when one has nothing. I thought it was nice to see three teens with almost no "golden days of youth" getting to be kids for a while.

WE BROKE DOWN THE GATE!

Think about your childhood for a moment; what was the cool stuff you had, growing up? Tennis courts, pets, bicycles, stereos, cars, vacations, Play Station. A computer. Think about every little thing you had.

Now, take it all away. All of it. No running water, no electricity. A front yard chiseled out of stone so there's no room to play, and a backyard that doesn't exist at all. No bathroom. A multipurpose room that also serves as a bedroom, one you share with your mother and a brother. You don't own a dog, but a pack of dogs roams the trash piles that litter the landscape in every direction. This is what you get to remember when, or if, you make it to your own adult years. And this is a step up from what you had a year or so earlier.

Just down the road from the home with the water barrels in the front yard, my peripheral vision caught a glimpse of a young boy jumping in the shadows of his decrepit house, ducking every time I turned in his direction. What does a child of about eight or nine do for fun in such an environment, and does he have any idea of the world around him? Soon, I stood at the front cutout to the house, recorder rolling, and found little hesitation from the young boy who methodically answered my questions about every kid thing I could think of, from cartoons to toy stores. The answers were mixed; he had seen some television but had never visited the kind of store where imaginations flourish. He provided stilted one- and two-word answers, whether due to his distrust of me or his lack of education—probably a mixture of the two.

While he struggled to give me what I wanted, I noticed his mother floating in the

At first glance these homes looked like wonderful Mexican villas but upon closer examination it was clear that many of America's homeless have it better.

background. And, trust me, if one of my children had a journalist asking questions, I can guarantee that my wife would be hovering too.

After a few minutes I was done—there wasn't much more I could get from the kid. I started to walk away, but by luck I decided to shoot mom a question, though I could barely even see her in the darkness of the house's interior. By divine intervention, perhaps, I got a short answer that was the nugget one prays for; it described the current U.S./Mexico illegal immigration issue perfectly. "Do you own or rent this property?" was the simple question I asked as I pointed the microphone in the lady's direction. She moved front and center to enthusiastically answer my questions.

"All these lots were given away for free."

"By the government?"

"I think so."

"And how many people are up here—up in this section? How many people live up here?"

"About thirty."

"About thirty up in this area? So they were all given away free?" I asked while pointing at all the homes—at least three hundred—that covered the length of the property.

"It was an invasion, and that's how we were able to get the lots."

"I don't know what that means. Invasion?" I asked.

"This used to be gated, and we just came up here, started living up here, and they just gave us the lots." With those words, the interview was complete and the two stepped back into the shadows.

President Lincoln signed the Homestead Act into law, a program that gave land—up to 160 acres—to someone willing to go into the wilderness, build a home, and live in it for at least five years. Though the program no longer exists here, I thought she may have used a similar Mexican program, so I started to ask around. The answer I discovered was the exact micro description of our national epidemic.

It had indeed been a gated area just outside the rather large city of Nogales, Mexico—private property that belonged to a wealthy landowner. The poor people in the city looked at it and decided that it was not fair that no one lived on the property, so they ripped the gate down, went in, and started living on the man's trails, rocks, and dirt road. The property owner was shocked when he discovered the trespassers and asked them to leave. They wouldn't. Tired of pleading, he went to the government. Since he was well-heeled, knew the right people, and could prove the land was his, the police removed the squatters and helped to reerect the gate. Days later, in the dead of night, the original invaders returned—joined by reinforcements.

Later, when the man returned to inspect his land, he found the gate was once again crashed, and this time the people were everywhere. Young, old, single, and married—humanity dotted his hill. This time, as he threatened to call the police to have them removed, the crowd started chanting, "We're not going to leave." The people declared the property to be theirs, and when the private property owner asked again for intervention, the politicians placated the squatters. "Give these people the land."

The government leaders felt sorry for the poor folks and worked a deal with the landowner so they could get a fresh start while building a new community. "Everyone wins," they declared.

Except those few turned to several and then to hundreds. The new community is now the most poverty-stricken in the region. Oh, and the political leaders got what they wanted since the poor were now out of their districts.

America's "gate" has been open to all immigrants; all we ask is that you get the proper pass and we will personally welcome you. Instead, millions have used the same philosophy as those poor people on the hill: "We're not going to leave." Though their verbiage is a little different, their chant is "Sí se pueda" and "Reconquista" (which means reconquest or reconquer).

In February 2006 about two thousand[1] people marched on Independence Mall in Philadelphia to accentuate the need America has for immigrants. When it was through, "A Day Without an Immigrant" signaled the beginning of a four-month series of protests from coast to coast. A month later, more than a million people hit the streets in cities like Los Angeles, Chicago, Denver, and Detroit. Another thirty days passed and illegal immigrants and their supporters walked the streets of more than one hundred cities with another million-plus total. Word spread through the Latino/Hispanic communities like wildfire as the protests became organized, routine, and systematic. Hundreds of thousands of young people left school, as bloggers matched up the school with the date and time for the walkouts.

I marched with the four hundred thousand through the streets of Dallas because I wanted to know exactly what was on the minds of the demonstrators, and I marched in Phoenix a year later when more protests hit cities big and small. "Why are you marching?" I asked as we stepped to the beat of thousands of footsteps.

"Because we were here first. This was our country before it was yours," was the answer from many—as though it had been rehearsed.

"But what about America's borders—our laws?"

"We just want to work. We are here, and you are lucky to have us. We make this country what it is. You discriminate against us because you are all haters."

"I'm not a 'hater,'" I said indignantly. "Seriously, I don't care what color skin you have or where you come from. I just want you to abide by my country's laws."

Each person I talked to and marched with refused to hear my arguments; all had made up their minds, and I was the odd man out. Yes, I did feel like the superminority on those days as one of a few "white people" willing to step into the streets with hundreds of thousands of brown-skinned people. "My parents brought me here when I was a child" was a routine argument from too many. "It's not fair that you want to kick my entire family out. You just want to break up our family," was another.

When I brought up the issue of law, borders, sovereignty, and a system that could not handle the overload that up to 20 million extra people brought with them, none of the marchers wanted to hear it. "Sí se puede" came the reply. It was the refrain from a few, the song of families, and the chorus of the multitude. Everywhere I went the people chanted, "Sí se puede," which in Spanish means, "Yes, it can be done!" or loosely translated "Yes, we can!"

I remembered the words to that phrase when the lady who helped "invade" the hill told her story. They rang loudly when the local officials described how the government finally relented by giving the squatters property that didn't belong to them, and the words scared me to my core when they were chanted in unison—by so many—without fear of reprisal. In America they screamed, "Sí se puede," and on that Mexican hill they shouted, "We're not going to leave."

Either way, the message means the same thing.

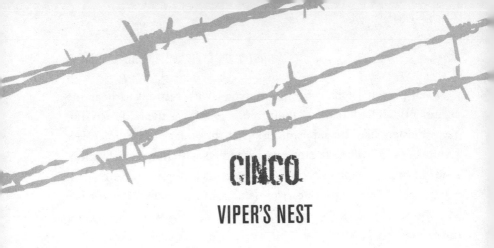

CINCO

VIPER'S NEST

I was hot, hungry, and headed home, but to get back to my side of the border I had to pass through the small, impoverished town of El Sasabe, Mexico, with a population in the hundreds living in the huts and broken-down buildings that housed them all. As my team and I drove our four-wheel drive down the road that routinely changed from dirt to gravel to pock-ridden concrete and back again, the first thing I noticed was the inordinate number of sets of eyes that tracked our every swerve, stop, and turn signal. There was zero doubt the gringos had pulled into a village where they weren't wanted; the squints, scowls, and glares were proof positive.

We had studied a variety of maps before we began our excursion and picked several of our border locations based on what we thought would allow for a quick retreat if we were put into any extraordinarily dangerous conditions. El Sasabe was supposed to be one of those spots.

We rolled past what had been an attempt at a gas station many years past on the left and a burned-out wooden-and-concrete square structure on the right, which looked as though it may have been a little store in a different era. This whole town was from a different time. The community cemetery was the only thing that looked as if it had been cared for. It was actually quite up-to-date, with Virgin Mary statues and memorials; a heaping mound of dirt awaited the newest occupant.

Before we got to the graveyard, we had to pass over the longest stretch of road in the area, and at first I thought the two young men—two young boys, really—were heading home from school or just kicking around until the day was done. We exchanged *holas* through the window as the vehicle crept slowly and carefully. I asked if they could point out any persons who might help a guy pass over the border, or if there were any people waiting to make such a trip, and they assured me I wouldn't find any here. I wanted to interview them, but as soon as they saw my digital recorder, they stepped up their pace and shut their mouths. We rolled on, down the block and onto the main drag. That's when we saw them.

The straightest street in town was lined with at least fifty or sixty men, women, and children who sat in door stoops and curbs and leaned against buildings, waiting for night to fall. They were clumped together as family, though the only real relationship they had was the common plan to sneak past our Border Patrol. They made no attempt to hide, because on this side of the fence, the patient congregants were law-abiding citizens; at the most, their only crime might be loitering, even though each one had gallon jugs of water, backpacks, and maps—all the trappings for an illegal immigrant's clandestine journey. Subtle whispers and finger-pointing followed us from the first person to the last in line. All stared as we drove past, some with a hopeful look of joining us, while most had a look of disdain—certain we would somehow thwart their planned assault on our law and order.

As we passed this cemetery in El Sasabe, Mexico I found it interesting that it was the only thing that had been consistently maintained. Just around the bend we would come face-to-face with the Mexican military and the automatic weapons.

I wasn't certain where to penetrate the border, so we decided to look for one of the highest peaks in the area. We chose a hill with a tower in order to get a better understanding of our surroundings. We figured there had to be a road that engineers use to tweak and repair the tower, so the hill represented the best opportunity to climb via vehicle without needing to jump out and push. So up we went, and though it was easier than others, we still had to fight hairpin curves, giant hanging boulders, and crevices that consumed our tires to the rims before releasing them again.

I had told the team earlier and felt the need to say it again, "You do not have to do this. You can stay at the bottom." I didn't expect any of them to walk away, but thought it was appropriate to offer, because I was sure this and any other moves could be dangerous, if not life threatening. No one flinched.

At the top, Adam pulled out his binoculars, or "binos," in a quiet, steady determination to get a better idea where things stood. Each of us took a turn because we needed the best possible route home. Suddenly he snapped, "We've got company." I grabbed the lenses, and sure enough, off in the distance—perhaps a couple of miles away—Humvees and military vehicles were kicking up a dust storm and heading in our direction. *Not good,* I thought. *We're in Mexico, I'm known for my tough stand on illegal immigration, and we've got a team of guys without a great excuse for being here.*

"They're packin' machine guns, and they look like they're in uniforms." I wasn't sure who said it, and I didn't care; I was consumed by the machine gun reference.

As they moved closer I confirmed that they did indeed have machine gun mounts on the vehicles, but they were armed with automatic weapons too. "Listen up," I shouted to our group as the troops arrived at the bottom of our hill, perhaps a quarter mile below us, "We are in Mexico as adventurers, and we selected this hill so we could decide where to go next. Period." I did not want anyone to suggest that we were a part of a radio or journalistic expedition, because I had no idea how involved these "Federales" were with banditos and drug lords. It is common knowledge that most of the police and military in this area are deep into the pockets of human and drug traffickers.

Once I was sure we were all on the same page, I nodded at Gary. "Let's start heading back down." While jumping into the Jeep, Adam added, "The soldiers set up a perimeter, pretty much waiting for us, just like, you know, they should have, so let's just be smart."

We started our slow descent. Alonzo and Adam stood on the Jeep's back bumper and did their best to appear casual and tough, but certainly not a threat to the awaiting military. I looked out the plastic window and noticed the Federales' fully automatic weapons, but more disturbing were the three or four with fingers crouching over their triggers. *This could go bad fast,* I thought.

When we were fewer than twenty yards away, their body language and stances adjusted to let us know this was as official as it gets. We did everything we could to set them at ease. Adam and Alonzo hopped off the rolling Jeep and, using universal signals, let the military personnel know we were not armed. "Stay right where you are. Keep your mouths shut. I'm gonna handle this," Adam said in his-fresh-from-Fallujah tone.

With their weapons drawn we were warned not to take pictures or record any sound. Oops, I guess I must have snapped a quick photo as I was putting the lens cap on! Notice the full military gear and weapons.

The uniformed men approached, and Alonzo immediately broke into fluent Spanish—telling the story we had concocted at the top. Adam had a few words for translation too, and after a brief moment, tension eased. Though still carrying AK47s, the soldiers were now pointing them at the ground or in the air. We started to breathe again.

"No," was the command when they saw our recorders, cameras, and microphones. We quickly obliged, though I managed to click the shutter at least once as I put the lens cap back on. "Do you work for a magazine?" one asked. We shook our heads. They clipped off a few more words in their native tongue, and I thought I heard them say, "Marine," so I assumed they were assessing Adam.

When Alonzo came back to where I was standing, I wanted to confirm my suspicion. "Was the soldier asking about Adam?"

Alonzo looked at the ground and then whispered—trying to look casual—"Yeah, he asked if our security was military, and I said, 'Yeah, he's a Marine.' And then he just asked if he was on duty. I said, 'No. He's off duty. He's on vacation.' They were less intense, but it really felt like they were trying to warn us."

"Like we are in no-man's land or something?" I asked.

"Exactly. That's exactly what it felt like. Like they were telling us, 'Look, we're warning you. You guys need to get out of here.'"

I tried to determine if the word of caution was coming from men who knew the things that could happen to naive Americans or from guys who would actually inflict the pain. Either way, we were ready to heed the warning. I found it interesting that once we confirmed that my son was a Marine—and built like one—the Mexican soldiers were a little less intimidating in their demeanor, kind of a mutual respect thing.

The soldiers exchanged a few more words with Alonzo and then walked away. Alonzo and Adam pounded on the Jeep top to let Gary know it was okay to take off; their manner suggested we should be quick about it. Those of us on the inside decided it would be smarter to drive for the checkpoint. Alonzo and Adam climbed in through the back flap. "That was intense," I said with just a little adrenaline kicking in.

Adam raised his voice to be heard over the noise of the tires ripping through gravel. "Alonzo was just kind of like, 'I don't like this.' And, if anybody is going to understand the feeling of these people, then it would be one of them. So, as I'm feeling his vibes and I'm feeling my own vibes, it's like, 'Let's just leave.'"

Rob's loud baritone voice boomed, "I was like, all right. Number one, the military is not marked. None of the vehicles are marked. And number two, if we don't have Alonzo, we're in jail or dead right now, because none of them spoke English. When we asked, you know, 'Hablas ingles?' and when they said, 'No,' I thought we were screwed."

"Well, because we're in another country now, aren't we?" My sarcasm dripped.

"Exactly."

"We don't expect the people here to speak Engl—oh, well, wait a minute. In the United States we expect everybody to speak Spanish. If I were pulled over at a checkpoint in America, and I'm Latino, I would expect them to speak Spanish or go get somebody who does—"

"Even more, I was reading on the U.S. Border Patrol Web site, if you join, you don't have to know Spanish, but you have to learn it as soon as you become a Border Patrol agent." As my producer, I expect Rob to store this kind of trivia—though I was amazed that he would have the presence of mind to remember it while engaged in such a harrowing experience.

We continued to analyze what had just happened as we navigated more potholes from hell on the way back to our border. We didn't have far to go—around a bend, past a few vacant buildings, and then off to the road leading to the Border Patrol station. That's when we heard the first siren blast. It sounded more like an air horn and was coming from an unmarked truck parked on the side of the road. "Policía?" I wondered.

We pulled next to the truck, and though the occupants had nothing to prove it, they were adamant that they were the police and wanted to know what we were up to. They wanted to know if we had been detained by the military, which we all thought was an odd question since they saw the trucks surrounding us and knew we had just left them.

"We're sightseers and adventurers. No more, no less." The men checked us as well and sent us packing.

Suddenly, a beat-up pickup was in front of us, and out of nowhere a trash heap appeared on our bumper. The car, a Crown Vic with deeply tinted windows, was rust and white.

I looked at Gary and told him to hit the gas. "That wasn't the police who stopped us—or maybe it was—either way, they were charged with slowing us down until the banditos could get to our location. We're being tracked by jackers." As soon as the words left my mouth, the rest of the guys backed up my assertion. Adam pounded on the roll bars and then kicked up the intensity, "Move it. We need to get out of here—now!" Gary punched it.

We swerved past a shack and a wide-open hole that looked as if it had been dug as the foundation for some building project that went awry; the town mutt jumped into our path, but we managed to miss it while putting some distance between us and the other vehicles.

Next, the road to the border, and we're out of here, I thought. Then, up ahead, a big passenger van was stopped dead in the road and parked to ensure we wouldn't be able to navigate around it. In the rearview mirror were our friends from the white car, with their trucker pals in hot pursuit. One wrong move and we were trapped, but this time our interrogation would be at the hands of the banditos.

Gary's survival training seemed to kick in.

"What are you doing?" Rob shouted as Gary jerked the steering wheel, popping us over gravel piles and mounds of debris while hugging the huge concrete dividers that separated in- and outbound traffic.

Tensely he muttered, "Getting us out of here!" We took off, swerved around a pole and back into our original lane, and did not slow down until the border officer asked for our IDs. The calm and typically quiet radio engineer showed a side that we hadn't seen before.

"What were you thinking?!" I asked, shocked by his reaction to the situation.

"Well, um, I was thinking, as we left town, 'we're on a two-lane road, there is a very high central curb that we cannot drive over, and a fifteen-passenger van with a very, very large luggage rack on the top of it stops, blocking the road entirely, and I'm not pulling up behind that van. No way. No how!'"

That town had every conceivable piece to the Mexico/U.S.A. immigration and crime fiasco. We had mules (the young men we first met—who probably tipped off everyone else), coyotes and jackers (on the side of the road and in the speeding cars), and corrupt police and military. (They had to be corrupt, because they did nothing to stop the congregating of illegal aliens and drug pushers.) Oh, and the problem wouldn't be so blatant without those fifty or sixty people (and millions more behind them) awaiting their chance to advance.

We regrouped on the American side as dusk settled in. A middle-aged woman who runs the only general store in the region gave us a better understanding of the history of the area. Although she stressed her disdain for the disregard for our laws, I couldn't help but notice much of what she had for sale were the exact items I had seen on the border crosser's shopping list when I was in Nogales.

"It's not my job to check the identity of my customers. If a person has the money, I sell to them." She sounded an awful lot like so many other American business owners who have picked up the knack of speaking out of both sides of their mouths.

When we explained everything that had happened on the Mexican side, the lady confirmed that we could have been killed. She filled us in on the details of a shooting a few days earlier that cost the lives of three Mexican policía—police who were actually trying to do their jobs. She told us we were smart for getting out when we did, because at night "anything goes."

After downing some of her reheated burrito-looking food items, we headed back to the border, armed with night-vision goggles to catch the evening's mad dash. This time, border agents were around every bend and on most hills. Every night, from fifty to one hundred illegal immigrants make the run for the border at this one spot, and the agents do their best to catch as many of them as they can. It is a game of numbers; if a hundred people all run in different directions, it is more likely that a greater number will succeed in their efforts.

We moved the Jeep at least a half dozen times and watched different sets of people zigzagging their way past agents and, we believe, to awaiting transport trucks about a half mile up the crooked road—just past the general store. Frustrated by the simplicity of the incursions, we drove from the region and back to our base camp.

—※—

The morning of our small-town visit I had been walking through the outlying area, just taking it all in, when I noticed a lot of little holes in the ground—snake holes. Since the habitat was theirs and not mine I walked gingerly, not wanting to wake anything up. It was direct foreshadowing for my El Sasabe experience: We were in a viper's nest. We thought it was a quiet town where a few illegals might cross, but we came to realize it was like mafia central and clearly one of the most used entry points between the two countries. Later investigations led me to believe everyone in this town is connected to the illegal immigration industry in some way, and our Border Patrol can only sit by and watch—since most of the preparation happens in a foreign country.

I knew the illegal immigration issue had been turned into an industry—but until this day and night, I just didn't grasp how many criminals it took to provide safe passage.

SEIS

THE BOYS ON A CURB

It was hot and soak-your-shirt muggy after the clouds dropped their load earlier in the day. My team and I made our way to a desolate section about twenty minutes or so from Nogales. I was already laying out the process I would use to punch through our border, and the thought of arrest kept revisiting the back of my mind. I had spent several days meeting the people who lived the illegal immigration issue in Mexico, but soon I would be heading to the border and then back home. Before I could slide back to our side, I wanted to bathe myself in a few more experiences from the other side, like the three young men who sat on a curb, eating from a bag of chicharrones smothered in throat burning super hot sauce, the kind where just the smell makes your eyes tear up.

We were in the resting center run by the Mexican government and the International Red Cross. They had already fed the boys, helped them call mom and dad, cared for their medical needs, and provided some bus money home after their latest attempts to cross were frustrated.

The boys stared at the ground as I walked into their vicinity, but I wanted their stories. They didn't flinch, budge, or acknowledge me when I stepped into their space, and so I just plopped right down in the middle of them. Over the years, I have worked with thousands of teenagers, not to mention the scores who always seemed to be hanging out with my own kids, so I didn't think twice about my actions. In the end, kids are kids. I pulled out my microphone and started asking questions.

"Where are you from?"

"Veracruz," said the haggard-looking young man to my left. They all looked pretty wiped out, and rightly so, because Veracruz is a lot closer to Guatemala than to the hole in the ground where we were sitting.

"You guys made the trip from way down there? How?"

"Sí," said the oldest, cracking the first smile from any in the group. "We walked, rode in trucks. We just looked for ways to travel." The pride that was on his face was swept aside by the stark reality of a mission that had just ended.

"How old are you?"

"Seventeen, twenty-one, sixteen."

"That's pretty young. Where are your parents?"

The youngest answered in a long-distance whisper, "At home in Veracruz." It was a mix between homesickness and failure. The father-of-four in me took over. "I've got kids older than you, and I would never let them do what you guys are doing! What did your parents say when you told them what your plans were?"

The seventeen-year-old, who seemed to be the quietest, stuffed another fried pork rind in his mouth and considered his thoughts. "We are so poor back at home; we have nothing. My mother cried when I left, but she knows what my life could be like if I could get to the United States." As I have made a living by interviewing people, I have learned to analyze people and their answers while the words are still coming out of their mouths. Though this kid was probably sincere, there seemed to be more going on with him—with all of them.

After all, Veracruz is a major Mexican port city and a popular tourist attraction with the cruise-the-world crowd. Like most places, those truly wanting to work will eventually find the opportunity, although its half million residents have had their share of illegal immigration issues too. Guatemala and Salvador let their poor slip into southern Mexico, and Veracruz saw a glut of people who were willing to work for less than the natives. When Nicaraguans, Panamanians,

These young men had been caught entering the U.S. They were delivered back to Mexico where they were given food and shelter, free phone cards, and an easy chance to step back toward the border once the shadows fell.

and Columbians joined the assault, prices soared and employment for locals crashed. These kids and their families were paying the price for their own brand of illegal immigration.

I studied the boy. His eyes were bloodshot, hair matted, and teeth caked with the remnants of a whole lot of days on the road without a toothbrush. "So jobs are bringing you to America?"

"Sí. And we want to get to know the place—to get ahead in life."

"And are you doing this, in part, because it's an adventure and it's, you know, something you do when you're young, or do you really want to get to America just so you can go to work?"

The twenty-one-year-old butted in, "For everything."

"For everything? So there's a little adventure to it, isn't there?"

"We just want to know." Earlier I had wondered why they didn't just get jobs on a cruise ship and ditch the gig as soon as it hit any U.S. port, but even though the whole Huck Finn lifestyle has a definite allure, the attraction has to get a little old if you keep getting caught.

As we sat together, the Bag O' Rinds made its way to me. The last time I had one of these puppies, drenched in fiery red sauce, was the day I jumped into the crowd of a half million marchers who had taken over the streets of Dallas. I literally felt tears run down my face then, so I was reticent this time, but they offered. I crunched into the circle-eight-shaped delicacy. *Hmm, not bad,* I thought. It's when I tried to speak that I recalled just how hot these things were. My vocal cords coughed and begged for refreshment. As my nose started to run, I neglected my internal screams and went back to the questions.

"And how much money did you pay to get to this point?"

"About two thousand pesos."

"So, two hundred dollars each?"

"Sí."

That's less than half the lowest price anyone had quoted for a single leg of the illegal trip, and since the fees increase the farther south a person starts, I assumed the three adventurers had been on their own since kissing their families good-bye.

"Have you been traveling alone, and if you are poor, how did you get the money?" I asked while moving my microphone to the face of the youngest for an answer.

"Yes, it's just us." Most of the answers I had been getting were usually short and abrupt, and so were his. "Our families gave us the pesos. We call our parents for money."

I surprised them when I laughed out loud, because they were sounding a lot more like my kids and a lot less like three strangers I had just met.

"How are you going to get home now?"

"We have bus fare." The seventeen-year-old boy transitioned from child to adult, midanswer. "We are tired of trying and getting caught, trying and getting caught. So, after so many times, we might go home."

"How many times have you tried to get into America?"

"Two this time."

"How many other times have you tried?"

"Two."

"So, you've been caught. Were you brought to this same resting center when you were stopped the other times?"

"Sí."

I had heard a few times that authorities were cracking down on repeat offenders, and I wanted to see their reaction to the news. "The police are throwing people in jail who keep getting caught. Eventually they're going to throw you guys in jail. Do you know that?"

"Sí."

"Are you afraid of that?"

"No. It's not for our whole life. It might be a couple of days."

"No. They say it's more like six months." I expected a look of shock or at least a little disbelief; not one of them offered anything close.

The middle child jumped in while staring straight ahead—eyes glazed. "Where's the problem in that?"

"That doesn't frighten you?"

"No. We have nothing back at home."

The guy on my far left, the oldest, added, "Life is better in the U.S. We have seen the pictures and heard the stories, and, well, the money is worth more."

"Don't you realize you will have to work hard when you get there?"

"We work harder at home, and we make less money."

"Do you miss your parents? You miss your family?"

All three answered in unison, "Sí."

I looked back at the seventeen-year-old and asked, "How many brothers and sisters do you have?"

"Seven."

"Seven?!" Do your mother and father work?"

"Sí."

"Can they support the whole family?"

"No. Of course not." As he spoke, I thought about the two hundred dollars he had spent to get to this point. That's almost all the wages his mother and father would earn—combined—for about a month. Was he so selfish that he would gladly take the family's living money, or was this the subtle hint I had picked up from him earlier in the conversation—the hint there was more to his story?

Perhaps he didn't want to be here; maybe this wasn't his idea at all. What if he had been seen as one of the greatest hopes for the whole family, perhaps even chosen in a vote as the most likely to earn the most U.S. currency so he could send half his wages back home, like millions of other border crashers do, to the tune of $50 billion a year?

"If you make it to America, what will you do with the money you earn?" I asked.

"Live a life better than we have now." Even though his words were being translated, his tone was sharp—almost angry.

"Will you send dollars back to Veracruz?"

"Well, of course we will."

"Because you want to or because you have to?" With that, the boy tuned me out. I was nonexistent.

"Do you like Americans? Are you afraid of Americans?"

The sixteen-year-old fielded this one. "I've never met them. I haven't made it over there yet."

"Well, my boy, you're meeting one right now. What do you think about me?"

They all looked at each other, then at me, then at each other again, and simultaneously laughed. They stopped. Then, the oldest rifled off some select Spanish words, and they all started laughing again.

"Wait a minute!! Alonzo, what did they say this time?" I smiled in the way we do when we feel like the odd man out—especially when a foreign tongue guarantees that you *are* the odd man.

Alonzo interpreted the words and laughter. "He says, 'Well, you won't take me back with you.'"

"I can't, I can't. Tell them I feel sorry for their condition, and I mean that sincerely. And ask any of the three, before we go—Are they not at all afraid of the coyotes, the banditos, the jackers?"

The oldest, clearly the leader, answered firmly, "All they'll do is take your money from you. You just have to hide your money good."

"You're not afraid that they'll kill you?"

"No, we don't run with them, and we have little they want."

And with that, the interview was over. I had more people to talk to and they had a bus to catch—or did they?

SIETE

MEXICAN BORDER PATROL AND OTHER SIDE-SPLITTING JOKES

After the showdown on the dirt road, the drug lords and coyotes abandoned any interest they may have had in us, and I persuaded our cab driver to cart us pretty much wherever we wanted to go. As he became our *de facto* tour guide, as should be expected, the persuasion came in the form of several Jackson-laden slips of paper.

He stopped the car at the edge of a huge open grazing area most likely owned by the people running the well-fortified ranch about a mile away. Butting up to one section of the ranch was the beginning of a half-wall–half-fence set-up covering this part of the border.

On the other side were Border Patrol and National Guardsmen perched in short towers and inside camps set up on the highest hills of the mountainous region. There they remained twenty-four / seven. It was comforting to know they were watching me as I swept the country-side with my binoculars, though I knew their hands would have been tied had I needed them.

Their shift changes follow typical civilian work schedules, including lunch breaks, which makes it that much easier for the bad guys to gauge their coming and going. That's exactly what we had seen demonstrated earlier in the trip by the coyotes who were preparing to cross their next herd. Our men and women are well trained to be the first level of defense against illegal immigrants and any of the terrorists who may have grander plans than to quietly slip over the border, but I was dismayed that politics or bureaucrats made their routines so easy to track. A case could be made that our elected leaders and their subordinates intentionally mix the two so D.C. can say, "We're doing our best," or some other mumbo jumbo.

Alonzo and I are on the Mexican side of a semi-secure border area. On our side there was no one watching our movements, but to the right of this building—part of a working ranch—U.S. National Guardsmen tracked our every step.

The information the Border Patrol and National Guard gather is relayed from behind their military camouflage, meshing back to a processing station several miles away. There, our agents watch movement via infrared, thermal, and high-definition cameras. Every agent or guardsman that I have interviewed or come to know is not in the least bit confused about their missions, but they also know their task is next to impossible due to the lack of support from their government, foreign leaders, and fellow citizens. Personally, the frustration associated with the catch-and-release program currently used would cause me to look for another line of work, but many of these men and women have been at their posts for decades. Said one, "I know my job, and I do it. I stop as many as I can and have a sense of satisfaction that a few less of them make it—at least on my watch."

I've already taken you into the heart of a U.S. Border Patrol compound and processing station, but to respect what we are working with, we need comparisons, so we checked out a Mexican Border Station. While the agents and guard on our side were watchful and vigilant, the men on the other side resembled Sunday football tailgaters more than law enforcement. The four or five "agents" sat back on ripped and bent plastic picnic chairs—the kind where summertime

The National Guardsmen, a few fresh back from Iraq, were proud to tell us how they had cleaned up and fortified the hillsides to stop nighttime entry. They also demonstrated some pretty cool night vision and heat sensing lenses they use to see everything in the area.

colors are woven in crisscross patterns so the bottom of your legs have the lasting impressions for the rest of the day. A filthy, oversized beer cooler propped up a smashed radio, circa 1982, that somehow still played the thumping Tejana music. The men didn't seem to care about its static-ridden sound because they were too busy stuffing their faces.

A long extension cord ran from the side of the dilapidated brown-and-white trailer that was their patrol station and directly to a hot plate strategically resting within arm's reach. As the men covered their camp with joking and laughter, they examined the pot full of chicken. The taco-making process was nearing completion. The difference between each country's approaches to border protection was stark: one prepared and one partied. This scene of haphazardness was replicated each time I spotted a new Mexican station.

Relaxing in the camouflaged patrol area.

On this day I tried to engage the agents in a dialogue, but the language barrier stopped that idea before I could get through. "Se habla English?" I asked. The reply, a simple head shake, was one I got many times in Mexico. I could understand a regular citizen not knowing English, but the uniformed agents too? What if I really needed some help? My mind raced home. Several miles before a person gets to the border between Arizona and Mexico, the language on the U.S. side shifts to a dual status because our agents are advised to learn Spanish. The courtesy is not reciprocated. The United States is a richer country but, to me, this is another example of the intentionally grave disparity between the two nations' commitments to the border issue and to the idea of fairness. If one country is doing more to bend than the other, I can guarantee it is not the one providing safe harbor and support to coyotes, banditos, and rogue Federales.

A hundred yards or so beyond the Mexican border trailer was a second trailer. It sported a familiar and inviting symbol, the Red Cross. I was curious about their status and stepped in their front door to understand what was up—thinking that I may have missed news of a recent disaster or something. The workers pointed to a big tent across the street and instructed me to look for "the Professor," because only he could answer my questions.

The Professor was introduced as a higher-level employee of the Red Cross, at least a higher level for this remote area. After speaking to him through Alonzo's translations for a minute or two, I learned that he could speak both languages well but preferred the Spanish tongue, so I obliged. "I want to know what you do here. How's this work?" I asked.

Chuckling, the Professor assured me there were no disasters. "I'm responsible for this receiving area. This is where we take in all the unfortunate immigrants which the North Americans send over this way."

"How do they get here?" I asked.

The Professor's face turned somber. "This is, uh, these are people whom the U.S. Border Patrol will release, and then they'll walk into this place, and usually these people are from south of Mexico."

"But why do they come to you? Why don't they just get on buses and go home?"

At a couple inches past six feet, I'm a tall man, but this guy towered over me by at least a half a foot. He gestured wildly with his hands as he attempted to drive home his point, "You are an American, and you don't understand a lot of things."

"Okay, so why not explain it to us?" I said, trying hard to keep my condescending thoughts in check.

"These comrades are people that try to cross to the U.S. in search of work, and they get caught by your law enforcement. Once they come here, we'll feed them, because the U.S. Border Patrol won't."

"After food, what else do you do for them? Do they get medicine and medical care?" I asked.

The Professor pointed to several younger people who sat on the floor of the tent. "We'll take care of their blisters after they have walked ten days in the desert." I could see two things with this guy: he was proud of his efforts, and he detested me and my fellow North Americans for putting these poor, pitiful people through the ordeal. In a roundabout way, the feeling of repulsion was mutual.

Though I knew I wasn't wanted, I had no intention of being set aside by this guy. I moved my microphone closer and asked, "Professor, when you are done feeding and tending to their wounds, and while the border agents over there do what they do best, which is look the other way, what happens next?"

He shrugged off the second part of the question but concentrated on the first, "We try to help them buy their tickets for them to go back to their original homes."

"How many will you help at this station today? A hundred today maybe?" I thought the nodding of his head meant that I was close with my number. "So aren't you wasting your time and Red Cross money, because you know these people will be right back here tomorrow—and the only difference then will be the number of friends they bring with them?"

It was suddenly obvious that my questioning wasn't to his liking, because without saying another word, the Professor turned and walked away. Then, from over his shoulder he set me straight, "A hundred a day? I see a thousand a day!" I couldn't tell if he was proud of the number or if he was trying to rub into my face the fact that this many people would be restored enough to take another stab at a border trip.

One nondescript dot on a map featuring two thousand miles of border sees a thousand people a day—even the least intelligent person can see this math equation leads to an answer that is not sustainable.

This was another crystal clear example of a broken border program and an equally broken government that encourages every bit of it. Who wouldn't repeatedly try to crash the border if the complicit politicians do nothing to stop you? Go. Get caught. Return. Return, not to discipline, but to free food, water, clothing, housing, medicine, and bus fare. Slap a child's hand when he reaches for candy he can't have, and he will learn not to do it again. Apply no pain and he will return as many times as he can.

New parents might want to teach our career politicians a thing or two!

OCHO

HOW I CROSSED THE BORDER—ILLEGALLY

S oon I would learn firsthand just how easy it is to sneak from one country to the other, but before I would get the chance, before an illegal entrant gets the chance, he has to go through a variety of machinations.

It can be as simple as a few kids from Veracruz who try to do it themselves to the more complex coyote-led plan. Most who make the trip choose the latter, because the leader has done it numerous times before. He knows Border Patrol watch schedules, locations, and who on the U.S. side may need a payoff. Besides, when it comes down to it, the law can't catch fifty of them at one time while they run in different directions. In the end, the Law of the Jungle rules: every man for himself. The rules are clear before the trip.

Typically, a crosser knows someone who has done it or tried to, and with a quick introduction, the newest member of the society of illegal immigrants is in the loop. The meeting may be with the actual coyote if he finds one of the smaller operations, but since the under-cover excursions to the U.S. have become a multimillion-dollar business, the small players are getting squeezed out. Either way, in the initial meeting the border crosser is told what is expected. Though I have yet to be allowed in an actual meeting, I have learned from former coyotes and illegal immigrants that it is a very intimidating process, one meant to control the mind and movement of every participant until they land at their drop house. Any deviation from the plan, and the alien is left behind.

After the nonnegotiable price has been set, the leader hands each participant a sheet of paper with a shopping list of things he will need on the multimile, multiday passage. "Have the stuff in your backpack and wait for us to contact you" is the order. The first handler begins securing the three to five coyotes necessary to get the trespasser from point A to point B. The going price in the summer of 2007 was between $1,500 and two grand to get over the border, but the fee can shoot up to as much as $10,000 to $12,000 if the starting point is in southern Mexico or Central America. The immigrant, or *centro,* is usually watched very carefully and guided along the way, because he represents more money to the illegal immigrant machine in the form of actual dollars for the trip and a lot more when kidnapped and held for ransom at a drop house.

While one of my many cabdrivers was driving us through a hotel and housing area, I asked about a rumor that was circulating. "I have heard that these hotels are run by the coyotes. Do they really have that kind of money?" Though I wasn't necessarily looking at the Ritz, the hotels I pointed to looked legitimate, with balconies, posted price rates, and even an occasional coffee shop. The buildings were run-down, with peeling paint and cracked window panes, but compared to the rest of this side of town, they looked somewhat inviting.

"The illegals will come, stay there; they'll get in contact with their family on the U.S. side, or the family on the U.S. side will get in contact with them." My driver pointed at the buildings as he weaved in and out of traffic. I dug my feet into the floorboard as though somehow I might have control of his brakes. "Some people from deeper in Mexico make it this far, so they can rest before going into the United States and over there." He was pointing again as our cab veered toward an oncoming vehicle. He caught himself at the last minute, but didn't stop the tour or his pointing. "Over there is where some coyotes have the people go with their shopping lists so everyone can leave together."

"How many of these hotels are there?" I asked.

"About fifty," he said as though he had personally counted them all. Based on his tour guide abilities, I wouldn't doubt it if someone told me he had. Another proof positive that no one in Mexico cares about the issue was the fact that everyone in the area knew about these locations, yet no one wanted to stop them: the little mayor, policía, citizens—no one.

"Hey Alonzo, since the driver just pointed out fifty hotels and houses the human smugglers use, ask him what would happen if I had you knock on the door and say, 'I'm an illegal, I'm lost, but I was told to come here, you could help me.' What does he think they would do?"

Alonzo looked at me like I was out of my mind, "If I did it?!"

"Yeah, if you did it!" Now, I was mostly joking but, just in case Alonzo was nuts enough to try it, I was going to try to open the door.

Alonzo and the cabbie rattled through their conversation, and finally my translator told me what would happen if we tried it—while the driver stared at me in the rearview mirror. "The cabdriver says they will charge me for the room, and then I'll ask for the coyote, and then he'll say, 'All right. I'll find the coyote for you.' They'll give me the coyote. Process starts."

"So right now, if I dropped you off there, they would let you in? No problems?"

"If I go by myself, yes," Alonzo said while watching me for some sign that I might be kidding. I did my best to keep a straight face.

"Ask him what happens when they find out you're working with 'that crazy American journalist.'"

The driver started laughing almost hysterically, "Oh, boy! Then, you're going to find some trouble. You're going to find some real trouble!"

I laughed with him, and then, in my best deadpan approach, I arched my eyebrow and asked, "Alonzo?"

"Yeah. No. *You're* going to find some trouble, not me!"

"Oh, never mind," I said and asked the cabbie to keep going. "Can you take us to the store where all the people buy the items for their trip?"

"We don't have any of those around here," he said.

"No, that's not what I hear. I've heard that they're everywhere."

"Nope. You would be wrong. They are not everywhere to be found. There are a few, but not over here."

"Come on, man, I wanted to see some of the shops."

"I can give you the shopping list. Usually, in this section of Mexico they'll just tell you to go to the store and give you a list of things to buy."

I wasn't giving up just yet. "I was told on this side that there were actual stores that catered only to illegals and that they have everything right out in the open—in some cases, fake IDs too."

"Yes, those stores do exist, but not here. You can find them in Altar and Sonora because that's where a lot of the people who cross the desert come from."

"Do you have a list?" I asked. "The list of the things that people need to make the trip?"

Again, the driver's eyes connected with mine via the mirror, and I could see he was trying to decide if providing this information would hurt any of his countrymen's plans. Deciding it wouldn't, he ticked off some of the items. "I don't have an actual list on me, but I've seen a few of them. The immigrant will need a backpack, cans of tuna, iodine tablets, bottles of electrolytes, at least a full gallon of water since we're so close to the border, light clothing for the day, and thick clothing for the night, to fight off the cold and the sharp cactus needles, because the people run through the desert at night. There are some other

This is a container of electrolytes usually given to a child who is dehydrated. In the desert, we saw these at every turn.

things, but I can't remember what they are. A lot of times the immigrant will bring other things besides what's on the list."

The driver continued his tour, pointing to tunnels, scouts, communications systems, apartments where coyotes live with buddies—similar to the set-up airline flight attendants use—and even pointed out a couple of drug deals going down, all from the comfort of his shredded and springless seat.

Little did I know, I would soon see the items on his list—and then some!

There it was—the U.S.-Mexico border. I was no more than ten feet away from it and minutes from a major illegal entry sector. Everything

I had been doing and seeing was leading up to this border crossing moment, and when it was done, my investment was six seconds.

It took six seconds for me to walk up to the mangled, antique barbed-wire fence, take one last glance for border authorities, and then climb through from Mexico to America. Obviously, though I wanted to experience the trip in much the same way as one of the invaders, there were certain things I couldn't do. In those instances, I spent a valuable amount of time and effort learning from people who had actually done it. But when it came to actually crossing—I was determined to touch every piece of it.

Though we almost got killed by banditos and had Federales aiming weapons at our heads, I was now standing only feet from the border fence, and it was weird. It all seemed surreal. So many lives change for better or worse, depending on their actions around this little clump of land.

I had spent several minutes walking back and forth along the line just to see what kind of reaction I would get from either side's law enforcement. Earlier in the journey my team and I had been back in America via a checkpoint, and our Border Patrol stopped us a couple of times. I'm sure five guys weaving their Jeep through sand and weed pockets looked a little suspicious, especially since we didn't seem to have any particular destination in mind. The agents were pretty cool about things, and I was up front about my plans. They warned me that banditos would love to grab an American at the border for nothing other than to create headlines by kidnapping someone like me. Snatched. Arrested. Creating an international incident. I walked through each scenario, as I had done numerous times before, and wanted to be sure that poor planning wasn't going to put any one of us into the hands of a band of bad guys.

I thought about the coyote who caught our attention when we

were on the U.S. side. We were in Arizona, near enough to the border that we could see movement in the brush over in Mexico. At first I thought it was a wild animal, because it was just a rustling bush that drew my notice. Then I recognized the outline of a man gesturing to us. We were in no-man's land due to the terrain, and if anything were to happen, our border agents would be useless. The only trail to follow to prove my fate would have been the long, deep lines in the sand made by my dragging and struggling body. I looked at Adam to get his security-minded take. "My guess is he's getting our attention because he's the friendliest unfriendly looking person we've seen. So, as we look at him and talk to him, I'm concerned that we may have people coming from our right or left behind us."

Look at the center of the picture. This Mexican man, who was waiting for his chance to pop over our border, tried his best to lure me to his area. We were later told that he would have been a hero (and paid handsomely) had he been able to kidnap me.

We approached the man from our side of the fence, and Adam called to him, "Where's your other friends?"

I studied the man; he was hiding his face from our lenses and video cameras, which was peculiar since he was still on his side. I managed to catch a glimpse of his scruffy face, dirty white T-shirt, and filthy jeans as he popped out from behind a small desert tree long enough to shout, "Viva la Mexico," but that was it. His yelling caught me by surprise, and all I could do was laugh. *Viva Mexico?! How goofy is that?* I thought. Some of the guys thought he lived in the junky two-story house we could see through the tree limbs and bend in the earth, but he had all the markings of the coyotes the Border Patrol had warned us about. I stepped carefully.

My eyes shifted between the guy—as he kept asking me to come over and talk to him—and the *casita* a few hundred yards away. The latter had a few broken-down cars scattered in its front and side yards, paint that had lost its color years earlier, and covered windows that refused to offer even the slightest welcome. There were at least three small, decrepit trailers off to one side, and the path and trash leading to their doors suggested they were still being used. "More places to crash while the occupants wait for nightfall" is all I could consider, as righteous anger covered my thoughts. How is America supposed to stop a corrupt country that either helps or allows aid to lawbreakers at every possible juncture? The best gambler in the world will confirm that it is nearly impossible to beat a casino if the deck is stacked; the same holds true for countries engineering a silent invasion.

The casita's second floor shade moved enough to show a person. As I trained the lenses of my binoculars at the window, I saw a glare and a reflection that looked like the person or persons on the top floor were checking me out with a telescope or lenses of his own. In an instant I felt violated—as if my group were the only one that could

How is America supposed to win the border battle when houses like this operate in plain sight on the Mexican side? Illegal immigrants will hole up at places like this until the coast is clear.

investigate or spy or do whatever it was that we were doing. As I swept the area with my eyes and mind, there was no doubt that this was the perfect safe house for any person ready to make the jump from one country to the next—it was so close to the border. I wondered why someone hadn't investigated the property and then grinned sadly—this was Mexico, after all.

The Mexican man kept doing everything he could to lure one of us over to where he set up a makeshift base. Then he shouted, "Are you Border Patrol?"

"No," I yelled back. "Come talk to me; I want you on the radio. You can stay on the Mexican side. We'll stay on the American side. We could be friends." I flashed a "You can trust us" smile.

He moved a little closer, "No camera!"

I had Alonzo tell him the camera was off, which was true, though I had one of the other guys shooting some footage, and I certainly kept the microphone on. Since he could be planning to snag one of us or break over the border, I figured I had a right to mislead him a little.

When he felt satisfied the camera was off, he stepped a little closer but stayed far enough away that everyone was yelling to be heard. "Señor, what are you doing out here?" I tried to get him to trust us a little.

"What am I doing?" he asked combatively. "I was going over there, but I seen you guys."

What are the odds of our stepping into this nondescript area just as this guy was trying to cross—in broad daylight? I started laughing. "You were heading for America?"

"Sí. So could you please leave? I need to get over to your side."

"You're not a coyote?" I shouted.

"No."

"How do we know you are not lying? Come closer to the fence, and let's talk."

He laughed at me. "If you want to talk to me, then come over here. Come to where I am."

The hilly area and about forty or fifty yards of separation told me he could have people waiting at his feet—to be seen only when it was too late.

"I don't think I'm going to do that," I responded. He let out a sigh of exasperation and suddenly bolted for the horizon with no advance warning, just as the group of coyotes had done in my first encounter with them. Was he a coyote or simply one of many border crossers? What would have happened had he lured one of us to his side? I didn't have these answers, but we felt a new, subtle respect that the border was a breeding ground for danger and that this time around we had dodged an incident that could have had untold consequences.

Two vantage points tell the same story—border protection is non-existent in most areas. Notice the poorly maintained wire fence on the Mexican side. It has been completely cut away so entrants can move swiftly and in large numbers! The U.S. side has railroad ties that are meant to keep trucks from merely driving right through.

I thought of that earlier encounter as I paced and scanned the territory for border agents. My pockets were intentionally empty of money and documents. If I got caught, I wanted the same treatment another illegal trespasser would get—though, like them, I hoped to pass uneventfully.

The barrier between the two countries was two-pronged. On the Mexican side was mangled, broken, snipped, rusted, and defanged barbed wire erected decades ago. In most cases there was little reason to spread wide the steel in order to pass, because the strands were permanently set that way due to the years of wear and tear and zero upkeep by the country that erected the fence.

Next came a gap of about two feet; this I suppose was international territory or a DMZ like the space between East and West Germany—

Part of the cut fence. "This is just too calculated," I thought.

without the machine guns, watch towers, or manpower to keep watch.

Then, it was America's turn to provide a fence that looked more like a fortified crash test site, one a test car might ram to see how good its safety features are. The car would lose. Every time. Ours was constructed of thick, crisscrossing, *iron railroad ties* that were bolted and welded in place. I climbed up to an unobstructed ridge; sure enough, it kept going—as far as the eye could see. I later learned from border agents that the railroad-tie creation was developed to stop trucks, busses, and all other vehicles loaded with drugs, guns, or people from simply driving from one side to the other. There are ample other places where that can happen.

As I prepared to climb through, under, or over, I noticed the types of trash were different from what I had seen in earlier Mexican fields and some U.S. desert trails I had scouted. Instead of backpacks and water bottles, the piles consisted of Gatorade bottles, limited articles of clothing, cigarette packages, beer bottles (a *lot* of beer bottles), and wrappers from snack foods. I surmised that the travelers must have been feeling more relaxed and comfortable, believing their journey had ended and their only concern was how quickly nightfall would come.

The U.S. border fence—made up of soldered and bolted railroad ties stretches into the horizon.

Later in my expedition, I would encounter tons of other debris, so only one of two things could have been in play at the crossing point. Either the trespasser knew he had a truck waiting within walking distance in a small nearby U.S. city, or he was about to confront the biggest shock of his life when the cockiness of a trip completed turned into an endurance race or rotting bones in a sun-baked Arizona desert.

I glanced up from the trash at my feet, gave one last cursory check of the area for banditos or agents, and then took off for the waiting fence just yards away. Sand stung my eyes and face as a wind spout kicked in. I inched past knee- and shoulder-height trees, down into a gully, and landed at my destination. I'll admit that my heart was in my throat as I reached the no-turning-back zone, knowing that agents could be right around the corner. I walked through the already-cut

I told my crew and my radio audience I was going to cross back into the U.S. just like millions of illegal aliens before me.

A Latino newspaper was monitoring my movements and had called the Border Patrol to inform them of my plans.

I told my team they did not have to follow me, but to bail me out if I got arrested!

My entry took all of six seconds. Six seconds!

Looks serene doesn't it? Within a few hours night would fall and this area alone would see hundreds of people climbing over and under the fence. I should know—I was out there with night vision goggles.

wire fence, crawled under the railroad ties, and popped up in America.

Six seconds and I was home. It was almost anticlimactic. In fact, once I realized no one was waiting for me with guns or cuffs, I went back into Mexico and came back again. And again. It was just too easy.

Since I was broadcasting our efforts back to my radio audience, I shared these thoughts: "As I am now walking in Arizona, in a brisk wind, in the dusk, I have decided that I am going to change jobs. This radio stuff is for the birds. I'm buying a casita in Mexico, and I am going to start delivering human property to the border fence—nothing wrong with that—and let them get across. Man. I'm an idiot. I could've been making all this money all these years. I'm also a stinking idiot for continuing to believe that the Mexican government cares or that my country is going to do anything about it. God bless the border agents—too little, too late to ever have a chance."

The frustration level brought on by this leg of the journey hit its peak with those few brief seconds. But, as I was soon to find out, this was nothing compared to the things I was about to see.

NUEVE

300 BIKES IN THE DESERT?

There is no comparing the day desert versus the one at night; your feet may be planted in the exact same place, but you are in a different universe altogether when the shadows cease to exist. I have heard this reference many times through the years, but it took the actual experience to drive home the point. Add the location we chose for this night's sleep, and an evening on Mars seemed like a better choice. We were in no-man's land somewhere in Arizona, and something told me my exploits on the Mexican side were just a foreshadowing of things to come.

While the terrain was still being bleached by the blazing sun we scouted the territory in teams of two and soon realized others had been here too—were they watching us as we looked around? There was just no way to be sure. Off in the distance, about two hundred yards away, was a gully that had been carved by years of flash flooding. In fact, there are places in the desert that fill up like a swimming pool after the briefest period of rain, and if you get caught up in one, you will drown. It sounds weird to think a person can drown in the desert, but these gullies are the traps that remind you it can happen.

I climbed down through a vast eroded area to get to the bottom and came upon my first tracks of the day, three sets. The first belonged to two-legged creatures. From the appearance of the dirt, there were several, and it wasn't long ago that they had congregated where I stood.

The second set belonged to four-legged coyotes, the ones with tails and sharp teeth—which I suppose could also describe the ruthless wilderness guides too. There were a few of these tracks in the outlying area; Gary and I surmised they may have been attracted by the smell of food and probably sat on the perimeter, waiting for a chance to pounce.

The marks of the third were different—ones that I didn't understand at first. Something with a fair amount of weight had left a deep, long, and narrow trail. It resembled snake tracks, but they slither back and forth and not in a straight line. These tracks were many and straight, and Gary and I were both at a loss to determine what would leave them in the middle of the Arizona desert.

As I climbed out, I noticed that the side of the sand- and dirt-filled gully had been hollowed out in a couple places. Stepping closer, it was clear we were in a makeshift holding area. Here some family had made a shelter from the heat of the day or, maybe, to trap the heat for the night. Inside were a couple of empty cans of beans, crudely opened by a knife or screwdriver, and over in a little partially covered hole was a backpack—the first I'd found on the trip—and I stopped to wonder what kind of story it could tell me. Little did I know there would be plenty of opportunities to analyze many more trash heaps for their stories.

We popped back into the Jeep while Gary pointed out the numerous snake and scorpion holes—they were everywhere. Moments earlier I had been obliviously surrounded by them, but now that I knew what they were, I just wanted him to step on the gas and get me out of there. He laughed the hearty laugh that a twenty-five-year survivalist veteran and river rafting captain would be expected to offer up. *I'm going to die out here,* I thought, as Gary's devilish smile flashed broadly.

We continued to investigate when we got back to the area we had chosen for base camp, and the third set of tracks suddenly made sense. There, behind the old wall of an even older building were bicycles—hundreds of bicycles: every color, shape, size, and condition. "Bicycles in the desert? What's this about?" I asked of the person who allowed us to wander her multithousand-acre property.

"The illegals use those for a lot of things. Some try to ride across the desert, but that doesn't last long. A few put their belongings on them and then push the contraption until it becomes impossible. But, mostly, they're used for drugs." This quiet rancher had seen tens of thousands of uninvited visitors, so her story was simple and emotionless.

"How do you use a bike for drugs?" I wondered aloud.

"If you look at that big stack over there, you will notice something most have in common. Go ahead, boy, take a look."

"They're missing handlebars and most are spray painted black."

"Sure thing. The drug dealers take two bikes, rip off their handlebars, and connect them with two-hundred- or three-hundred-pound pallets of drugs, and as partial payment for desert passage, two or three illegal aliens will push the bikes into the U.S. They paint them black so there are no reflections for border trucks or planes." One of the ranch hands explained later that pickups would blow into the area in the middle of the night, take the load, and leave the bikes and people behind. The Border Patrol can't stop what it never sees. I was still days away from visiting the Border Patrol's drug evidence room, so the enormity of what I had stumbled upon didn't completely resonate.

Later, I would think deeply about the toys-turned-crime-machines and about all the people and pain attached to them. But now evening was calling, and I hoped sleep was too.

As dusk moved in, we used our feet to spread the sand until it was level, and then threw our sleeping bags on the ground, lined up side by side, and systematically put other essentials in place. For me that included a small Mag flashlight, my mace/tear gas canister, and a six-inch hunting knife that could gut a man with a couple flicks of the wrist. At least I would have a fighting chance if I had to protect myself.

Night arrived. The moon was huge, and though it did provide some light, when you are away from city lights, you realize how dark

Some of the hundreds of well used and worn bikes tossed into the Arizona desert after they haul drugs and contraband to awaiting vehicles. Handlebars have been painted black to minimize the sun's glare and to hide them from the watchful eyes of agents in planes and helicopters above.

night really gets. I pointed my Mag at my sleeping bag to be sure nothing had climbed on or in it, unzipped it, and ran my hand quickly through the fabric for the same purpose. I climbed in, finished a few running conversations with the guys, and felt exhaustion sweep over me. Here I was, a mostly city slicker talk show host, bedding down in the midst of snakes, coyotes, scorpions, and more, and all I wanted to do was sleep. That was a short-lived plan.

When you are in the middle of an area full of tracks from aliens, bandits, and drug runners, the ears hear and the mind examines everything, which provides for a less-than-restful night's slumber. It was actually very funny; every time there was movement or a sound of any kind, our heads all popped up like puppy dogs do: "Okay. Did you

Rattlesnakes. Scorpions. Coyotes—the human and animal kind—we are oblivious to most of them. Just a few more minutes rest on this hard desert ground!!!

hear that?" "Yeah, I heard it. Did you hear that?" Each of us repeated those words far too many times that night.

I went to bed afraid of snakes, thinking, *Because of the desert's night chill, one of those freakin' things is gonna slither over to my heat, crawl into my bag, and eat me, and in the morning they will find me dead.* If that's all I thought about earlier, now all I could consider was the kind of trouble the human animal might be planning.

The sound of a muffled snore killed the silence. I squinted to see that Alonzo was gone—out cold. Rob was next, and then, apparently I slipped off, because I was startled by Adam asking, "What was that?" What he heard was kind of a *pfff* sound—the noise the lips make when air slips out just before a snore develops. "Uh, I think it was me. Sorry." And with that I was out again.

A few minutes later and we were at it again. This time I saw Rob's head up and his neck arched back because he heard something. Adam—responsible for my safety—was braced on the other side of me. Adam was motionless and quiet and moving a millimeter every ten minutes at the most. He was in his stealth mode—the kind that guarantees you won't see or hear him. As a Marine sniper, this talent is hard-earned; the truly good ones can take half a day to crawl a few yards and can move right under your feet and you won't know it.

Okay. Something's up, I thought. My eyes refused to focus, and all I really wanted to do was rub them. But I knew if those guys were immobile as scarecrows, I had to be so as well. All three of us, senses on high alert, stayed braced as we watched and waited. After half an hour or more, with my head propped on my hands, I watched as Rob's head slipped a little; then it was down. Moments later, Adam dropped his too. So I thought, *Okay, false alarm. We're okay.* Back to sleep.

Then it happened again, ten minutes or an hour later—no idea. I just knew it was pitch black outside, and this time it was Adam alone who scoured the landscape to assess our risk. "Are you going to stay awake all night, Son?" I asked.

"Over in that direction," he whispered. "Shh." I could barely see his body, let alone the direction he was pointing out with his head tilt, but if he thought someone was nearby, then I believed him. "Get the NVGs" (Night Vision Goggles), he ordered, knowing that I had put them between us, and they were closer to me.

Several days earlier, while I shopped for trip necessities, more than a few people laughed at me for picking up military-strength NVGs, but now, as the noises grew more likely to be human caused, I was the hero for thinking of them. The speed at which I picked them up and handed them to Adam seemed like fast-forward compared to his ultraslow-motion movements as he popped the cover and flipped the power switch. Unless a person was right next to us, he never would have found us based on our movements, because there weren't any. I had an all new respect for the patience of military men and women.

After he came up empty, Adam passed the NVG to me for fresh eyes and a better angle. Suddenly his guttural whisper caused my pounding heart to try to dig its way out of my chest. I've heard of "fight or flight," but at that moment I'm not sure that I had an option; being paralyzed will do that to you! "Movement. There's movement to your south. Check it out, now." Adam brought me back to the present with a whisper so low a dog would struggle to hear it. "Take a look over there; is it the two- or four-legged variety?"

I put the NVG back to my left eye and scanned back and forth. The goggle, a sophisticated piece of equipment most of us recognize from the green television footage of Baghdad's early assaults, uses the ambient light of even the darkest night to give the viewer the sensation of broad daylight. "I've got something."

"What do you see?" Adam asked again. "Two or four legs?"

"I don't know what we call it out here, but back at home I would call it a cat." I laughed as I said it.

"So there's a cat out here in the middle of nowhere; that's all you've got?!" He was frustrated that we had wasted what seemed like hours on nothing. We dropped our heads to take another stab at sleep, only to have the same scene play out at least another half dozen times. We grew more irritated each time.

At about 3:30 AM, the pitch-black desert setting put us on edge again with a different kind of start. Adam was on alert again, ready to spring into aggressive action. That wasn't new, but this time he was certain the movement was human. "Are you sure?" I queried quietly. "Which way?"

"To your left," he muttered. As an aside, he knew he had to say left or right because he knows if someone says north, south, east, or west, I am completely lost right out of the gate. My wife says I'm "directionally handicapped" and has often kidded that I should apply for one of those wheelchair parking stickers. It really is pretty bad. "Now! To your left. Look!"

I squinted and then cast my eyes in every direction, but I wasn't seeing anything. Then I smelled a very familiar odor. Cigarettes. "Do you smell that?" I asked.

"Yeah, that's what woke me up." He whispered even lower than before.

"Really? We're wasted from exhaustion, and tobacco smoke woke you up?" It was a little unbelievable to me, because I was taught that odors are the last thing that will wake a sleeping person unless it's something powerful, like smelling salts. No matter; I was happy his nose worked.

"Yeah. It had to be, like, just way out there, but I smelled it. A hint of cigarette smoke, and then it smelled like an ashtray. So I knew it had to be close; I guess, whatever it was, they put it out. I don't know, but I smelled it, and I wasn't sure, you know, if we had other people out here besides—"

"Right. Besides us." The interruption was set in motion by adrenaline as my brain gripped the situation. We were multiple miles from civilization, so the odor coming from our left dropped humans too close for comfort—in the middle of the night. His words were more deliberate as he turned his head in the other direction, "Alert! To your right."

At first I thought I was seeing flashlights—high-powered flashlights. "What was that?!" Every muscle in my body was ready to jump as the lights went on and off—like someone was giving a signal.

"I think those are trucks. I think those are vehicles," he exclaimed.

"No way."

"Just watch." His voice grew more certain. And then, they came closer and brighter, and suddenly we could hear the sound of rocks and gravel hitting the wheel well of the unidentified vehicle. "Why would a truck, or trucks, be out here?" I wondered.

But, there they were—two trucks—white. I could see them as they passed within twenty feet of our little set-up. I arched my back and neck to see all I could without completely exposing my location to the oncoming lights. *Anybody driving out here at this time of night has to be running on the other side of the law,* I thought.

Their fast speed signaled they had been here before and knew when to turn and when to slow down—two things they weren't even beginning to do now. Within seconds, the pickups blew past us—kicking dust everywhere. "If they see us, it could be problematic," I whispered to Adam, surprised that our three other team members weren't roused at all.

They were gone just as soon as they arrived, one—two—ten football fields away. The red lights flashed as they hit the brakes. Since I was making this trip to get to all the stories of the illegal immigrant, I wanted to jump up and run—quietly—to see what they were up to. My son and security expert stopped that idea before I had the chance to finish it. "We've got eyes on, so we'll watch from right here," he said, as he shoved the binoculars into my chest.

Just as they were becoming dots on the horizon the trucks stopped. Dead. A few men climbed out and walked to one of the many old fences that ran through the desert. It was difficult to determine exactly what they were doing, but it appeared as though they were fiddling with the chains holding the gates shut. Soon, the gates swung open, and the trucks entered and disappeared.

The next day, as Adam and I shared what everyone else had slept through, we took the Jeep out to see what they may have been doing. There we found numerous tracks made by feet and bicycle tires—and freshly cut chains that a landowner had used to keep his gates secure.

Since more than a million people illegally penetrate our borders, and 40 percent of them come via the Tucson sector, there is little doubt the sights, sounds, and smells that night belonged to people who would have hurt us if they'd had any idea how close we actually were.

Thank God we were quiet, motionless, and reserved that night in the desert, because with drug money on the table, and our remote location, any kind of confrontation could have easily ended in disaster.

But we were not immune to potential disaster—it was waiting just down the road.

DIEZ

DEATH'S EMOTIONAL DRAIN

It's called "Dead Man's Tree." With those few words my guide, Bob, from the Arizona Minutemen, had my undivided attention.

"Is that a figurative or literal 'dead'?" I asked.

"This is a tree that, at the first part of one of our operations, we found a guy that had died probably twenty-four hours or so before. His head was over here at the stump of the tree; his feet were down across where you're standing right now." Bob was matter-of-fact as he drew an imaginary chalk outline in the sand mixed with weeds under one of the many mesquite tree varieties found in the great Southwest.

"He just crawled under the tree and died? Was he hurt—did he just give up and die?"

"Yeah. We think he had a broken leg. He had two tourniquets— one below the knee and one above the ankle."

"Was he wearing boots, tennis shoes, or something else, and were they on or off?" It sounded like a good question when it rattled in my head.

"He had one boot off, off his good leg, that we think was his good leg, and the boot was underneath him, and—"

"Why would he do that?

"Uh, who knows? When you die out here, sometimes you do funny things. I can tell you this—he died of exposure."

And with this short exchange I again saw—firsthand—how ruthless and uncompassionate the coyotes can be. The injured person knows he's in trouble and hopes for just a little time. If he's traveling with family, they are no doubt begging for a morsel of help and understanding, but these forty or fifty people are nothing more or less than cattle to him. The callous leader is not about to slow down the pace for one wounded or infirm—he needs the cash from the many.

As I began my movements through the Arizona desert and on toward home I faced my first hard dose of reality. On the ground, just to my right, was the outline of a man's body. He had been left behind by his coyote after hurting his leg. The man died while waiting for someone—anyone—to help him.

Why is it, then, that when I say we need to do something about the massive invasion, I am the one who is labeled as having no compassion? At least, if the people are stuck in their own country, they won't be suffering to the point of death in mine.

"Well, he had to be left by the entire group, then? So, at some point, the coyotes say, 'You're either moving with us or you're dying here, because we're not waiting,' and everyone else just lets it happen." I was beginning to get an idea how the crime against humanity worked.

"I don't even think they say that. I think they just leave," Bob said. "Just get up and go."

The Minutemen are U.S. citizens who are tired of the lies, games, and politics presented by Washington. Following the current laws, they do whatever they can to spot illegals at the border and stop them on our soil. From what I saw, they work closely with law enforcement. Though this kind of group has a long and powerful history of service to America, they are currently under fire in the U.S. because some liberals and left-leaning media groups suggest they step outside the law. "You guys are taking some heat; some even refer to you as 'vigilantes.' Is this unfair, and what is your policy if you had seen the man under the tree before he died?"

Bob replied, "Sure, their assessment is unfair—and wrong—but how do you fight that stuff? Mike and I are both on the search-and-rescue team, and that's part of our jobs, as we see it—to help people like this."

I looked down again at the place where a stranger lost his life. "The sad part—there's a life that was lost—"

Mike, our second guide, interjected, "If we would have been there a day or so earlier we would have probably found him, because this is one of our posts right down there."

Though signs are clear, in English and Spanish, fresh tire track surrounded us on every side with evidence of numerous people walking to vehicles that would whisk them off to America—the land of plenty—and drop house horrors.

Mike and Bob are retired men who volunteer their time and operate at their own expense in an effort to somehow slow the ocean rumbling in our direction. They are fairly inconspicuous, with gray beards, walkie-talkies, and canteens, though their requisite sidearms would probably startle the faint-of-heart ideologue. Their grandfatherly, quiet mannerisms didn't make them seem like the vigilantes the news media had made them out to be, that's for sure.

I stopped him. "Mike, but at the same time, you and I both know, he's hiding out. He's trying to get into the general population of America. If he sees you, he's ducking. He probably saw you guys go by thirty times and he's like, 'No way. That guy's going to get me.'"

"Yeah, but they need to change that attitude. Basically, when they get to the point where they can't function anymore, they need to get help. We'll give them that help while handing them over to the Border Patrol."

I know—U.S. citizens who are fed up with the constant encroachment will get all the blame for trying to stop the illegal aliens from coming in, but at the end of the day, five groups are responsible, and we're not included: (1) the illegal himself; (2) the coyote; (3) the fellow travelers; (4) America, for keeping the door open; but most important, (5) Mexico. If the dead man's home country would get with the program and shut down the borders and do its part, Mexico wouldn't have killed that guy. America didn't kill that guy. Mexico and those who are complicit in this kind of crime are the murderers. His death is on their heads. Like so many other times during the trip, I felt my anger bubbling to the surface. Bob, Mark, and my team watched me as I was visibly shaking; the senseless death had rocked my world. It wouldn't be the last time.

Two thousand fellow humans have been found in all stages of death in the Arizona deserts, and another fifteen to twenty thousand are wandering through the cacti, thorns, and small trees at any given time. I looked around. *The population of a small town is out here with me right now.* I wondered if I would see any of them along the way. To put it in a better perspective, in March 2007 the Tucson Sector turned away fifty-six thousand illegal immigrants. When one is caught, the others scatter; so how many did we miss? How many was I missing as I scanned the terrain?

As I gazed down at the floor of the desert, I called for Bob to come over to where I stood. "Explain the tracks down here."

Bob bent down and examined just one of the many near my feet. "These tracks are fresh. It's real windy today, and it's dusty here, so tracks like these usually disappear within moments of making them. We just picked them up in the last few yards."

I knew what that meant; the travelers had just left the place where I was standing.

"Is there a chance that a while ago when I thought I heard somebody yell "down" or "duck" or "move," they could have come around this corner? When we were going one way, looking, they came around this way?"

"Entirely possible. These prints are minutes old."

It was disturbing to think eyes were checking me out. We were the ones in a vulnerable spot, since they would have the drop. I wasn't so concerned about the families; it was the banditos. Their reputation as ruthless has been earned for a reason. I felt better knowing that we had guns and we all knew how to use them. We may have left the weapons behind when we went into Mexico, since it's illegal for a common person to own a gun there, but we were back in America now. Unlike our southern neighbor's citizens, we get to carry weapons.

"Hey Bob," I called out as we walked away, "do they have spotters watching us?"

"Yes, they do. They have scouts. Sometimes scouts go up the front; they see somebody, they'll come back, warn the entire group. They'll do a detour or they'll stop, or whatever."

I looked around and then, with no advance notice, took off running up the little hill in front of us. I thought I would try my hand at the element of surprise and see if my fast-moving presence might spook one or more into the open. If they were surrounding me, they did a great job of hiding, because the only movement in the area belonged to a cactus mouse as she ran for her hole.

It was a shock to the system to be standing in the wilderness, with no civilization or help for many miles, and to see hundreds of footprints branching out in every direction. Even though I have seen the same pictures on Fox News or NBC, where the illegal aliens are running in large numbers through our borders by cover of night, until I saw the proof up close, it just didn't compute. Anger, sadness, perplexity, curiosity, and about twenty other emotions hit me all at once as I looked at the variety of children's and adult's prints.

Up ahead it got worse.

There we came upon the first of many holding areas; these actually represented the smallest and most nondescript of any that I would see, but for my first exposure, they still had a major impact.

Under a small tree I found the place where three or four dozen people must have stopped to catch their breath. Quietly, they left their lives for strangers like me to wander into and dissect. Glass, baby bottles, and tequila bottles were semiburied in the sand.

I moved one of the tequila bottles with my foot, and Bob yelled from behind me not to pick it up. "Diseases," he said. "And do you know the rest of the story on the booze? Do you know how many U.S. citizens drunk Mexican drivers kill in America every day? More than twelve people a day. And if you can't make it up here without drinking, you're pretty damn likely going to be driving on our highways and drunk and kill somebody."

I moved away and on to the next trash-strewn areas.

Every ten to fifteen yards displayed yet another water jug, backpack, blown-out tennis shoe, or shirt literally tossed off and left behind. And tuna cans everywhere. It took a few minutes before I realized the aliens would pack several cans of tuna to pop open and eat on the go to avoid the bother or light of a nighttime fire. In this section alone there must have been four or five hundred of them—tossed aside with the rest of the junk. It was unimaginable to me that some people could be this desperate, but the proof was everywhere.

Just as evident was the vast number of pieces of broken fences,

We all laughed at the sign! There, out in the middle of absolutely nowhere, the U.S. government felt it needed to erect a "no dumping" sign! Right around the corner we would step into more than 25 tons of junk left by illegal aliens.

There, with my hat, boots, front-loading hydration pack, tape deck, and binoculars I paused to wonder what would cause people to drop everything they wore or carried and run. "How do you just discard everything you have left?" I wondered.

many ripped up as soon as they were erected or repaired. In many cases, the trespassers would kick the wood post until it broke and use it as a tool to spread the barbed wire wide enough for multiple people to pass through swiftly. Sometimes they would hollow out the dirt and sand from under the fence; once it was twelve to eighteen inches deep, all but the most rotund passer could simply roll from one side to the other and get on with the trek.

"Hey Bob," I said, swamped by a sea of trash, "take a look at these sweaters. Obviously, they would be fresh crossers, because we're still very chilly at night. So they've been told on the southern border, 'Make sure that you've got something to take care of you at night.' They get here, and during the course of the day I wonder if they're thinking, 'Okay. It took me four or five days to get to this point. I'm close to

"Oh, the humanity!"

civilization. I'm just tossing off whatever I don't need. I'll be home by tonight,' or 'I'll be to wherever I'm going by tonight.'"

"Yeah, it could be that. It could be they get hot and when they're hot they throw the things off. They could have things out of their backpacks and the coyote says, 'Go,' and you either leave the stuff there or you get left, so how many of these people are actually forced to leave some of their stuff behind?"

What an existence—on both sides of the border. Think about it: On one side they've been told, "Go after the shopping list. Buy everything that you're supposed to buy on this list, things like clothes, water, specific easy-to-eat food, backpacks"—all the things we were seeing.

The literal list provided in Mexico runs for almost a full page, and once the illegals put it all together, they go to their homes or a hotel and wait for a quick knock at the door or the magic phone call that says, "We're leaving." Once contacted, they have to grab what they have and run. If they are not ready, they risk being left behind or leaving without everything on the list, which can be deadly.

But then, when they get to the U.S. side, they're hustled and herded. "Hurry up and walk. Hurry up and run. Stop. Drink. Stop. Go to the bathroom. Stop. Eat." And then they're told, "All right, get going. Now, now, now, now!" And they just drop everything in the desert. And they permit this kind of treatment because they have heard about the Dream that is America, and they want a piece of it.

Bob watched as a couple of us prepared to climb between the barbed-wire fence. "Don't cut yourself, because they could cut themselves too, and then you've got blood, blood transfer. You can get AIDS, hepatitis, and who knows what else."

We had already been stepping carefully, but had never even considered that we might pick up a disease from a fence. Every little thing, every single step, just seemed too important—too real.

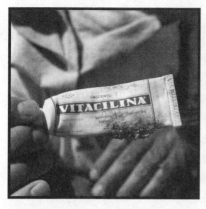

This tube is meant for diaper rash but crossers will also use it as skin protection against sun and wind.

The uniform is U.S. army issued. I have often wondered how it ended up in a mound of discarded waste from illegal aliens.

I was rummaging through the leftovers when a little bottle fell out of one of the many plastic bags the aliens use to make the trip. A bottle of moisturizer. It seemed surreal that at one moment I was thinking about dying of AIDS or hepatitis, and now I had to consider the mind-set of someone who would stow skin care in her very limited bag. I poked a little more and found hair conditioner, a full bottle of shampoo, some mousse, and other standard makeup items. Was this a person careless in her packing, or so sure she would make it that she wanted to look pretty when she met her friends and family already waiting for her? My emotions conflicted between wonderment and rage.

It's fascinating the way the coyotes manipulate their flock. According to many witnesses I spoke with, if the young man in charge of passage believes he is running behind the timetable set for him, he will tell his people they are less than a mile away from an awaiting truck, which causes most people to abandon their belongings in favor of a swifter arrival at the destination. What they soon learn is that once again they have been deceived, and they can still be ten, fifteen, or even twenty miles from the pickup location. But now they travel with nothing, and even a short distance is enough to kill.

Many acres in the Arizona desert are working ranches and ranges, some of them owned by the state, so it wasn't unusual to come across watering holes or tanks where livestock or horses stop to drink.

The ones we saw were dry and cracked, so I could imagine the broken spirit of the traveler who long ago ran out of water but was holding out hope because the leader said, "A place for water is just ahead." As they see the tank from a distance, their hearts leap, and then they plunge just as quickly when they realize it offers nothing. To borrow a line from one of my team members, "It has to completely take the wind out of their sails when they find no water." The location where I was standing may have represented the difference between someone's living and dying.

But what if the hole had water? Could they drink it?

"It's nasty stuff. Cows wade in here—whatever you imagine goes on here. It's so dark you can't even see through it. I mean, so opaque—" Bob interjected.

I studied the area, and the best comparison I could think of was pools on the ranches and farms I had seen while growing up in the Midwest, complete with thick, green scum on top and animals wading in while urinating and defecating. "Do they bring iodine tablets or anything similar to process the water?" I asked Bob and Mike.

"They're just scooping it up. I'm sure they bring some purifying agent—some of them—but most of them, no. They just take whatever they can get."

"That's one sick hole, man," I said.

"Yeah. It's bad news. That's another reason why most of them are sick when they get up here," Mike added.

I thought about it all for a brief moment. "Maybe it's a blessing that it's completely empty."

"Yeah. They may live longer. Diarrhea will do you in a hell of a lot faster than anything else." Bob kicked his boots in the dust bowl as he answered.

Included with the items tossed aside were numerous plastic bottles typically used by athletes in the U.S. "Maybe the electrolytes that we saw earlier—the little containers of electrolytes—maybe those have something to do with this."

I scraped the crusty top of the bottle to see if there was any moistness underneath. There wasn't. "If you get diarrhea out here, you're wiped out. I mean, that's it. That's the end of it."

Gary had seen some of this before in his nature trips. "The predominant danger in an area like this is cattle feces that contain giardia. Giardia has about a two-week incubation period inside the intestine before it becomes a problem. So, they would actually drink their water, get refreshed, and be out of here before the onset of the disease."

"What I think I'm hearing you say, if it's two-week incubation, Gary, is that means they've made it to Phoenix, Tulsa, Flagstaff, or Chicago or wherever, and now they're sick. And this is a sickness that can only be fixed with antibiotics, right? So, they're immediately going to our doctors, I would imagine?"

"That is correct," Gary answered, sounding very much like a professor on the matter.

"And I would have to imagine that if they're carrying any kind of diseases with them, and they don't get the medical attention they need, other people are just picking them right up after them."

"Exactly."

Another reason my health care costs so much, I thought.

Just then, Mike reached down and picked up a weather-worn ski mask.

"What the heck is that?"

"Some bad stuff. This is a drug guy," Mike said.

"How do you know that?"

"They're [the ski masks] always black, and they dress in black—they carry drugs."

I was certain this was another urban legend. "The kind that you'd see from a PLO terrorist or a mugger? But, again, how do you know?"

Mike followed up, "Yep. Yep, that's right. That's what I think of when I see them too. We've been told by illegal immigrants, law enforcement, and Border Patrol that the masks are used by two groups: people trying to avoid slashes in their faces from tree branches and cactus thorns and by drug runners who don't want to be recognized." He waved his finger in a direction over my shoulder, "There is another one there on the ground."

Bob completed the thought. "A lot of time they'll force the people that they're bringing to carry the drugs, basically; but if they're dressed all in black like this, it means they're hired by somebody else and they're dressed all in black and they don't want to be photographed, so that's why they wear the mask over their face."

"And how often are you finding these masks out here?"

"All the time," Bob said. "You'll see a lot of them before the day's over."

How right he was. Every camp, hole-up site, and dried-up ravine stored at least one. With the millions of dollars in drugs coming into America via this one sector, I now believed the story. The images of these masks, with eyes and mouths crudely cut out by pocket knives, lingered in my mind as we hiked.

I thought I had seen everything after walking through so many resting points, but I think I slipped into a state of shock when we walked through a field of cactus and low-hanging desert trees and up a ridge. There, for as far as I could see, were mounds and piles and more mounds of tossed belongings. It was the first and largest of this kind of mega holding area, and I think everyone in my team was absolutely stunned. We just looked without saying a word for the longest time. It was later confirmed that this area alone had at least twenty-five to thirty tons of castoffs. Tons!

Alonzo was the first to speak. His voice was trembling. "Man, this is, uh, this is a disgrace, man. This is a shame. This is just a big shame."

I walked next to him and said, "I've been watching you, and you look like you want to cry."

"Yeah, man. I mean, there's

We learned that ski masks are used by drug smugglers and illegal crossers to protect against thorns, stickers, and cactus pricks during nighttime runs.

Even though I was warned not to handle the discarded items, mostly because of disease, something lured me to certain items as I searched for clues—stories and a better insight into "why?"

about maybe sixty little kids' backpacks. I mean, the kind of backpacks that I buy for my daughter and for my little boy, and—it's just amazing. I can't believe people would actually put other people in a situation like this to where they just don't care about them. Rape 'em. Bring little kids across sixty miles of nothing but desert, and if they get lucky,

Cocaine?

they make it to the other side. If not—well, you tried. Too bad. And the Mexican government, once again, is doing absolutely nothing about this. Maybe we should mail them all this. Maybe pack all these backpacks, put them in a big box, and just send them off to them. Send them off to the Mexican president and see if maybe it touches his heart."

I was already physically and emotionally drained, but to see Alonzo's reaction—his anger at his fellow Latinos—broke my heart at another level.

"I think that's one of the most insightful ideas I've heard in a long time, Alonzo. You're right, because some of these lives are in the States right now, and they'll end up getting a day labor job, and they'll end up spending the next ten, twelve, fifteen years as an illegal citizen in the country.

"Some of these people are dead right now, or will be soon dead. Maybe we get a variety of coffins, big coffins, baby coffins, and the kind that you see in streets of third world countries—wooden coffins. And we load those up with some of these items. And, we take them to Mexico City, and then on to Washington, D.C.

"Think about the image: 'Mr. Politician, you're allowing death to occur. You are complicit in death. You are complicit in suicide, in murder, in death, so we thought we would let you grieve at a makeshift funeral.'"

Repulsed by it all, Alonzo kicked the junk. Several pieces went flying. "All these condom wrappers, all these tequila bottles, beer bottles, baby bottles, shoes, sandals, bras, panties, toothpaste, tooth—" His voice trailed off. We all felt it—but it was his emotions that sealed the moment. "Really, man. I mean, what else can you say after seeing all this?"

Every great revolution starts with a seed that says, "I am not going to take it anymore."

ONCE

A MOTHER'S PRAYER

Señor Dios Todopoderoso te hago presente el camino por donde vamos a pasar niñito, niñito de Belen, niñito, niñito de Belen, niñito, niñito de Belen. Bendice el camino igual por donde vamos a pasar. Bendice el camino igual por donde vamos a pasar. Bendice el camino igual por donde vamos a pasar.

San Miguel Arcangel con tu espada con tu manto nos haz de hacer invisibles, flecha dorada de la tribu piel roja, haz que el camino sea corto contando con el auxilio de la corte espiritual vamos a llegar sanos y salvos halcon dorado abre el camino por donde vamos a pasar que no haya ninguna barrera en el camino.

Doctor gota de la garza bendice el agua que vamos a llevar pon una gota de tu divino balsamo para que no nos vallamos a enfermar. Doctor gota de la garza te pido que nos pongas un suero para que puedamos resistir ese camino. Doctor gota de la garza y doctora les pido que me ayuden y bendicen esta agua.

He elevado mis ojos hacia ti eterno me he sentido fortificado tu eres mi fuerza oh Dios estoy devorado por una sed ardiente haz que brote un manantial de agua viva y esta quedra apagado que no se abra mi boca para murmurar las aflicciones de la vida si no para contar tus alabanzas. Soy débil Señor pero tu amor me sostendra por que tu solo eres grande excelso por los siglos de los siglos. Amen.

I am the proud father of four great kids and know the deep love that runs in the heart of a dad or mom. We worry, complain, argue, and lead our children, yet no one will know the sleepless nights; those are between God and our own hearts. Parents' skin color and nation of origin have no bearing on those innermost thoughts and desires for their kids. I was about to be confronted by that fact in a very real way.

The sun was doing its best to dehydrate us, and I was thankful for my Marine Corp Boonie hat and the sunscreen my wife, Laurie, carefully planted in my backpack. They kept me reasonably comfortable as I stepped into another hole-up area. I had seen so many and was used to the subtle smells associated with used, sweaty clothes, feces, and food containers left behind, but this camp had an odor that almost knocked me down. When the very aggressive flies—the kind with the deeply muted rainbow colors—attacked from every direction, I was sure I was going to find a dead body. The smell, the flies, the trash—I was sure of it, and each step became calculated and deliberate—just in case.

This was by far the worst of all the areas I had come across. Instead of little stations of leftover bleach bottles that once carried water, tuna cans, and random items of clothing, I now saw tens of thousands of these and other remnants. I came to learn that, even though miles from civilization, the illegal immigrants used this area as their final stopping place before the mad dash to avoid ranchers, Border Patrol, and rogue banditos. They left everything they did not absolutely need for their perceived final leg of the journey. An estimated twenty-five tons of toss-asides left the stench hanging in the air as it would if you visited a U.S. landfill on a one-hundred-degree day. It was just foul.

My team wandered the area for almost an hour as we tried to take it all in, and each of us seemed to be touched by something different.

Adam was overwhelmed by the enormousness of the trash heap; he struggled to think of such desperation while flashing back to the people in Iraq who had solicited him and his fellow Marines for a little help while he walked in their midst.

Alonzo's eyes welled up as he held up one of hundreds of children's backpacks—with Spiderman, Superman, and Scooby Doo characters emblazoned on the fronts. His daughter was the same age as some of the kids forced into this hike, and his emotions were raw. Rob held up bottles, crayons, and writing materials and shared the same loss for words as the rest of us. Gary's gaze was far-off—he knew an illegal alien or two and was suddenly struck by the suffering they endured to get to popular U.S. cities. My compassionate side wanted to cry; my humanitarian leanings struggled with a desire to help all of them if they had been standing in front of me. The thought of such monumental human anguish brings that out.

Look very closely where the fabric touches the ground on the left and you will see a man's legs and tennis shoes. This make-shift tent would cover him from the elements until it was time to run.

But I would be a liar if I suggested that anger did not sweep over me like giant waves at Hawaii's North Beach. I was mad that people felt they had to flee their homelands because their countries were so incredibly bad. I was crazed that they had so devastated my state—my country. How dare they?! And I was distraught over the fact that so many parents had forced their children to make a journey that easily kills many an ill-prepared adult, let alone a kid.

I kicked the empty tequila bottles with the boots Adam had once used in a different pile of sand, in Iraq. Lucky for me, those were the ones I wore—because a needle from a buried syringe stabbed into the side of the shoe, perhaps saving me from a waiting disease. As I yanked the plastic tube by its base, it crumbled in my hands.

I swiftly moved from the team to a remote area a few hundred yards away. I stood without moving for several minutes, seething with anger that felt as though it had turned my heart and lungs inside out. As deeply troubled as I was, another emotion—one of thanksgiving—was also emerging. *How lucky am I?* I thought.

I pulled a plastic bag out of my pack and methodically placed a few items into it as reminders of this area and the stories it could tell: a hand-embroidered hand-

Finding so many things that belonged to little kids was really an emotional drain—on every single one of us.

The statistics are troubling when it comes to alcohol and drug-related traffic fatalities caused by illegal aliens in the U.S. Here, to help take the edge off the desert trip, are just a few of the things some continue to use and abuse when they arrive at their destinations.

kerchief, a young boy's soccer shirt, a button with porn stamped on the inside, an ID badge, and a letter. At least I thought it was a letter. But, as Alonzo translated it, I soon realized the Spanish words that had been quickly scrawled on the crumpled and weathered piece of paper were really a mother's prayer.

As Alonzo read it aloud, a quiet kind of reverence covered the camp: "Dear God All-Powerful, I'm making known the journey that I'm about to embark in. It's going to be me, my little boy—my other little boy. Bless the road where we're going to be going through as we're going through it. . . ."

"Was this a last will and testament?" I wondered aloud. "You're from the Mexican culture, Alonzo. What do you think this represents? Is she thanking God for safe travels, or is she saying good-bye through prayer?" I asked.

My translator's voice was shallow. "She's—she's praising—she's doing a lot of praising here."

I asked the same question in a different way, "Is she praising because she thinks she's found the Promised Land? Think about this: She's gone for days and days and days. She's given up every last penny she's got. She's left her family behind, other than her boys there in the note, and she's saying, 'Praise God! I've made it to America! Free at last!' Little does she know, huh?"

A work or bank I.D. badge from one of the illegal crossers?

Alonzo just stared at the words. "Man, she did not know

nothing of what she was about to embark—because, by the—I mean, why would she leave this behind? So, that means that whoever had this probably left it here because they didn't make it."

I looked over at Adam, who was doing his best to stay disengaged. "You know what? I've got to tell you. I can't handle this stuff. You've been to Iraq, you've been to Fallujah, and you've been in the middle of all that crap. What do you think about all of this?"

He didn't have any answers. "It's the world we live in. I don't know. It sucks. I can't really tell you any—"

"You can't even articulate it?"

"No." His voice was choked.

"I mean—you're married. You don't have kids yet, but you're going to one of these days."

"Yeah."

"So, what's this doing to you?"

"I don't know. We're blessed."

Here we were, a half dozen men in the desert, and to a person, we all tried our best to be men, macho tough men. It wasn't working for any of us. "Man. You know, I've got to tell you, I can't even handle this, man." No response was necessary; I was just saying what we all were thinking.

Every step that we took was a life we were walking over or on top of—a life that was running from something, running to something. Each was a life that was trying to snatch something that most Americans take for granted every second of the day, and here they were, grasping at it.

"Does this mother say anything else, Alonzo?"

"Yeah. I've been reading and translating the rest of this. I was having a hard time reading it, because it almost seems like she's delirious because it sounds like she's praying to a gentleman by the name of Gora el la Gasa, unless that's a saint that I've never heard

While I paused for this picture I had the eerie feeling that we were being watched...

of. But it sounds like she's just writing and writing and writing without really knowing what she's writing, because of whatever she is going through . . ."

"But what is she saying to him?" I asked.

"She's saying to help her get through, get through everything that she's been through, and just to continue blessing the water that she's taking with her. That she's raising her eyes toward him, his eternal being, 'You're my strength.'"

"I've got to tell you, I've prayed those prayers, man. I've prayed that kind of a prayer.

"'Lord, I've only got so much money left. What do I do?' Or, 'Please help me have enough to feed my family.' So I get the prayer, and I respect that, and I respect the human desire to do better. Look. I would jump. Guys, I'm telling you, I would jump over this border, and I would come to America if I thought I could get away with it too. All day long, you know what I mean?"

No other words were spoken on that mound of human leftovers. I folded the paper into a little square and tucked it into my pocket—a reminder of the human will and the power of a mother's prayer.

DOCE

ARMONDO

The Arizona desert in springtime offers hot days and cold nights, and with the change comes a pesky fiend known as the rattlesnake. And if you see a little one, then there is usually a bigger one not far away. I know this because "momma" wasn't happy that my team and I had just stepped over and on junior. She let her presence be known loud and clear. The little guy didn't make any noise, so it was by luck that we realized he was more than just a piece of cloth or a snapped twig—since we were still making our way through some of the left-over debris from the illegal travelers.

"Momma" was a different story. I was second in line as we walked single file along a pathway created by thousands of other uninvited and unwanted guests. The leader passed by without incident, but not I; no, for some reason she decided to teach me a little lesson. The coiled beauty went into full rattle mode as I came by, and for a city dweller, that was enough to send me flying backward and upward all in one very convoluted motion.

It's amazing how quickly the brain can process the sight and sound of something that can do more than just scare you. Her head was cocked, and her rattle made a continuous "I'm gonna get you" sound; there was zero doubt she was angry. After we settled down, the brave men (that's us) decided to play with the noisemaker (that's the snake) by stepping close and then jumping away. For five minutes we were snot-nosed adolescents again and not leaders of enterprise and industry. And at no time during the exploit did "momma" back off.

The rattle was shaking and the snake was poised to strike! Did we run? Are you nuts? We taunted it!

I've seen my share of snake, shark, and spider specials on the Discovery Channel, so I knew her "alert" was really meant as protection to let us know she would strike if necessary but she preferred we get the message and move along.

After the thrill of taunting the sister of Lucifer wore off, we were on our way again—but only after I took out my microphone and audio recorder so I could share the scare with my

This was taken a few moments before I moved to the front of the line and ventured off to investigate some noises...

radio audience. For the record, they thought we were adolescent as well.

Since I was the one who finally said we should leave the poor thing alone, it was I who somehow took point on the next leg of our excursion; the rest of the group walked several paces behind and whispered in little one-on-one teams. As I came around a corner, I was sure I heard something, so I stopped to be sure. For a moment I thought it may have been Alonzo speaking Spanish. But I wondered who he would be speaking to. Everybody in my crew speaks English. After I listened awhile longer, it was clear the voice I heard was not that of my translator. I stepped around a bend, completely out of sight of the others, and the talking grew louder.

Suddenly, I saw legs—under a little desert bush. The same senses

I felt good that because we were in the right place at the right time we saved "Armondo's" life.

that made me jump from the rattlesnake halted my feet midmotion. My breathing went shallow, my eyes focused, and I was on high alert. I didn't know if I was facing one or a hundred, and I didn't know if he or they were armed.

Slowly, I crept around some rocks and near the tree where the shoes were protruding. There I found a single man—a "quitter," as the Border Patrol and Minutemen like to call them, because they have given up on their desert trek or have become such a burden that their coyote has left them behind.

Once my group caught up with me, I signaled for them to stop talking and listen. If you've seen any of those B movies where cops, undercover agents, or military people stick their fingers to their eyes while pointing and counting—that was what I did. Suddenly, I had become gifted in sign language so the team would look, listen, and know what lay ahead. I laugh at it now, but it was dead serious stuff then. We moved within thirty paces of the man, and then I shouted, "Hola. Do you speak English? Do you have water?"

He looked both startled and relieved to see us. "No. No agua."

I had hoped to find someone in the wilderness, and here he was, so I had a lot of questions.

Bob wasn't sold on the idea. "You guys, hey. Stay back. Stay back away from him. Stay back. Get away from him now!" His pitch was a mix between a tough drill sergeant and a father who knows what could happen if we let our guards down.

"What are you doing out here?" I asked as Bob yelled again, "You guys stay back away from him."

When I politely but pointedly let Bob know that we'd moved "back," he yelled again and again—certain that our discovery would knife, shoot, or attack us with some other unknown weapon. My mind said, "The guy's been doing this a lot longer than I have, so I'll listen to him," while the journalist in me said, "Get the story; that's why you're out here."

"How long have you been out here?"

"Three nights and one day." I knew that was mathematically impossible, but I wasn't about to correct him or quibble over times and dates—not at the beginning of what was sure to be a great interview.

"Why are you here?"

"The coyote left me." The man was dark complected with equally dark hair and looked well fed—not overweight, just well fed.

"He left you behind?! Why?"

Alonzo saw the cell phone in the man's hand and patiently listened as a voice was still talking on the other end. Then he whispered to me, "Oh, that's 9-1-1 on the phone right there."

I was at a loss as I looked at Alonzo. "9-1-1 on the phone?" Not waiting for his reply, I asked the question again, "Why did he leave you behind?"

As the words were being translated Bob barked out the orders again, "You guys, stay back over there, please." I wanted to tell him to lighten up; we weren't punk kids. But the stupid rattlesnake game may have sealed his opinion that we were, so I just whispered to Adam, Alonzo, and Rob that the guy needed to back off—we had a story to get. It didn't accomplish anything but made me feel a little better.

The lost alien started speaking at a thousand words a minute. He lost me with the second or third one, so I waited to hear what he was trying to convey. "I got lost, and when I tried—I stayed a little behind them, and then, when I tried finding them, I couldn't locate them anymore."

"So did you finally give up? You were calling 9-1-1 to get help?" I asked.

"Yeah. I called 9-1-1."

"Where'd you get the phone? I thought y'all are searched for phones and weapons before you leave?" I had learned while prepping for the trip that a cell phone will get a traveler left behind or, in drug-related cases, killed. Coyotes and banditos want to control everything about the trip and also want the option of forcing the illegal immigrants to go into a drop house where they can collect more money, so any communications outside the group are strictly forbidden.

"I hid it where they couldn't find it," he said, sort of laughing. "I would have been in real trouble if they caught me—probably would have left me behind." I wondered if he fully comprehended that his leaders had already done what he was most fearful of.

"Are you in this area alone?" We had been wondering if he may have had lookouts or accomplices waiting in the bush.

"Yes. This is the only place where I could get a signal."

"Did you come on this desert trip alone, or did you come with family?"

"By myself." I didn't really understand anything he was saying, but his body language told me that he was a long way away from his family, and the look in his eyes said he was done, finished, through. In that moment, he was transformed from one of a million people breaking through my country's borders to a single soul, lost and ready to die.

"Where did you come from?"

"Hidalgo. The state of Hidalgo."

"Hidalgo, Mexico. Do you have any weapons on you? Nada, nada?"

"Nothing."

"What is your níquel?" I was quite proud that I actually knew a word in his native tongue until Alonzo's head tilted—just before he started laughing.

"What are you asking him? If you want to know his name, try 'nombre'; you just asked him what his 'nickel' was." We all laughed, which set everyone at ease just a little.

Our lawbreaker piped in, "Nombre? Armondo."

"And, uh, Armondo, we've been trying to understand why all the backpacks and everything have been left out here. Why do people leave everything behind?" I was pretty sure I knew the answer, but to get it from the actual source was something I wasn't about to let pass by.

"That's when you can no longer carry anything. That's the reason that I was here by the road, thinking that somebody was going to cross by here."

"Why the ski masks? We have seen several ski masks. They are black with the eyes cut out—what are those all about?"

"You wear those so that you don't get any splinters in your face— see the way I'm getting splinters on my face?" He pointed at cuts and scratches on his cheek and forehead as he dabbed at the blood with a little rag.

"Splinters? Is that because you're moving at night and you run into trees and cacti and stuff out here?"

A desert guide once told me that to avoid detection, many illegal immigrants run through the desert at a fairly fast clip, and though they often run directly into cactus fields, they are so afraid of getting caught that they won't stop to pull out the needles or clean the wounds. In fact, tens of millions of dollars of tax money are lost every year in places like Organ Pipe National Monument, Coronado National Park, and other national parks because the football stadium-sized crowds trample everything in sight as they run from the law.

The man's eye turned to a far-off gaze, and in a whisper he responded, "Yeah, we walk at night."

"So, do you sleep in the day under these trees, or do you keep walking during the day too?"

"You walk day and night and rest for an hour."

"So what's next for you?"

"I would like to make it to the other side. I've been walking for this."

In a matter-of-fact tone I let him know what was next, "You're going to go home to Mexico. You know that, right?" He nodded. "Are you hungry?" I asked.

"It's been two days since I've eaten anything."

I looked at the guys. "Well, give him something to eat. We have food for you. We will give you food. Have you had water? Has he had water, Alonzo?"

For some weird reason I felt a panic hit; I was mad that he was disregarding our border laws but wanted to make sure that he was going to be okay. And then Bob, the barking guide, exploded into the conversation, "Please stay back away from him. Move a-w-a-y."

I ignored Bob completely.

Glancing at Alonzo, I said, "Ask him if he's had water," and then over to Bob, "We're away, Bob. We're away!"

"Okay. I'm sorry," Bob said.

"Did he say that he's had water?" I asked.

"No. He said—"

I cut into Alonzo's words as I attempted to finish the sentence. "He would like some."

"Yeah, he would like some more water."

"Armondo, what do you think is waiting for you in America?"

"I was going to go to work."

"Where?"

"Tennessee."

I used to live in Nashville, so that answer took me by total surprise.

"In Tennessee. Do you have a job already waiting for you?"

"My family, my children—my wife and kids."

"Are where? In Tennessee? They're already there. So, they went through before you? Why did you wait? Did you go before?"

"I've been in Nashville for a long time, but a family member got sick, so I went back to Mexico to go see him, and now I was on my way back to Nashville."

"So what do you do in Nashville? What kind of work?"

"I'm a butcher."

He was a young guy, probably in his mid to late thirties. He was hot and hungry, and since he wasn't sweating much I figured he was dehydrated. Here he was, stuck in the desert with a bunch of strangers who had one singular ambition: get him out of the country. Before that could happen, I had more questions—besides, I had no clue when the Border Patrol would respond to the call we had made to them.

"Do you have a Tennessee driver's license?" (Tennessee used to issue drivers licenses to illegal aliens.)

"It's suspended."

"Why?"

"I ran a stop sign."

"Did you run away from the cops when you did that?"

"No, I'm doing my community service." He was almost proud to let me know that as a pseudocitizen of Music City, he was doing what any responsible, community-minded person would do.

"Do you have a Social Security card?"

"No."

"Come on! Not even a fake one?" Even the most naive American knows that one of the first things an illegal does once he gets to town is buy one or more of the magic cards that open all the right doors. I wasn't buying his answer.

He interrupted me. "I work with a fake one."

Bob interrupted. "Ask him what his name is. His assumed name in Tennessee. What name does he use?"

Armondo answered, "Another one."

Bob asked again, " What is it?"

"Juan."

"Juan what?"

"It's just a different first name, but I use my own last name."

He broke the law to get here. Broke the law while staying here. Broke the law by using someone else's identity. This is the standard method of operation of most who bust the border. It's like the old adage our parents used to tell us, "Once you lie, you have to keep lying, or you get caught." This guy knew the game. "How much did you pay for the Social Security card?" I asked.

"One hundred dollars."

"And if I went back to Nashville with you, how fast do you think you could help me find one?"

"Quick."

"*Rápido*? Five minutes?" He nodded in the affirmative.

Apparently Bob's loud warnings from earlier were planted in my mind, because I started to wonder what my newfound stranger/buddy would do if I gave him a chance. "Now that you've had food and water that we just gave you, would you just like to take off running and see if you can get away?" I was halfway joking, halfway curious if this guy had anything left.

"Well, if you gave me a chance—why not?"

"Okay, I'll give you one hundred yards. Is that enough?"

The man paused, looked at me, glanced off into the one-hundred-plus degree, cactus-strewn desert and then back at me. "No. I want to just pace myself." I guess he figured at least one of the seven or eight guys that surrounded him could catch him in no time. His body slumped in defeat.

"So what happens after you get shipped off to Mexico? How soon are you coming back?"

"My family depends on me."

"Have you thought about bringing your family back to Mexico and living with them there?"

"But my children were born here—in America."

More than three hundred thousand "anchor babies" are born on U.S. soil every year. Foreigners, mostly illegal, view having a child in America almost like winning the lottery, because our U.S. Constitution has been improperly interpreted to say that any child born in the U.S. is a citizen, even one born to illegal parents who have come intentionally and fraudulently just to give birth. All have been given the gift that keeps on giving: citizenship for their child.

"Did you intentionally bring a pregnant wife to America so that child would be born here?"

"No. She got pregnant over here."

"Oh, she was over here. And were you aware that when the children were born here they would be U.S. citizens?"

"Yes. And, yes, they are."

"Do you think that's unfair to the American taxpayer?"

"Well, I file every year."

"But that doesn't change—it doesn't change the complexion at all, Armondo! So, will you return to Mexico and try to raise the money? Will you get it from your family, or will you have to wait in Mexico for another year until you've got the money together?"

"My boss was going to pay for me to get there."

"So, your American boss knows that you need to get back from Mexico to Tennessee." I had a rush of anger, not so much toward this guy but at the thought of yet another traitor of a citizen willing to fund a liar, cheater, and thief—one who is willing to financially support a person who is helping to destroy this nation's middle class.

The man stopped me midthought. "Yes. What happened was I just had to leave because of necessity."

"And will the American boss expect you to pay the money back, or is this his gift so that you'll keep working for him?" What boss would just give someone a couple thousand dollars so he can go home to see family? Very few, unless they realize that by paying the person a deeply deflated wage, their business grows and they become wealthy.

"Oh, I've been working with her for ten years."

Ten years?! I thought. A decade! And this guy hasn't tried to become legitimate? I was losing my patience.

"You've been in America for ten years?"

"No, I arrived in Tennessee in 1990."

"Nineteen ninety. It's—what?—2007. So, seventeen years ago?"

"Yes."

"You've got to be kidding me," I said in a manner in which the recipient knows there's anger in the air—no matter what the language is. "I'm frustrated. You've been in America for seventeen years. One, why are you not a U.S. citizen already? Two, why don't you speak one ounce of English?"

"Oh, the reason is because I work with nothing but Mexicans at the butcher shop."

"Wait a minute. For seventeen years you've been in America and you can't speak any English?" As I was pounding home the point, a rush of wind blew dust in our eyes, and the limbs of the surface trees bent backward. Within seconds the noise arrived too. The Border Patrol helicopter was finally arriving, so I knew my time was short with him. "We've got a helo; let's hurry—I have great compassion for your plight in Mexico. As you can see, we gave you food and water here because our hearts hurt for you. But you are exactly what is wrong with this story. You come to America, you have children in

America, you don't try to become an American, and you don't try to learn the language. You understand how that makes us feel?"

"Like I said, I'll repeat it: nothing but Mexicans go into that store." It was in Spanish, but I could tell he, too, was becoming indignant.

"No way! You have never run into a United States citizen who speaks English one time in the last seventeen years? I'm having a hard time with this."

"No."

"So you are not even trying to assimilate."

"Huh-uh." That's a "no" in any language too.

The copter landed; the blades swirled. "Have you even tried to become a U.S. citizen? Have you—"

"Hey guys." The Border Patrol had landed, and they wanted our attention. Now.

"Would you rather be a U.S. citizen or a Mexican citizen? You have to pick only one," I said.

We were both rushing our conversation; we were seconds away from things becoming very official, very fast. "Well, with my children over here, I would like to be a resident, if I can."

"Would you like to be a U.S. citizen?"

"Of course. More than half of my life I have been over here. I've been here since I was young."

"So what! In half your life, you have not tried one time to become a U.S. citizen or even blend in—even become a part of the beautiful fabric of America."

When we first spotted Armondo, we put in a call to the Border Patrol. Though we knew where we were, it was impossible to tell anyone else. Even though we eventually provided GPS coordinates, it still took about ninety minutes before they were able to find us. I was getting impatient at first, but then started thinking about it: thousands of other illegal immigrants were also in our sector, everything looked identical for miles in every direction—nothing but sand, rugged terrain, and cacti—and we had no idea of knowing how close or how far away the agents actually were. Finally, a helicopter went over, then planes, and then the Border Patrol arrived.

Through some simple but direct questions of our uninvited guest, the agents determined that there were about seventy-five persons who had gone ahead, including at least five little children.

Two agents stayed back to process Armondo, while a third tossed his gear on his back and slung a rifle over his shoulder. It should be noted that the U.S. Border Patrol issues each of its agents a Berretta handgun and touts the fact that they do not carry rifles. Had I known that piece of trivia before the trip, I would have examined his rifle a little more closely. Some sources say they use paintball rifles, though it appeared to be the real deal to me. As soon as he was geared up and ready to go, the young agent with a military build was off like a tracker of old, following the many footprints in the desert.

A couple of days without food and water can waste a man when the desert heat kicks in. Although we had given Armondo water and food, he asked the agent in Spanish if he could have more, and he began drinking nonstop with the gallon jug braced in both hands.

He seemed like a nice guy, with a wife and kids. My compassionate side had a broken heart, while the citizen who sees his country's sovereignty constantly ripped and assaulted was glad to see him in Border Patrol custody.

As he stood quietly, waiting to be placed in the patrol truck, Armondo motioned for me to come closer. "You are my guardian angel." I laughed at his comments and said, "You know we saved you." And I was actually kidding with him when I said it, but then his eyes kind of misted up, and he said, "No. I would have died. Had you not come along, I would have died. You saved my life." And he was sincere about that. The lump in my throat almost choked me.

That said, an agent ordered the lawbreaker to follow him to the side of the truck. They began pulling each item out of his light backpack for examination. A couple of T-shirts was about all he had. After another routine pat-down for weapons, they opened the door to the truck. Part of me expected to see him tossed in the holding area in the back, or at the very least, cuffed. Neither happened. Instead, they offered him a Powerade and a sandwich to go along with the gallon of water.

Everyone's reality is their own, even when they make it all up. And that is true in the illegal immigration dispute. Only a day or so earlier, while I was in Mexico, officials and some humanitarian groups told me that our agents would do nothing for the people they captured—no food, water, or genuine aid. That's why these groups said they had set up shop on that side of the border; they wanted to help people that we had refused. I thought it was bogus when I heard it, but after I saw how our agents treated Armondo, it was evident just how deceptive and distorted the stories from pro-illegal immigrant groups had become.

Just before Armondo was led into the truck, the agent asked for permission to go through the wallet he had found in the pat-down. As he started pulling items out, Armondo was all too similar to me again: a couple of bucks, a picture of his family, and some coupons. A smile brushed my face as I thought how certain things are just universal—a man's wallet being one of them.

With that I gave Armondo one of those guy kind of salute / waves, and he shot one back as he climbed into the vehicle to be whisked to a detention center and back to Mexico. My fleeting thought was that he would probably make it back to Tennessee before I made it back to Phoenix. I felt good that I and my band of radio guys had saved his life. In the end, a life is a life, and it should be valued.

We resumed our trek through the desert, because there were still miles ahead of us before sleeping bags and sandwiches.

As evening turned to night, we tossed the bags on the ground and headed to a paved road where a dive of a convenience store stood out as a place for chili or similar food. Off in the distance was a Border Patrol bus, the kind that moves forty or fifty people at a time. On the outside, sitting on the ground, was a group of quiet men, women, and children. I walked over with a bounce in my step, kind of proud at the day's accomplishment. I was certain these were the same people Armondo had been traveling with. The agents looked at me with suspicion until I told them what my role was in the day. "Are these the people who were picked up earlier?"

"Yes." They shook my hand and they said, "Congratulations. You took twenty-five illegal immigrants out of America today."

Then I looked at them; their brown eyes begging for hope, begging for help, begging for somebody to reach into their souls and save them. And I will be honest—it broke my heart to the point that I had to look away. I don't condone their actions—not for a minute. But it was still a tough moment in time.

I often wonder when or if Armondo ever made it back to Nashville. I am also curious how he can watch Titans football and Predators hockey without a working knowledge of our language. Can the underground and very subversive illegal immigrant network be as established as he suggested—to the point where he and his people really have no need to even try to learn our language or our ways?

TRECE

THE RAPE TREE

I was a bit too sure of myself as I stepped through the brush of the blazing Arizona desert. Earlier in my investigative excursion, I had experienced third-world poverty inside the nation just south of us and mere steps from the good ol' United States of America. There I had endured my share of stares and glares from passersby, interviewed people living in homes constructed from trash borrowed from the local dump, and judged the threats from a just-released convict who told me to "get the 'f' out" of his country. So, I was prepped for whatever this day would bring—especially since I was back in my own country—less than three hours from my own home.

As we dodged rattlesnakes and cholla cacti (a funky little plant whose little arms jump at and attach themselves to you as you walk by) and had limited access to any cool, refreshing water, my certainty exploded into disbelief.

I had seen my share of clothes, backpacks, and discarded remnants of human life along the way—no doubt hole-up areas where quite a few people had stopped to catch their breath. But this place was dif-

ferent; it had a heavy, eerie presence lingering in the air. As usual,
I had stopped to better understand where I was, which put me
way behind the rest of the crew.
Examining the footprints, strewn
pictures, and flow patterns of the
people led my eyes to the trees
and what was decorating them.

I shouted for my desert guide
to stop the group and come back
to where I stood; there, digital
recorder running, I asked for the
backstory. He glanced in the
direction of my pointing finger,
and suddenly the affect on his
face turned to sorrow—gloom.
He sighed deeply, measuring the
words he was about to share,

These little suckers actually jump at you! They hook
their barbed spikes into your skin making them
difficult (and painful!) to remove.

and then matter-of-factly described what most will never see.

Deliberately tied to branches in the Velvet Mesquite tree were
worn, soiled, and torn bras and panties. Trees like this had but one
name: the rape tree—a name well earned.

To be completely honest, I thought he may have been repeating
an urban legend or exaggerating, so I wasn't really buying everything
he told me. I certainly wasn't going to repeat it to my radio audience;
it was simply too unbelievable. I whispered to a couple of my guys,
"I'm not airing this interview! There's nothing that we know that con-
firms the story to be true."

Later, other independent sources, including multiple Border Patrol

Thank God I took an expert's advice and wore long thick pants!

agents, confirmed the information just as Bob had described it. My soul was ripped wide open as I realized just how desperate many of the border crossers truly are.

What seems to be common knowledge in the illegal immigration industry south of the border is that coyotes expect more than just monetary payment for leading young women into America, and he will take what he wants if it isn't given freely. In spite of this ice-cold reality, the sweltering desert trips go on unabated.

Imagine—you are so hopeless in your own country that you risk getting raped during the heart-wrenching journey. Or, just as distress-ing, you agree to let the pig have his way with you. In some cases, the man—husband or boyfriend—is the one who agrees to this price by turning his back while the act is performed. Oftentimes all parties know it is going to happen before the trek begins; they just don't know exactly when or where. Think about it. How desperate can a person be to allow such a thing to happen to his best friend and greatest ally!

"I want to be sure I tell this story accurately, so explain what we're seeing, Bob, and give us the details," I said.

"This is a real thing. For some reason, the coyote gets macho. I don't know what the hell it is, but they hang women's underwear. They rape them. They can be doing it just because they're mean, they can do it as part of the pay to get up here, but I'll bet that almost every woman that gets into the United States has been raped once."

"We've never heard that. So what is he doing by hanging this stuff, showing his trophy or something?"

"Why does a dog pee on, you know, on a tire—the same thing." Bob's disgust was palpable.

"But, wait a minute. The crossers know this beaten path—it seems everybody knows about the path—so I would have to assume the word is out all over Mexico and beyond. They know about the water, clothes, and what kind of utensils to bring. If that word is on the street in Mexico, it has to be, 'Hey, if you do this, here's what's going to happen.'"

"Darrell, this is the real thing; it's unbelievable what they go through to get here."

"But man, this is just brutality. How do people do this to other people? It's brutality." My breathing was heavy, as though my backpack now weighed three hundred pounds. I was more than overwhelmed; I was devastated.

Bob was just as defeated in his spirit as I was. "You're right, it's inhuman."

"Not only inhuman, Bob, but let's consider the rest of the story: Those pigs who raped these women or young girls are in our midst out here, because they're the ones who are bringing them into America, and they probably live in our cities too!"

"That's right. They're not just coming up here to work."

While investigating this story I learned that the coyotes, the punk criminals that they are, pull the women of their choice from the group of travelers and rape and sodomize them. It doesn't happen too far from the other men, women, and children. That's by design: the coyote needs the security of knowing where everyone else is while he abuses the woman, but he also chooses his spot carefully, guaranteeing that a very clear message has been sent and received: "Don't mess with me!"

After he has had his way, the criminal peels off any remaining underwear the woman may still have on and ties them to the nearest tree—the rape tree. It is his own monument to his power and prowess and a firm reminder to all who follow the trail later: the coyote rules the wilderness.

Too many trees told the stories of the price women paid for passage. Of all the images and stories—these are the ones that haunt me to this day.

I was poking the dangling bras and panties with the nearest stick I could find even as the guide outlined the sad and nasty details. I was not sure why I was doing it. Fascination? Investigation? Uncertainty? All I know is that the anger bubbled up inside of me as I had never felt before, drenched in the tears and cries of thousands of women, muffled cries that would never be quenched.

"What did this lady struggle through?" I asked myself as I

prodded. "How can your life really be so desperate that you would risk this kind of assault?" Ever notice that many illegal immigrant women always seem to be looking down or away as we cross their paths? Perhaps this is why. It was certainly too steep a price to pay for a "fresh start" in the Promised Land.

As I have already mentioned, this was such an unbelievable story that I wanted to verify it by more than two independent sources, which I did while visiting the country's biggest detention facility for illegal immigrants. There I heard even more elaborate details about the crime and the participants. I was told that many of the women coming up through South America actually take a birth control called Depo-Provera.

A doctor administers the Depo injection, which stops a woman from ovulating. No one is willing to provide stats on how many women crossing into this country use this method, but the Border Patrol agents I talked to said it appears to be routine.

As we stood in the intake and holding facility for the illegal immigrants, I asked a high-ranking Border Patrol agent to tell me more. His answers mirrored those of my guide.

"Tell me about the rape tree. What does it signify?

"Well, what it says is that you have smugglers working in cahoots with bandits, and what they'll do, once they rob people, either on the south side of the border or on the north side of the border and further in, they will pull the females aside, and they will sexually assault them; they will rape them."

Alonzo was looking at all the caged women in the holding cells. "Did you guys ask any of those young ladies if any of them were victims of rape, or . . ."

The agent replied, "We'll ask them, but a lot of times they won't say anything because of the shame."

I stopped him. "Although we've been told a majority have been, somewhere along the way, raped. Can you confirm that?"

"Exactly. Many of these women also take the Depo shots, but I can't confirm how many. They take it before they ever leave their home country."

With each telling, the stories shared the same details, yet I still couldn't fully comprehend it all. "In other words, the lady knows what's coming, so she had better get ready for it. Is it payment?"

"In some cases, yes. You have to understand, when people are paying that large amount of money, they may not have that money readily at hand. If they are not paying their debt through forced sex, they may play in the drug trade instead. Somebody may say, 'Well, go pick up those bundles of marijuana and walk through to the desert. Drop them off at a certain point. They'll pick you up and take you to a stash house, and you're free and clear.'"

"Now, that innocent lady who is coming just for a job or just to be reunited with family is now confronted with doing the work of a felon or a prostitute. And she may be raped on top of it all?!"

"Exactly. Or, here's another side to the same story—they get to a stash house and may not have the sufficient funds, or they're lacking money because the coyote is demanding even more money. The illegal immigrant is given keys to a vehicle. 'Drive down to the border. Pick up X amount of people or pick up this load of narcotics. Then get back here and you're good to go.' But they don't tell them what the consequences are."

"I asked my guide earlier if it is some sort of a badge of honor to dangle the women's undergarments from trees, or is it a message to the followers, 'You better watch out. This is going to happen to you'?"

"It's probably a way of showing the people that are walking the desert, 'This is an area that you don't want to be in. This is a danger area.' But it also could be a machismo thing for them that this is, you know—they're the top dog; they're the alpha male in this area."

Alpha male?! What a way of putting it. The lowest common denominator is to dehumanize a person—make them a thing, an object, or at the most—an animal. And in the process, the people perpetrating the attacks become animals too, though I'm not sure what other animal on the face of the planet rounds up others of its species and molests them for pleasure or warning.

In the end, what does this make the coyotes, jackers, banditos, and other thugs of the desert? And at what point does the illegal crosser ever get to feel like a mother, daughter, grandma, sister—or woman—again?

DROP HOUSE HORROR STORIES

I had heard the stories, on both sides of the border, but it took observations at two drop house locations for me to fully understand just how badly illegal immigrants (in this case, Mexican illegals) are treated by people from their own race, culture, and shared histories, and how these traitors to their own people blatantly operate in the open much of the time.

The first house had a main floor that looked immaculate—minus most of the usual furniture pieces. Except for some filthy dishes in the sink it looked like your neighbor's house. But the upstairs level was a different matter. Clothes, shoes, cell phones and other personal property were all bunched into hall closets. Plastic milk bottles that had been cut in half were brimming with human waste while another five-gallon bucket of the material sat conspicuously in the corner of one room. This bucket had been used to torture illegals who the kidnappers believed were holding out.

Human smugglers rent out nice houses in nice areas and maintain the exteriors so nothing seems out of the ordinary. When owners get them back they are in shambles.

Many of the fifty captives were able to get family members to cough up a little more to insure their release but a young husband and wife weren't budging—they had no more to offer. The jackers weren't buying it and grew tired of the begging and pleading so they grabbed the husband, wrapped a plastic bag around his head and started suffocating him. When he was gulping his last breaths they allegedly punctured the bag allowing the man to sneak some air into his lungs. Then they plunged his head into the bucket of urine and feces and performed their own version of water torture. As the bag filled with human excrement the man sucked it into his nose, throat and eyes. His body convulsed from the shock as he vomited. Still, the jackers were sure he had money.

As they threw him to the floor they grabbed his pregnant wife—in her last trimester—and smacked her in the face. The husband screamed for them to let her go. They hit her again. And again. And again. When they had finished with her beating, the young lady lost the baby as vaginal blood streamed down the legs of her once dark blue jeans. In the end, the couple was telling the truth—they had no additional funds.

Jackers take shoes and often all outer garments of the victims to ensure they won't try to escape.

The second house was a two-story, single-family type located in a quiet middle-class neighborhood in Arizona. It sported the usual suburban trappings, like a small playground, a hillside flash-flood wash for any mountain rain runoff, and a Starbucks within

Men and women are forced to relieve themselves in bottles like this—usually placed in the corner of the room where all the victims are kept.

walking distance. The house had a two-car garage and a nicely maintained exterior that most certainly made some proud homeowner association members quite happy. From the outside, it was the perfect American home.

Once inside, the story turned dark as soon as the door swung open. Torture had visited this place—and more than a few people had felt its sting. The windows were completely covered with large particle-board slats nailed to their frames.

In a couple of instances, cardboard and heavy burlap had been used

Jackers tortured at least one kidnapped alien by wrapping his head in plastic until he almost suffocated and then plunged his head into the bucket or urine and feces until he choked on the excrement.

The young illegal immigrant who wore these blood soaked jeans and underwear (top right) was seven months pregnant at the time. She was tortured and repeatedly beaten when she and her husband could not provide more money. Her unborn baby died.

to block out any sights and to muffle any sounds. My sources later told me that the drop house kidnappers definitely had at least one guard in these rooms at all times, because victims have been known to tear through the material or, worst case, dive directly through the covering and glass in an attempt to escape. Seldom did their efforts succeed.

As I scanned the rooms, I saw the same kinds of things, albeit in limited numbers, that I had in the Arizona deserts—discarded shoes, shirts, diapers, and other personal items. The raid that led to the arrest of a half-dozen banditos and the liberation of at least forty people had happened several days earlier, but the stench of rotting food still hung in the air, combining with the stench of human waste that had collected in buckets or been deposited onto the carpet in several rooms. The illegal aliens were herded to the home in the middle of the night via several large passenger vans. The victims were told to be quiet or their families, on either side of the border, would be harmed or killed. The same method of operation plays out in cities large and small throughout the Southwest and California.

The walk-in closet in one bedroom had been turned into a whipping area, and the evidence would have provided CSI investigators with all the details necessary to convict: shoe scuff marks on the walls, damage to the wooden clothes rod caused by the full body weight of several who had been tied there with belts while receiving their beatings for not following directions or to make sure the victim realized how serious the situation was. And on the back and side walls of the closet was the most damning evidence—blood. Lots and lots of blood. I was later told that no one died in the house, but the beatings were severe.

Kidnappers usually force detainees into a specific area of the rented house and seal off the windows with plywood so escape is almost impossible.

Banditos kidnap the people from coyotes and hold them against their will until someone pays for their release—and payment always comes! In the rare instance that it doesn't, and the illegal aliens refuse to run drugs or sell their bodies for sex as payment, lifeless corpses turn up on the sides of roads or in desert areas frequently traveled. The bodies are meant to be found because the message guarantees cash from the next load of humanity.

The third drop house gave me the chance to actually see the occupants and kidnappers and set up my interview with one victim's family member. It was late in December 2007, and most people were making their way home through the evening commute. My phone rang. It was one of my sources within the county sheriff's office. His team was raiding a house, and if I jumped in my car right then and there, I could watch events unfold in real time. I flipped my cell closed midsentence and jumped in my car.

The skies turned dark as I used side streets to make my way to the address I was given—an address that tipped me that I would arrive in a lower-class neighborhood. Deputies and ICE agents were escorting the occupants of the home to the sidewalk as I drove up. A woman and four or five accomplices were cuffed and tossed in the back of a sheriff's van. My source explained that this lady, dark and quiet, was actually the ringleader.

Inside, the home looked and smelled like most other drop locations after a raid, but this time only two windows were covered, since all seventeen victims had been kept in one or two rooms. Outside, I watched as a man in his twenties paced back and forth in front of the house. I called my sheriff's office pal over to the side to hear the backstory: the young man's brother had been in the home, and it was this man's call that brought the police to the scene. I grabbed my cell phone and summoned Alonzo, my trusted translator, to meet me. There, I heard the firsthand account of the terror Raphael shared.

"What happened?" I asked. "I understand this was a drop house, and you had relatives in here?"

"Yeah, they had my brother and two friends here."

"How did you find out?" The slight man paused at the question and then launched into an account that would scare most of us to death. "Yesterday morning I received a phone call where they were demanding three thousand dollars apiece to let my brother and his friends go."

I wanted to be certain of the facts. "So they called you and said, 'We're being held for ransom for three thousand dollars'?"

"A lady called me and she told me that if I wanted to see them again, I would have to pay."

"And what did she say she was going to do to them if you didn't?"

The man looked puzzled at my question, so I rephrased it for Alonzo's translation. This time he understood, "What would happen? I would never, ever again be able to see them alive. They were giving me until Wednesday to pay them the money."

I tried to put myself in his place for a moment—panic would set in if I thought a loved one of mine might be hours away from being murdered. I felt sorry for the guy.

One of the arguments against immigration enforcement is that it drives these people underground, which leads to unreported crimes. My long-held belief is that if an illegal alien sees a crime he can anonymously call a Silent Witness program or contact a friend who is a U.S. citizen who can report it. So the next question had to be asked, "Are you here illegally?"

"Yeah, I'm not legal, and neither were my brother and his friend. That's right."

"So you called the authorities to ask for help?"

"I called a friend who is a citizen, and he told me to go ahead and call the authorities, that we will receive help from them." I quietly smiled to myself; my theory held up.

"Did the lady say what was happening to your brothers and their friends? Did she say that they were getting beaten or anything like that, and did you hear from anybody else in the house?"

The young man's eyes darted up and down, as if he was trying to remember all the particulars. "I spoke to the woman and another man that was working with her, and I did speak with my friends and my brother just for, like, two or three words, just to know that they were . . ."

Illegal aliens are searched for cell phones before they make the desert trek and then again when they arrive at the drop house so the only possible communication with the outside world is very controlled. The gun keeps victims in line.

"So what did you say to them and how did they respond?"

"They told me that I needed to get the money if I wanted to see him again. My brother said just to go ahead and get the money, but I shouldn't worry if I couldn't get any." Raphael's eyes slipped into a comalike gaze, "How was I supposed to not get the money and just leave him there? By then the authorities were already searching the calls and investigating into it."

"How did they sound when you talked to your brother and friends? How did they sound?"

"They sounded really scared, as though they were being threatened, and they never did let them speak too much."

As I spoke to Raphael on a silent sidewalk, I noticed one lady in cuffs sitting on the curb. Next to her were three other illegal immigrants. All were awaiting transport to a holding facility. The woman, an accomplice, was in charge of bringing food to the drop house and was caught as part of the raid, which caused me to wonder if Raphael had seen his brother while the vans loaded the aliens.

"No, by the time I got here, they were already in the bus."

A deputy slammed and locked the front door of the small cookie-cutter Arizona ranch house, so I knew my time with this witness was almost finished. Soon he would be whisked away to answer questions, or perhaps be detained on immigration charges. "What would you like for us U.S. citizens to know about drop houses and what happened here tonight?"

Raphael's answer was intriguing. On one hand he clearly appreciated and respected the work of a coyote: "I know these men work hard to get the money, they risk their lives in the desert also, along with immigrants, but once you get here and they kidnap you, well, that's a kidnapping. It's no longer work."

"What should happen to them?" I asked.

"These people want to take my family from me; they wanted to kill my brother. I think they should do a long prison term."

"Is there anything else my listeners and readers should know?"

The young man's countenance changed to a slight smile. "I think the borders to America should be opened. All we want to do is work. Let us come and live here, and the need for drop houses would be gone."

"You know I don't agree with open borders, don't you?" I asked.

"I didn't know that." Raphael paused and then looked me in the eyes. "But we can still be friends."

I grabbed his hand and shook it. "I believe we could probably be good friends, but you must respect this nation's laws."

As I walked away, I glanced back over my shoulder. "Hey."

Raphael stopped midstep and glanced over at me.

"I just wanted you to know I'm glad your brother is going to be okay."

SECCION DOS
TO KILL A COUNTRY
(AKA SOVEREIGNTY TERRORISTS)

Deserts. Poverty. Illegal immigrants. Border Patrol. My travels opened my eyes and mind to just how complex our border issues are, while one thing kept returning to my thoughts time after time: this issue may be big enough to kill a country. Before it can get there, it must attack our very foundation. By now, we have all heard that terrorists want to sneak into our nation to wipe out complete cities, but what if we are also contending with sovereignty terrorists—people who have the capacity to blow up our ideologies—too?

Let's start there.

Sovereignty plus autonomy equals freedom; it's that simple. Let's dissect the words: Sovereign is defined as "independent of all others" and "free from external control," while autonomy means "having the right or power of self-government." Besides the answer that a bleeding and dying soldier may provide, the book definition for freedom is "absence of constraint in choice or action" and the "liberation from slavery or restraint or from the power of another." So, if my formula holds up, by design and definition, then, anything that interferes with the parts ultimately changes the answer—and there is surely an effort to change the parts.

Our borders, government, laws, culture, morality, language, education, and more have been created and grown around a simple quest to have and maintain freedom. The single common thread that has always pulled our diverse people together is our enduring need to own that freedom. Then we were attacked.

After 9/11, Washington gave us the Patriot Act and Patriot Act II, as well as numerous other programs to protect "We the People" as terrorist acts exposed our susceptibilities. Certain freedoms were lost or damaged in the transaction, while our nation struggled to find the proper balance between liberty and security. Later, added laws allowed the government to tap our phones, read our e-mail, and track our license plates as never before. An uncomfortable uneasiness settled in. In very real ways, terrorism, an outside influence, started whittling away at our rock-strong foundation.

While our eyes focused on the next suicide bomber, millions of people—mostly from Mexico and Latin American countries—amassed in cities large and small. Many

Americans realized there was a new threat to our foundation—only this one was already on the inside. In the end, left undeterred, these people now threaten our way of life as much as anyone who dares to explode a suicide belt in the name of their god. They bring their own lawlessness, poverty, and tribulations for us to solve, but instead of our helping them, they are slowly disintegrating what we have strived to maintain for more than two hundred years.

We can only endure for so long the barrage of assaults on our laws, language, workers, cost of living, and Constitution, and the added crimes perpetrated by their worst, before it causes irreparable damage.

An assault on a nation's sovereignty usually involves military might and bloodshed unless there is an internal, nonviolent coup by people who seize power in the dead of night. Though a threat from military or police forces is almost always needed to ensure a takeover, there is another way to seize control of a nation—flood the landscape with enough people of like minds to change the will of the masses. This is America's quandary today.

Major societal building blocks, such as our courts, language, laws, work ethic, economy, and health care, are all under siege, and as never before, the attack is hitting each area at the same time, threatening the autonomy, freedom, and, ultimately, the sovereignty that made the U.S.A. the world leader it has been.

CATORCE

WHY THE FEDERAL GOVERNMENT WANTS ILLEGAL IMMIGRATION:
A FEW MOMENTS WITH DR. JEROME CORSI

Political assistants and handlers did all they could to make the Waco, Texas, meeting between the heads of North America's three power-base countries look like a public affair, but they had one glaring problem with which to contend—it wasn't.

It was a chilly Wednesday, a few days after the official start of spring 2005, and President Bush had invited the heads of Canada and Mexico to summit about the trinity's future. When finished, the Security and Prosperity Partnership (SPP) was born, and decisions that impacted each country's laws, economies, and other citizen advantages had been made—minus any input from Congress or voters.

Later, as government "working groups" converged on our well-crafted and well-thought-out rights, they documented their strategy:

The notes for the presentations document the need to overcome popular opposition to North American integration: To what degree does a concept of North America help/hinder solving problems between the three countries? . . . While a vision is appealing[,] working on the infrastructure might yield more benefit and bring more people on board ("evolution by stealth").[1]

When governmental agencies suggest doing things by "stealth" so We the People don't become enraged, red flags should be flying all over the place.

According to documents obtained through Freedom of Information rights, several groups, including Judicial Watch and author Dr. Jerome Corsi, uncovered proof that the leadership has plans to synchronize and "harmonize" immigration, national security, trade, transportation, energy, and law enforcement, among others. In March 2006, U.S. commerce secretary Carlos Gutierrez told his Washington insiders, "Work must continue to formalize a transnational labor force that could work in any North American country on a temporary basis."[2]

Mexican president Vicente Fox was bolder with his words, saying the "long-range objective is to establish an ensemble of connections and institutions similar to those created by the European Union." Many wanted explanations—was this new three-country relationship going to undermine commerce, transportation, salaries, political structures, and national securities? Answers have remained "stealth."

Though a better relationship between the three countries has many advantages, it is the proposition of the integration of cultures, laws, courts, and unique systems—not to mention the incremental loss of each country's sovereignty—that trouble so many. Especially since it's being done in the shadows. It's almost as if politicians believe citizens are simply too stupid to help make such epic decisions. National security expert Frank Gaffney addressed that risk:

> Such rules are intended to govern tri-national trade, transportation, immigration, social security, education and virtually every other aspect of life in North America. There are new institutions being proposed, too, such as a North American Tribunal with authority to trump rulings of the U.S. Supreme Court.[3]

Though details are still few, one scenario depicts a voting system similar to the European Union, which puts the U.S. on par with Canada and Mexico and gives each country an equal vote. If this ever became reality, there is a very real possibility that the U.S.A.'s systems could be outvoted two to one by lesser countries. That could cause a loss of control of everything from immigration to redistributed wealth.

President Bush grew tired of the questions posed by members of the media and responded by attacking the questioners: "You know, there are some who would like to frighten our fellow citizens into believing that relations between us are harmful for our respective peoples. . . . I just believe they're wrong. I believe it's in our interest to trade; I believe it's in our interest to dialogue."[4] Smart strategy on the president's part, but if there are no side deals in the works, why do news agencies require a Freedom of Information Act (FOI) request to get the details? And why has the president kept the SPP under executive branch jurisdiction, effectively shutting out oversight by Congress?

British scholars have called the European Union a nonmilitary coup d'etat. In polls, a majority in the affected countries says sovereignty was stolen by leaders who flatly rejected any "union" plans. Those leaders opted instead to call the program the European Coal and Steel Community in an effort to sell it as a simple way to develop better avenues for trade. Reread the president's lines about "trade" and "dialogue." The same words were used in Europe.

Remember, in public the players tell us we are overreacting or using "political scare tactics," as President Bush calls them, but in private and within planning groups, it is a different matter. In October 2006, former U.S. ambassador to Canada Paul Cellucci slipped up in an address to the Canadian Defense and Foreign Affairs Institute when he said:

> Now, I don't believe that we will ever have a, in name anyways, a common union like the Europeans have . . . but I believe that, incrementally, we will continue to integrate our economies. . . . I think . . . 10 years from now, or maybe 15 years from now we're gonna look back and we're gonna have a union in everything but name.[5]

Citizens, politicians, and commentators all make note of the immigration issue in the U.S.—but what if it cuts far deeper than people crossing a border? What if we have intentionally left the doors open in order to entice millions to make the move to America? Think about it—we have known about the invasion for several years and have never attempted to fully secure the borders. We have the most sophisticated technology, military, and skills in the world, and we can't figure out how to secure ourselves? Doesn't this strike you as a little unbelievable once you really think about it? U.S. citizens would never allow politicians to steal the sovereignty their family members spilled blood and died for, but with sixty million Mexican people in the U.S., including first-generation citizens, the sales job is easier.

Let's look at some other road signs. One of the rankings used by The Heritage Foundation examines a country's "economic freedom." Currently, the United States is the fourth freest nation in the world;

Canada is tenth; Mexico drops in at number forty-four.[6] Imagine all three countries on the same playing field, an SPP idea—wouldn't the one supercountry need to massively digress for this to be accomplished? Former Federal Reserve Board Chairman Alan Greenspan suggested as much in March 2007 when he said, "Our skilled wages are higher than anywhere in the world." Then he added, "If we open up a significant window for skilled workers, that would suppress the skilled-wage level and end the concentration of income."[7] If left without checks and balances, the SPP could create such a system.

In addition, the Heritage study places Mexico with a seventieth place (out of 163) in a "freedom from corruption" category.[8] And, if that country's southern neighbors continue to illegally immigrate, what is to prevent them from moving completely through Mexico and into America without fear of reprisal?

When speaking about the new opportunities the people of Mexico could enjoy in an open America, former foreign minister Jorge Casteneda told his country's press,

> I like very much the metaphor of Gulliver, of ensnarling the giant. Tying it up, with nails, with thread, with 20,000 nets that bog it down: these nets being norms, principles, resolutions, agreements, and bilateral, regional and international covenants.[9]

The SPP follows a testing of the waters suggestion offered by the Council on Foreign Relations when it used the term "Creating a North American Community." Besides foreign and inland ports, foreign customs stations in mid-America, and a superhighway from Mexico to Canada, there was also a trial idea to "re-educate" U.S. students by having them embrace the term "North American" when they consider their personal identities. Would this ultimately replace allegiances to sovereign names like American, Canadian, and Mexican? Time will tell.

To get a better idea of the SPP concept and the packages, I went directly to one of the sources who has reviewed the documentation, Harvard-educated and respected author and investigative journalist Dr. Jerome Corsi.

ANKARLO: SPP, to some it is a conspiracy theorist's perfect dream, but to others, like you, this is the real deal. Take us on a trip; what is it?

DR. CORSI: SPP is a secret government program. The letters stand for Security and Prosperity Partnership in North America, and it was declared at a summit meeting in Waco, Texas, with little more than a press statement—no law, no treaty. But at the end of the summit, Vicente Fox, then president of Mexico; Canada's prime minister then, Paul Martin; and George Bush came out on the stage and they say, "We're in the Security and Prosperity Partnership of North America." And, from what I've been able to research and document—and everything I'm writing and saying is thoroughly documented at government Web sites, so citizens can go see the original sources themselves and read the government documents and validate what I'm talking about. But the Security and Prosperity Partnership, I think, ends up being an agreement by George Bush with Mexico and Canada that he's going to progressively open our borders with Mexico and Canada.

ANKARLO: All right. I've read some of the links and documentation that you're talking about and, from what I've seen, they're pretty innocuous—suggesting that we need a good relationship with our neighbors, and we do. One says, and I quote, "In March 2005, the leaders of Canada, Mexico, and the United States adopted a Security and Prosperity Partnership of North America, SPP, establishing ministerial-level working groups to address key security and economic issues facing North America, setting a short deadline for reporting progress back to their governments. President Bush described the significance of the SPP as putting forward a common commitment to 'the markets and democracy, freedom and trade, and mutual prosperity and security.'" Et cetera. What's wrong with that?

DR. CORSI: Well, it sure sounds like it's all good for you.

ANKARLO: Yeah, sure.

DR. CORSI: And I know, if you really click those words, maybe it plays Bobby McFerrin music and says, "Don't worry, be happy." Then, I go into the working groups and what are they going to do; there are twenty of them with our bureaucrats meeting on a regular basis with the bureaucrats of Mexico and Canada. That catches my eye, so I file a Freedom of Information Act request to find out what this is all about. I get back a couple of thousand pages of documents; I get the names of all the bureaucrats, their e-mails, and I also get a formal organizational chart of these working groups, which the government has never before published. I publish it on page 81 of my book *The Late Great USA*. Now, we've got a North American transportation working group, North American health working group, North American environmental working group, North American movement of goods and food and agriculture, four different working groups, and all the little boxes on this chart report up to three cabinet secretaries: Secretary of State Rice, [Michael] Chertoff in Homeland Security, and [Carlos]

Gutierrez in Commerce. Then the next level of little boxes report up to the—in the White House—the Homeland Security Council and National Security Council, and then up to the office of the president. Now, this organizational chart is an organizational chart of a shadow, trilateral bureaucracy that isn't defined in the Constitution.

ANKARLO: Wait. Slow it down.

DR. CORSI: Darrell, this isn't supposed to exist.

ANKARLO: Go back to the shadow trilateral thing. What is that, Dr. Corsi?

DR. CORSI: You see there is the transportation working group and it's got Department of Transportation, U.S., Jeffrey Shane. Well, Shane is the undersecretary for policy. He's a very high official in the Department of Transportation. And the Mexican and the Canadian counterpart of this group have Mexican and Canadian Secretaries of Transportations or Undersecretaries in comparable boxes reporting to the three cabinet-level officers in Mexico and Canada.

ANKARLO: I'm hearing you describe a flowchart that starts with the president, goes through the various secretaries and moves on down. Not only do we have our transportation secretary, but we also have these other secretaries included in the flowchart.

DR. CORSI: I put it all on the Internet at StopSPP.com. If you look there you'll see the lists of who the comparable bureaucrats in Mexico and Canada are by name, phone number, and e-mail address, who are assigned each of these working groups.

ANKARLO: And you say this is not something that is constitutional. It seems that for the last thirty or forty years our Supreme Court has been using laws from other countries to dictate laws in this nation, and that has scared me, and now we have these quiet groups, created in a stealth mode, without a single vote by Congress or U.S. citizens.

DR. CORSI: And, Darrell, you've got to read these thousands of pages of documents on the Internet and the Freedom of Information Act requests. Many of them boring, arcane, legal, but within them, you see these structures where our bureaucrats are knitting together into a new, a trilateral, bureaucracy that exists and functions and is making agreements—those 2005, 2006 reports of the leaders document some 250 agreements that these working groups have formed, most of which are not published anywhere. And the agreements that—we now have a North American Health Policy, a North American Transportation Policy, a North American Energy Policy, and they supersede the U.S. National Energy Policy and replace it.

ANKARLO: And that's the part that scares me, because once fully implemented, the sovereignty of the country is gone.

DR. CORSI: That's right.

ANKARLO: To have relationships and policies, to have, you know, a variety of, "I'll scratch your back, you scratch mine," I think we all get that, and I think most of us would say, "Yeah, that's smart." But to do it in a way that supersedes the laws and the policies we already have, that's pretty, not just unconstitutional, but some would say it's treasonous.

DR. CORSI: Well, it's just like what happened in Europe when the EU, the European Union, went through fifty years from a coal and steel agreement and ended up being a full-fledged regional government, the European Union with its own currency, the euro, this was a bureaucratic coup d'etat. And, to give you an example of what the working groups are doing: These working groups— Mary Peters, secretary of transportation, on April 27, 2007, in Tucson, held the first North American Transportation Trilateral. And she called the meeting a "trilateral meeting." Her counterparts—Secretaries of Transportation in Mexico and Canada— attended. They announced that we have built, under the SPP working groups, five wide-area augmentation stations from Mexico and Canada. Those are the stations you need to download our GPS (global positioning satellite) data that's at the heart of our air traffic control system. So, we've given Mexico and Canada the U.S. Air Traffic Control System, including the ability to know where all military aircraft are over the United States.

ANKARLO: Why would we do that?

DR. CORSI: Because Mary Peters announced that shortly, Mexican and Canadian airlines are going to be able to operate in the United States out of our domestic terminals, because we're all North Americans, and they can compete on domestic U.S. routes—New York to Los Angeles, Denver to Las Vegas, you name it—without any connection to Mexico or Canada, and, since we're all North Americans, we all now share the same air traffic control system continentally, and all—

ANKARLO: But Air Mexico and Air Canada both operate out of American airports already, don't they?

DR. CORSI: Well, yes, but they operate out of international terminals, they have their own air traffic control system, and they hand off the airplanes at the borders to U.S. air traffic controllers. This gives Mexico and Canadian air traffic controllers our air traffic control system, so they're integrated into a North American air traffic control system, as if Mexico City were just like Detroit or Phoenix or any other U.S. city.

ANKARLO: Wow. If they gain access to all of our ATC programs, are they going to fall under the FAA regulations, or are we going to have something else that supersedes that?

DR. CORSI: Well, I think the whole idea [of] the SPP working groups, as I read them, is to go to a new regional air control structure, because we're really developing regional air traffic control rules, and I believe the FAA will be superseded by, ultimately, another organization. You know, Darrell, I spent hours and hours reading all the details from these groups—the FAA Web sites, the Department of Transportation Web sites. There are actually literally thousands of Security and Prosperity Partnership pages. They're just very boring; they're very detailed; they're very administrative; you have to pore through the rules. If I didn't have a PhD. in political science at Harvard, I don't think I could make it through half of these. And I think the government's planning that the American people won't put the time into seeing the administrative work that's being done to create a regional framework.

ANKARLO: And so, what would happen if this new trilateral deal is put together, and let's say all the airlines and trucking companies are floating in and out, as you're saying—what changes and pressures are applied to United States military then?

DR. CORSI: Well, it's a good question, because the long-term prospects are frightening. And, I talk a lot about NORAD (North American Aerospace Defense Command), and increasingly—we're involving Mexico and Canada in our continental emergency plans. NORAD has created the whole USNORTHCOM—which is a new command structure that's devoted to using the U.S. military in domestic emergency situations. And the definition of those domestic emergencies in NORAD are continent-wide. Mexico has not yet chosen to participate, but Canada is interfacing with the USNORTHCOM command, with Canada command and, of course, in NORAD itself is a bilateral command, which has traditionally involved Canada. So, Canada's sitting right at the command tables in Peterson Air Force Base.

ANKARLO: I believe it is a smart idea to involve our friendly neighbors in a protection strategy, but you seem to be describing something more involved. Foreign countries with their military personnel routinely setting up in our command centers is unfathomable. And so, here we are, as a sovereign nation, men and women have died for this country, for the boundaries—

DR. CORSI: Right, go to Arlington. They didn't die for North American Union, but—that's why, in the book, I call it the "Late, great USA" because they say this is a bureaucratic coup d'etat.

ANKARLO: All right. Hang on. When you say "coup d'etat"—I always think of machine guns and guys who are shouting "death to" whoever the leader is of that country at the time. But this seems so clandestine that bullets may not be necessary.

DR. CORSI: It's all being done by the bureaucrats.

ANKARLO: Let me change gears from the air to the ground. Where does the proposed superhighway, the Trans-Texas Corridor, fit into the SPP program?

DR. CORSI: Well, the NAFTA superhighway is going to be started with a trans-Texas corridor. It's going to be a new, four-football-fields-wide highway. I have the architectural drawing of the highway. It's going to tear up the center of Texas and extend down to the ports in Mexico like Lazaro Cardenas, for Mexican trucks to bring containers from China, off-loaded onto the Mexican ports because it's cheaper without longshoremen, Mexican trucks because they're cheaper. The Mexican trucks now are going to come on up through our nation's heart. The Department of Transportation pilottested one hundred Mexican trucking companies with their long-haul rigs. Both Texas governor Rick Perry and the Department of Transportation are ignoring the will of the people. Perry just vetoed about six pieces of legislation the Texas legislature overwhelmingly passed that would have placed a two-year moratorium on this highway. Texas legislature is now out of session for two years, and the Department of Transportation is ignoring the House of Representatives, which 411-to-3 passed a bill which would have shut down the Mexican trucks; but the Department of Transportation is saying, "Well, it's not been passed yet by the Senate, so we're ignoring it." And the Bush administration lobbied the Senate Department of Transportation Committee, telling that committee not to have a comparable bill. And so, what's happening, the Mexican trucks are being brought into the United States to undercut U.S. trucking. Plain and simple. They are still holding meetings on it—especially in Texas.

ANKARLO: Yeah, and besides all of the security and infrastructure issues, the bottom line issue will result in U.S. truck drivers watching their paychecks dwindle—yet another sector with less of a likelihood of having a solid living in America.

DR. CORSI: That's right. The multinational corporations are winning these global and regional agendas, and they're going to reduce the cost of shipping, they're going to push down the cost of trucking a third to a half, and U.S. truckers are going to suffer directly as a consequence of this.

ANKARLO: Let me tell you what frightens me the most. I'm thinking ahead twenty years from now. There will be no middle class. There will be the minions—who won't have a shot at negotiating how many dollars they should make—or pesos or ameros or whatever the company pays. If you don't like it, then you're screwed, because the multinational companies will control the destiny of the world. America, or this North American Union you speak of, will have the poor slave types grinding it out for the super, super, superrich, the conglomerates who own everything. There will be no middle class. That's what I see.

DR. CORSI: Well, that's the way it's headed. I mean, Mexico's shipping its impoverished masses to the United States. President Bush admits there are 12 million illegal aliens here, three-quarters of which came under his term. He says he can't secure the borders. No, that's not correct. He won't—he doesn't want to.

ANKARLO: You link the lack of our border protection directly to the plans of our leaders as they work to make a North American Union.

DR. CORSI: Certainly.

ANKARLO: Louie, one of my radio show listeners, asked what I think is a fair question on the SPP deal. The gist of his point was "Why don't we try the European Union route? Why are we so into keeping everybody so separate? America, Canada, and Mexico are all in the same area, and it would be a good thing to cooperate together." Pick up on that, Dr. Corsi, because his question is an interesting one. With all the crazy, militant, radical Islamic extremists, the crazy ones, all forming their unions and getting ready to play their games, if we have Mexico and Canada with us, maybe we become a more powerful player now?

DR. CORSI: Well, in fact, Robert Bartley, who was then the editor of the *Wall Street Journal*, in an editorial published in the *Wall Street Journal* on July 21, 2001, agreed. He said, "Vicente Fox thinks we should have a European Union in the United States." He said, "The *Wall Street Journal* is all in favor of it." They endorsed the North American Union. The problem is this: the United States has uniquely defined rights under our Bill of Rights and Declaration of Independence. They are defined as "given to us by God." They're not defined as "given to us by some kind of a European Union-style bureaucracy." These are rights that are basic to human nature that we have from God.

ANKARLO: Is your point that this country is God-inspired or that our guaranteed rights as citizens are being dissolved in favor of something more global?

DR. CORSI: Good-bye, Second Amendment. Good-bye, First Amendment. And our founding fathers believed that the whole definition of our institution's government derived from natural rights; in other words, given the human nature, this constitutional-limited republic, in which the powers are balanced off against each other, the executive, the legislative, and the judicial, the fundamental form of government that is needed to protect these inalienable rights granted by God.

ANKARLO: Fox News reporter Bret Baier asked the leaders of our three leading North American countries a very interesting question after they concluded their August 2007 summit. This is what he said: "As you three leaders meet here, there are a growing number of people in each of your countries who have expressed concern about the Security and Prosperity Partnership. This is addressed to all three of you. Can you say, today, that this is not a prelude to a North American Union, similar to a European Union—are there plans to build some kind of superhighway connecting all three countries, and do you believe all of these theories about a possible erosion of national identity stem from a lack of transparency from this partnership?" And they answered with ridicule and even more questions; none wanted to address the real issue. Canadian prime minister Stephen Harper responded, "A couple of my opposition leaders have speculated on massive water diversions and super-highways to the continent, maybe interplanetary, I'm not sure, as well." President Bush was equally as elusive:

> We each respect each other's sovereignty. Um, you know, there are some who would like to frighten our fellow citizens into believing that, um, relations between us are harmful for our respective peoples. I just believe they're wrong. I believe it's in our interest to trade; I believe it's in our interest to dialogue; I believe it's in our interest to work out common problems for the good of our people.

DR. CORSI: The interesting thing, Darrell, the president was given an explicit chance by Fox News to deny categorically that there was any thinking about a North American Union or any NAFTA super-highways or any erosion of sovereignty, and he didn't take that route. Instead, what President Bush did is he went the route of ridiculing and calling us names—you know, conspiracy theorists—and unfortunately, since the time of the ancient Greek rhetorical, you know, Demosthenes, and all the Greek learning and training on debate, it's been well established that somebody in a debate or an argument who reduces to ridiculing their opponent or calling them names has already lost, because they can't answer the argument on the basis of fact and argument.

ANKARLO: It certainly sounds like he's taking that route. Here's the rest of his answer to the North American Union question,

I'm amused by some of the, some of the speculation, um, some of the old, I think he called them political scare tactics, etc. If you've been in politics as long as I have you get used to that kind of technique, where you lay out a conspiracy and then force people to try to prove it doesn't exist. That's just the way some people operate. Uh, I'm here representing my nation. . . .

DR. CORSI: What is it about the Security and Prosperity Partnership that causes them not to want to answer? Number one, the entire way the SPP is conducted is behind closed doors, in secret. There was a North American Competitiveness Council, thirty companies from North America hand picked by the Chambers of Commerce, meeting with the president, the three leaders in closed doors. The media were not allowed in. No detailed reports were given on what they discussed, and it's that lack of transparency that, itself, is a problem. Then, you know, I begin the book by saying, why do we have a war on terror for six years and we've not secured our borders with Mexico and Canada? We're six years into this war on terror, and there's proven cases of Hezbollah terrorists coming across the border with Mexico; they set up shop in Dearborn, and they're in federal prison.

ANKARLO: And you and I both know that we simply have not wanted to secure the borders because the Republicans will say, "We need to make sure we have all these people to work here for the rich companies." Democrats will say, "We need those people to vote for us. Leave those doggone doors open."

DR. CORSI: First of all, there was no discussion. I'm saying that illegal immigration is the symptom. And the cause, the reason why the borders have been left open, is that Bush and Calderon and, before him, Fox, and the Canadian prime minister, have all been agreeing to increasingly open these borders and to move towards economic integration. And that's the exact path that Europe went down, in a stealth fashion, only saying it was economic—opening of borders—but it ended up necessitating political arrangements, and ultimately, a regional state—the European Union—and the elite and the multinational businesses in Europe now admit—you know, we've got the memoirs of Jean Monnet, one of the chief French architects of the whole European Union scheme, who admits it was a stealth plan from the beginning, and he was always lying to deny that his goal was a regional government. And the argument is: When you've got that strong a model from Europe that ended up with the European Union and a euro, it is not unreasonable to say, that, you know, we now have a tenth of Mexico's population living in the United States as Mexican citizens. By 2015 or so it's going to be one out of every five people born in Mexico living in the United States as a Mexican citizen, with some forty consular offices to protect their civil rights as Mexican nationals living in the United States. That's already becoming a dual country.

ANKARLO: And you bring Canada into it—and I find it interesting that they see it as a trade opportunity. We became their number-one trading partner as a result of NAFTA—and Mexico benefited from the arrangement as well. So what do you say—if you were to take the crystal ball out, is it twenty years, thirty years, forty years, that we're no longer the U.S.A., we're now the North American Union?

DR. CORSI: I'd say twenty years [is] going to be a lot closer, and it will not take the fifty years it took Europe. There'll still be a United States, as the same way there's still an Italy, but, you know, Italy can't pass a law that the bureaucrats in Brussels and Luxembourg, the working groups that run the European Union, don't first give the Italian Parliament to pass. If they pass a law that the European Union working group bureaucrats don't want, that law's overturned.

ANKARLO: Is what we're seeing now a precursor—started way back when—to get us used to working within the framework of other countries' laws?

DR. CORSI: International law, or a law from a higher regional authority, is going to supersede U.S. law. We have Chapter 11 tribunals in NAFTA that already can overturn state and federal laws in favor of NAFTA investors. So the question is, will, in twenty years, our laws remain supreme? No. I'm waiting for the challenge to come to the First and Second Amendment. Let me just run this scenario by—and we know the Mexican consulates have protested and demanded the prosecution of Border Patrol agents like Ramos and Campion and Gilmer Hernandez.

ANKARLO: Okay, let's go there.

DR. CORSI: Okay. So, now let's just assume that some Mexican national in the process of committing a crime in the United States—a rape, an attempted murder, a robbery—a U.S. citizen takes a gun and, in self-defense, kills them. Okay, the Mexican Council, the first thing they're going to say is: That violence using a firearm was in excess of what was needed for this unarmed Mexican national who really didn't intend to hurt anybody, and there's too many guns in this community. So, the guns allowed in this community are threatening the civil rights of the Mexican nationals, and in Mexico, we do not have a Second Amendment. We're going to challenge the Second Amendment in this community on the basis that this Mexican national was killed, and we're going to charge that . . . U.S. citizen who shot him, with murder.

ANKARLO: Mexico, in particular has played that card several times. They won't allow certain people to be extradited back to the United States because they say, "Well, you're going to kill them. We don't do that here." And let's remind everybody: in Mexico, they have some of the most severe gun regulations in the world. You're not going to own a gun if you're just a private citizen there, so all sorts of ramifications.

DR. CORSI: How about this one: someone goes to a city council meeting, all upset that, you know, Mexican and illegal immigrants have taken their job at a construction site. And they start railing about the Mexican illegal immigrants. The Mexican Council comes in and says, "We want this person prosecuted for hate speech, because he's trying to turn the city council and this community against Mexican nationals."

ANKARLO: Let me give you a quote from Mexico's president Felipe Calderon, "Now, this meeting allows me to reinforce the conviction that North America as a region still has not developed the enormous potential it has, and I'm more convinced about this today than ever before that it has to be developed. There's no doubt that the globalization process that we are currently experiencing is definitely pressuring the competitiveness of countries; and not only countries, but the competitiveness of the countries that have joined into regions." That's interesting, because he is already tipping the hand: Hey, yeah, the plan is the regionalization of this world.

DR. CORSI: Not one word has been said about getting the illegal aliens controlled. It is presumed by Bush; it is presumed by Calderon; it is presumed by Harper that the illegal aliens are staying.

To check the will of the people, Grassfire.org, a popular Web site dedicated to informing and calling citizens to action, posted a petition online. "The response is overwhelming," Steve Elliott, president of Grassfire, told a news agency, adding, "The petition has been up on the Web site for less than a week, and we have been getting as many as five hundred signatures an hour." In fact, the petition, posted in August 2007, had a goal of 100,000 signatures by December 2008. Less than two months after its inception (October 29, 2007), it was up to 219,984 and counting. Will the president, congress—anyone in authority—care what the will of the people is? Stay tuned.

QUINCE

THE POWER OF A LANGUAGE

How many times have you dialed a service number or bank customer relations line, or tried to get business of any kind done on the phone, only to have the automated machine tell you to press 1 for Spanish and 2 for English? I was on an Arizona driver's license and voter registration Web site, paid for by the state, and before it would let me review the pages, I had to select between the two languages. It ticked me off to the point that I had to turn off my computer and walk away.

And why is Spanish always the first option? Why can't the voice say, "Since you are obviously a citizen, or at least somewhat educated, you may continue on, but if you can't speak the language of the citizens of this country, we're going to do you a favor and translate for you"? Obviously, I would prefer no such options, but why can't they do that? And why are there only two? If I am from Saudi Arabia, France, or Russia, I would be feeling pretty discriminated against by the government or U.S. companies. I wonder why a couple ambulance-chasing lawyers haven't turned this into some sort of class-action lawsuit.

The current controversy isn't the first time America has debated the words her people use. In 1906, with more than 1.2 million new immigrants coming to America, President Theodore Roosevelt stated, "We have room for but one language in this country, and that is the English language, for we intend to see that the crucible turns our people out as Americans, of American nationality, and not as dwellers in a polyglot boarding house."[1] He clearly understood that it would be the end of progress if every person in the country kept the luxury of speaking only in his own tongue.

During the nineteenth century's European immigration wave, numerous programs were developed to help legal immigrants get along until they knew enough to swim on their own. In the mid-1800s German and French were spoken and taught to help citizens in Ohio and Louisiana assimilate, but by the end of the century, bilingual education and government offerings were all but eliminated because our newest citizens loved their new country enough to want to participate in her national language.

Fast-forward a century, and once again citizens are debating the need for a unifying language for the country—even though such laws have been on the books in more than half the country for years. It is interesting to note that eighty-five member nations of the United Nations have "official" languages, and yet America has failed to follow suit. Former Republican House Speaker and renowned historian Newt Gingrich provided his perspective:

> In an America where there are over 80 languages taught in the California schools as the primary language, not as the secondary language but as the primary language, in a country where in Seattle there are 75 languages being taught, in Chicago there are 100; this is not bilingualism, this is a level of confusion which if it were allowed

to develop for another 20 or 30 years would literally lead, I think, to the decay of the core parts of our civilization.[2]

The difference between early acceptance and tolerance for foreign languages at the turn of the twentieth century and now is tied up in the way today's courts interpret civil rights decisions from the 1960s, most notably Title VI of the Civil Rights Act of 1964. It prohibits discrimination based on race, color, and national origin, and shrewd lawyers were swift to run to a judge every time another immigrant claimed "discrimination" because his language wasn't supported by government programs. The end result: more than three hundred languages are currently spoken in America.

Eventually, the Supreme Court stepped in and the landmark 1974 case of *Lau vs. Nichols* ruled that school districts must ensure that all students have equal access to standard lessons no matter what language they speak. Once these floodgates opened, the natural by-products were opportunities for the limited and non-English speakers' parents to receive communications in their native tongue. Once the U.S. took that step, the practice spilled from the schools to town halls, departments of motor vehicles, voting booths, and countless other avenues into mainstream America.

Multiple languages lead to confusion and added costs to taxpayers. Massachusetts offers driver's tests in twenty-four foreign languages, including Turkish, Finnish, Farsi, and Czech. The California test is worse, with thirty-one official languages. These two states underscore a national trend that placates instead of challenges, which results in a growing trend that keeps average people from excelling, communities from uniting, and costs taxpayers billions of dollars. Rep. Joe Knollenberg (R-Mich.) says, "By teaching young people in their native languages, we are handicapping their performance in a highly competitive arena. Bilingual education may make the school day easier for children speaking English as a second language. However, it creates another class of student unable to read, speak, and write English in an English-speaking society"[3]

According to the Population Reference Bureau, "nearly 50 million Americans spoke a language other than English at home in 2004—nearly one-fifth of all U.S. residents age 5 or older."[4] Even though many assert that today's young non-English speakers are picking up the language faster than people did in the past, they still represent a burden to U.S. taxpayers ($3 billion for bilingual education in 2006 alone[5]).

Susan Headden writes in her "One Nation, One Language?" column,

> Of the children returning to urban public schools this fall, a whopping one third speak a foreign language first. "It blows your mind," says Dade County, Fla., administrator Mercedes Toural, who counts 5,190 new students speaking no fewer than 56 different tongues.[6]

Not only is there a cost to U.S. citizens for classes, but think of the extra manpower hours for Web sites and phone systems to be diversified, and the actual labor and hard costs associated with multiple languages are staggering.

Since America is the destination of choice for so many immigrants wanting a fresh start, it is only natural for many of them to bring their native languages with them, but when they were allowed to keep their language without repercussion, the welcome mat came out for all takers. Currently, the U.S. government estimates the number of illegal immigrants at approximately 12 million,[7] while other population trackers like Californians for Population Stabilization say the number is up to three times that number.[8] Even with such wildly differing numbers, the costs borne by citizens are incalculable.

In 1986, shortly after President Ronald Reagan granted amnesty to 3 million illegal aliens and while U.S. citizens protested the various languages forced upon them, the Linguistic Society of America held their regular business meeting. In it they resolved:

> The English language in America is not threatened. All evidence suggests that recent immigrants are overwhelmingly aware of the social and economic advantages of becoming proficient in English, and require no additional compulsion to learn the language. American unity has never rested primarily on unity of language, but rather on common political and social ideals.[9]

As the number of illegals in the U.S. has soared to as many as 38 million, with another 37.5 million here legally, there is little doubt the assault on this country's language attacks her political and social infrastructures as well, and to report otherwise is foolishness.

Alexis de Tocqueville, the great French writer who analyzed America's democracy in his book *Democracy in America*, said, "The tie of language is perhaps the strongest and the most durable that can unite mankind."

Hijack a country's language, and soon you won't have to take her sovereignty and autonomy—she'll give it to you.

DIECISÉIS

IMPORTED CRIMINALS

A sk yourself how you would respond to this scenario: You are twenty-two years old with little education, making thirty-nine dollars a week—for a seven-day, fifteen-hour-a-day job that you will lose if you are late. A friend says he can get you into America safely for free; the only catch is that you will need to deliver a few packages every now and then. You jump at the chance but soon realize the "packages" have drugs in them. Your "boss" says your debt will be paid with the next delivery, but if you continue with your deliveries, you will be paid two to three hundred a day, and that figure could easily multiply by ten times if you work hard.

This scene plays out thousands of times a week all across America. With each passed bag, envelope, and package, the young person takes another step toward more minor illegal activities, soon to be dwarfed by major ones. The response should be swift and powerful; instead, our city fathers respond by designating their communities as "sanctuary cities," and politicians massage our laws so our guests feel even more welcome.

Why would cities welcome illegal border crossers and some of their more demented counterparts? In a word—power! The growing base of Hispanic persons in America can change the political land-scape in cities across the nation, and our elected leaders know it. *The New York Times*, citing U.S. Census Bureau data from July 2005 to July 2006, said, "Nonwhites now make up a majority in almost one-third of the most-populous counties in the country and in nearly one in 10 of all 3,100 counties."[1]

Heather MacDonald writes in "The Illegal-Alien Crime Wave,"

The Hispanic population numbers represent the majority. The immigrant population has grown so large that public officials are terrified of alienating it, even at the expense of ignoring the law and tolerating violence. In 1996, a breathtaking *Los Angeles Times* exposé on the 18th Street Gang, which included descriptions of innocent bystanders being murdered by laughing *cholos* (gang members), revealed the rate of illegal-alien membership in the gang. In response to the public outcry, the Los Angeles City Council ordered the police to reexamine Special Order 40. [Special Order 40 is a police mandate that originated in 1979 by the Los Angeles Police Department and City Council to prevent police from inquiring about the immigration status of arrestees.] You would have thought it had suggested reconsidering *Roe* v. *Wade*. A police commander warned the council: "This is going to open a significant, heated debate." City Councilwoman Laura Chick put on a brave front: "We mustn't be afraid," she declared firmly.[2]

To mollify a large Hispanic voting bloc, New York City mayor Rudolph Giuliani defended his beloved sanctuary city platform by suing all the way up to the U.S. Supreme Court to protect it. Later, on September 5, 2001, a committee he selected ruled that immigration information could be kept confidential to protect the line of trust and communication between illegal immigrants and city leaders. Giuliani and his constituents had won. Less than a week later, some of the members of New York's illegal immigrant community flew planes into the World Trade Center buildings, the Pentagon, and a Pennsylvania field, and—some would argue—helped to cause the U.S. military wars in Afghanistan and Iraq.

In early 2007, New York governor Eliot Spitzer wanted to join a half dozen other states that have elected to give illegal immigrants driver's licenses. Said Spitzer, "The facts show that restricting immigrants' access to driver's licenses does nothing to improve security. All it does is drive immigrants into the shadows." Later that year, after an outcry of public opposition, the State Senate voted 39–19 to overturn his policy. Regardless of the outcome, the new power base had flexed its muscles just enough to prove they have the numbers to get the political wing nuts to do as they are told.

According to a *Chicago Tribune* story, U.S. Rep. Luis Gutierrez (D-Ill.) encouraged illegal immigrants to register to vote. Rep. Gutierrez told participants they must focus on electoral strategies after mobilizing hundreds of thousands in the Loop and elsewhere. Gutierrez said he has given up hope that Congress will pass immigration reform before the November elections. "It's nice to have marches. I go to all of them," Gutierrez said. "But there is something that has to happen after a march. You register to vote. Congress will only move when it is in fear of losing power." As impossible as that sounds, it has been done numerous times in recent elections as many illegal alien supporters don't just want their people to drive as though they are citizens; they want them to vote like us too.

In 2004 elections, Massachusetts, Illinois, North Carolina, California, and other states watched as noncitizens walked into polling places and pulled the lever for the candidates of their choice (politicians who defended an easing of restrictions on illegal aliens, no doubt) as on-lookers were powerless to do anything.

Gutierrez told his followers that the Motor Voter Registration form merely asks the applicant to sign it, state he is a U.S. citizen who is at least eighteen years old, is a resident of the precinct for the last thirty days, and is not a felon. When the lawbreaker is asked for a Social Security number, he uses a stolen one. For those who are fortunate enough to live in New York, Governor Spitzer's people have said that voters need only show up. The governor suggested that it was too difficult to ask a person to prove citizenship. Perhaps someone can explain to the former governor just how difficult it was for a military man or woman to fight and die so bona fide citizens have protected rights.

As Gutierrez and Spitzer were watering down the laws of their states, presidential candidate and New York senator Hillary Clinton, was voting against the Help America Vote Act of 2002, because providing a proof of citizenship ID would "disproportionately affect ethnic and racial minorities, recently naturalized American citizens, language minorities, the poor, the homeless, the millions of eligible New York voters who do not have a driver's license, and those individuals who otherwise would have exercised their right to vote without these new provisions." Huh?! The bill allowed citizens to use Social Security cards, utility bills, government issued IDs and checks, and numerous other typical IDs, but it was too difficult for her and the only other person to condemn the act, Senator Chuck Schumer, also of New York. Both elected leaders recognized the short-term bonanza that so many welfare-reliant "voters" would bring, but the long-term disaster will cost taxpayers billions as the effects of decisions to pacify instead of fight are realized.

—✳—

While we're waiting for another attack by terrorists already living here, we need to focus on the crimes perpetrated on U.S. citizens by illegal aliens on a daily basis. The number and economic impact is unparalleled in our country's history. Edwin Rubenstein chronicles the epidemic in *Criminal Alien Nation*:[3] In 1980 our state and federal corrections system housed fewer than nine thousand criminal aliens, but in a little more than a decade, that number shot to more than a quarter million.

Rubenstein also points out that almost 27 percent of all prisoners in federal custody are in the country illegally, and of that number, 63 percent are Mexican. The government spent $1.4 billion to incarcerate the criminal alien population but required local jurisdictions to pick up the tab for 75 percent of any costs. No wonder so many cities and towns are finding it difficult to balance the books, let alone hire any new police or firefighters; they simply can't afford to.

On May 9, 2005, the federal government's General Accounting Office (GAO) released "Information on Criminal Aliens Incarcerated in Federal and State Prisons and Local Jails,"[4] a report that tracked 55,322 illegal aliens to better understand their patterns of lawlessness. Remember, we are constantly reminded that "these poor people come to find work." Some do. Many don't. And, when they choose to move to criminal activity, they don't stop at just once. Of the 55,322 illegal aliens studied:

- Researchers found that they were arrested a total of 459,614 times, averaging about 8 arrests per illegal alien.
- They were arrested for approximately 700,000 criminal offenses, averaging about 13 offenses per illegal alien.
- Nearly 50 percent had previously been convicted of a felony; 20 percent of a drug offense; 18 percent a violent offense, and 11 percent, other felony offenses.

- More than 80 percent of the arrests occurred after 1990 (after our first amnesty deal).
- Fifty-six percent of those charged with a reentry offense had previously been convicted on at least 5 prior occasions.
- Defendants charged with unlawful reentry had the most extensive criminal histories: 90 percent had been previously arrested. Of those with a prior arrest, 50 percent had been arrested for violent or drug-related felonies.

According to P.F. Wagner of the popular Web site The Dark Side of Illegal Immigration [http://www.usillegalaliens.com/], "In reviewing those numbers, note that the study only sampled about 21% of the incarcerated illegal aliens. To get the full extent of the collateral damage, we need to extrapolate the average number of offenses out across all 267,000 incarcerated illegal alien criminals. Doing so results in some 1,288,619 crimes!" Wagner continued:

One of the problems in identifying the involvement of illegal aliens in crime, is that NOBODY TRACKS IT as a particular demographic statistic. . . . While the Justice Department tracks nearly every conceivable aspect of crime, evidently, Congress only wants to know what crimes "White, Black, American Indian, and Asian" Americans are committing. Interestingly, however, ethnicity is very important for establishing minority status and preferences but totally unimportant for determining who is committing crimes. Crimes being committed by illegal aliens, aka foreign nationals, are not tracked. Thus, if anything, the FBI underreports crime.

In 1999, Centre College professor David Anderson created an abstract on the cost of crime on the average American. In "The Aggregate

Burden of Crime," Professor Anderson demonstrates the financial burden on the U.S. economy at more than $1.6 trillion (adjusted for 2006 inflation).[5] When coupled with the federal government's under-reported figures, it is easy to see that illegal aliens are creating havoc on our entire system. Wagner, in his studies on the subject, said, "Given that there are about 270,000 career illegal alien criminals currently incarcerated in federal, state, and local jails results in a cost of $432 BILLION. If so, that is $1,440 for every man, woman, and child in the United States."

Iowa Representative Steve King reviewed the warrant, arrest, prison, and crime records of illegal immigrants, and what he found causes serious concern. For instance King says:

- 12 Americans are murdered daily by illegal aliens
- 13 are killed daily by drunk illegal alien drivers
- An untold percentage of 2003's 42,636 U.S. road accidents were caused by illegal aliens
- 20 percent of fatal accidents involve at least one driver who lacks a valid license[6]

I was surfing the Web in early October 2007 while doing some research for my daily radio program, when I noticed a trend on one of the many news sites I visit. The headlines were all drawing my attention to tragedies fellow citizens endured at the hands of illegals— or those who support them:

- Police Arrest Illegal Immigrant on Sexual Assault Charges
- El Salvador Lawmaker Wanted on Money Laundering Arrested in OC [Orange County, CA]
- Fired Illegal Indicted in Crimes

- Border Patrol Agents Arrest 3 Illegal Aliens for Sexually Related Crimes
- Ritter: Colo. Will Be Friendly to Foreign-Born (and Unfriendly to Fourth- Generation Americans?)
- SC Senate Leader Wants Constitution Change on Illegal Immigration
- 6 Illegal Immigrants Arrested In Maury Co. [Tennessee]
- Hillary Clinton Talks Immigration, Housing in Kansas City
- 37 Foreign Nationals Face Criminal Charges and Deportation
- Dead Body Found in Abandoned Avondale Drop House

I opened my RSS news feeds, and even more flowed off the pages. A burning question demanded an answer: how can so many people be so gravely affected by this problem and most of the time we don't look past the headlines? I was ashamed of myself. So I decided to dig a little; I wanted to know the stories; I needed to know the true personal impact created by our imported criminals. Rapist Ricardo Cepates, an illegal alien from Honduras, was arrested in 1998 for attacking a woman with a knife and ordered deported. He never left the country. In 1999 he pleaded guilty to a weapons charge and was released. Since then, he has been convicted of four rapes and is accused of raping four more, including a fourteen-year-old girl.

Police officer Nick Erfle, thirty-three, stopped three jaywalkers on simple charges of disrupting traffic on a Phoenix street. While checking the men's IDs, one, belonging to Erik Jovani Martinez, came back with an outstanding charge—which surprised Martinez because it was a stolen ID in the first place. Martinez bodychecked Erfle to the ground and fired several rounds into the officer's upper torso and face. The illegal alien then carjacked a woman and held her hostage until police put a bullet in his head. It turns out that Martinez, a gang member convicted on drug and auto theft charges, had been in jail and ordered deported once released. But as is routine these days, no one bothered to ensure that he was. I propose that we create a new law that requires the idiot bureaucrats who won't enforce immigration standards to be forced to tell the surviving family members that their loved one is dead. Perhaps if they see what they are doing to people like Nick's wife and two kids, they may grow a conscience—though that's highly unlikely!

A thirty-seven-year-old Huntersville, North Carolina, woman went to visit her friend at a trailer the man shared with several roommates. Once she was inside, the friend attacked her and then held her down. For the next six hours, the seven illegal aliens took turns raping her. Police said such rapes with multiple attackers are nearly unheard-of in the town of about 32,300 people, though the number of rapes has increased 11 percent from a similar time period in 2003. Coincidently, the illegal alien population has also been on the rise in the Huntersville area.

Maximiliano Esparza easily penetrated our U.S. border in search of "a better life"—at least that is the excuse most illegal immigrants entering America use. His "better life" consisted of robbery and kidnapping, which should have put him behind bars for no fewer than six years with a mandatory deportation once released. Instead, he was out in four and stayed around just long enough to see Sister Helen Chaska and a second nun conducting their walking prayers as they worked in Klamath Falls, Oregon, on a missionary endeavor. Esparaza attacked both women, strangling Sister Helen so violently that her rosary beads were implanted in her neck. Prosecutors offered a plea deal so the second nun would not have to testify. The illegal now gets three hots and a cot for the rest of his life—courtesy of U.S. taxpayers.

Phoenix police officer Marc Atkinson wanted to work in law

enforcement since his teenage years, and at twenty-three he finally made the cut and would serve proudly for the next five years. That's when he was cut down in a hail of gunfire after being ambushed by three Mexican nationals from the Acapulco area. The three later stated that they came to America to find work but were having a difficult time of it. Their Mexican village was a farming community, which may explain the pound of cocaine officers found in their car.

Members of a Salvadoran street gang liked to flex their muscle in the city of Somerville, Massachusetts, but when one father confronted them about the way they treated his son, three of them decided to teach him a lesson. While the man was away from his home, they snagged up his deaf daughter and her deaf friend and repeatedly raped the young teenagers. Gangs, especially brutal ones like MS-13, are growing in communities nationwide. By the way, the three rapists were illegal.

Gary Selby, an eighteen-year-old promising young man, had just graduated from high school when a tragic "accident" instantly killed him. An illegal alien, Samuel Avalos Gallardo, was arrested and convicted for causing the car accident after he was found to have a blood alcohol level three times the legal limit. While serving his forty-year sentence at a minimum security prison, Gallardo walked off the job and apparently slipped back into Mexico—where he has been living happily for the past decade.

Adriana Sanchez is a Los Angeles police officer who had no idea she was more than seventy-thousand dollars in debt because her Latino name made her the perfect target for identity theft. The thieves had every piece of her credit history covered, even though they were thousands of miles away in Atlanta, Georgia. Authorities have learned that one of the new cons is for cocky thieves to intentionally look for familiar names and high-profile job descriptions just to show how easy it is to do.

Los Angeles County sheriff's deputy David March pulled a car over for a routine traffic violation. He expected the driver to try to negotiate, but instead, as the thirty-three-year-old officer approached the vehicle, known drug dealer Arroyo Garcia opened fire. When he was finished, March lay dead from gunshot wounds to the head. Garcia took off for Mexico and remained there for more than four years while American authorities worked to find him and have him extradited. Once his location was discovered, Mexico refused to return him because the U.S. has the death penalty—especially for cop killers. After an agreement was reached to remove the death penalty option, he was delivered here for trial. The illegal alien had been deported four times before the fateful day when he decided to shoot a cop.

Troy Payton was living in a residence motel near Las Vegas while he struggled to put his life back together. One day, Abimael Azmitia, a fellow resident, began harassing and insulting a fifteen-year-old neighbor girl. When Payton stepped in to help, Azmitia plunged a butcher knife into the thirty-two-year-old man's chest, killing him. The murderer had a prior record for domestic violence and assault and had been ordered deported a month prior, but like so many illegal aliens, he simply chose not to leave. None of that mattered to the judge who gave him a sentence of a year and a half to forty-eight months in jail.

Armando Juvenal, Jose Hernandez, Victor Cruz, and Carlos Rodriguez joined at least five of their gang buddies and went looking for a little recreation. They spotted a forty-two-year-old woman as she walked near her home, so they snatched her for their night of fun and frolicking. For the next several hours, the men gang-raped and tortured the woman until she was near death. She was rescued by a police canine unit. Each deranged waste of life was an illegal alien with numerous arrests for weapons violations, criminal trespass, assault, and drug offenses. New York's sanctuary city policy kept them from prior deportations. The woman sent a note to the court that was read at their sentencing, ending it with "mourning of a life lost."

Policarpio Espinoza was twenty-two, and his cousin, Adan Espinoza Canela, was just seventeen, but that didn't stop them from committing a most heinous and brutal murder—of family members. Espinoza had an ongoing dispute with his brother and invited his cousin to help teach him a little lesson. The two men slipped in to where the brother's children were staying and tortured them to death. When they were finished, one child was beheaded and the others were nearly decapitated after they had been beaten and smothered to death. The parents of the children were illegal immigrants, as were the two murderers.

Vinessa Hoera said it was an answer to prayers when she landed a job at the local seafood market. It was there that she met coworker Faustino Chavez, an illegal alien from Guatemala. He took a liking to the twenty-three-year-old almost immediately and bought her diamond earrings as a Christmas present. The problem—Vinessa Hoera wasn't interested in him. While confessing to her murder, he told the woman's father to go to a local soccer field to find her body. Authorities said that her neck had been cut ear to ear at least five times in an attempt to decapitate her. Police weren't completely sure if he raped her before or after she died.

Officer Will Seuis, a motorcycle patrolman in Oakland, California, had thirty-three letters of appreciation—including one from a person he had just ticketed. His friends and family described him as a "good guy." He was killed when Carlos Mares slammed into his cycle with a fully loaded truck. Instead of stopping to help, Mares took off, only to be caught due to citizens' 9-1-1 calls. Mares, an illegal immigrant, had a history of traffic convictions but was never deported. In fact, he ran his own licensed commercial trucking business in the city.

Seuis, a sixteen-year veteran, never got to say good-bye to his wife or two daughters.

An illegal immigrant from Mexico, thirty-four-year-old Armando Martinez-Lozano, walked into Jason Okon's front yard in Phoenix, said something to him in Spanish, and proceeded to slash the three-year Army veteran and Bronze Star recipient with a knife hidden in Armondo's pants. Okon barely escaped with his life; he spent weeks in Arizona hospitals. Okon was preparing to move his pregnant wife to Wisconsin because too many illegals had taken the kind of job he did before leaving for the war.

Before killing forty-one-year-old Teresa Wright, Eustorgio Leonides Facundo worked as a roofer in Sarasota, Florida. He got the job with a fake ID (big surprise, right?). He was supposed to be back home in Mexico after serving sixteen months detention for burglary. After he killed Ms. Wright, he tossed her burning body into a wooded area.

Nashville, Tennessee, police detective Robert Swisher said, "In my twenty-two years on the job, I have never seen anyone executed, and I mean executed, because someone thought they had hit the person with a vehicle. It sickens me." He was talking about Tracy Owen. The young pregnant lady was standing on the side of the road when seventeen-year-old Antonio DeJesus Idelfonso grabbed the steering wheel from his buddy Eliseo Marcelino-Quintero and tried to run her over but missed. After she fell, the two illegal aliens thought they had actually struck her. When they turned their vehicle around, she thought they were returning to help. She begged for assistance. Instead, Idelfonso shot her five times at point-blank range and drove away.

Augustine Breceda went on a twenty-five-day armed-robbery spree in Reno that left several women, including a seventy-two-year-old grandmother, shaking in their boots after being carjacked, robbed, and attacked. This was after the twice-deported Mexican tried to run over pursuing police officers. This illegal alien had six felony convictions in California. While awaiting sentencing (for 216 years) he begged the judge, "I just wish you would find it in your heart to give me a release date where I'll still be able to be with my three children who I miss so much." I wonder how many of his victims begged for a little mercy?

Each life impacted by illegal alien crime becomes wrapped up in years of hurt and loss that never would have been felt had another nation's criminals not been imported.

Further reading in the 2005 U.S. Government study, "A Line in the Sand,"[7] reveals troubling drug-offense data that receives little to no attention except from border or drug agents who are overworked and outgunned:

- Drug seizures included 222,714 pounds of cocaine, which accounted for roughly 10–20 percent of all drug seizures
- 1,162,509 pounds of marijuana were confiscated
- Only 10–30 percent of illegal aliens are apprehended

Run the numbers for yourself. Using the highest figure the government provides for seizures (20 percent), you will calculate that 4,840,000 pounds of cocaine and 25,520,000 pounds of marijuana arrived at their various U.S. destinations. If an ounce of cocaine has a street value of two thousand dollars, the dollar amount of the white powder equals at least $9,680,000,000 while pot, at a rate of $800 a pound, sells for $20,416,000,000. Remember, illegal aliens only come for work— too bad many of them want to work in the drug trade.

The "Line in the Sand" report explains why they have picked America:

While many illegal aliens cross the border searching for employment, not all illegal aliens are crossing into the United States to find work. Law enforcement has stated that some individuals come across the border because they have been forced to leave their home countries due to their criminal activity. These dangerous criminals are fleeing the law in other countries and seeking refuge in the United States.[8]

No matter the laws on our books, from the mundane to the extreme, illegal immigrants have little difficulty in breaking them. Few will argue with the assessment that the ones causing the most suffering and scars are sex crimes. Researcher Deborah Schurman-Kauflin, PhD, of the Violent Crimes Institute, studied 1,500 violent crimes from January 1999 through April 2006 to provide a glimpse into the cold, dark world of sex crimes in the illegal immigrant camp, and her numbers are staggering:

- 617, or 41 percent were sexual homicides and serial murders
- 525, or 35 percent were child molestations
- 358, or 24 percent, were rapes[9]

Schurman-Kauflin further states that it is after the data have been crunched that the impact can be clearly seen, "This translates to 93 sex offenders and 12 serial sexual offenders coming across U.S. borders illegally per day." Her numbers show an average of four victims for each sex offender, or 5,999 per 1,500. "This places the estimate for victimization numbers around 960,000 for the 88 months examined in this study."

As I reviewed Dr. Schurman-Kauflin's information, one of her stats baffled me at first until I looked further. Her research showed that in 82 percent of the cases, the victims were known to their attackers. On the surface it appears that a lot of incest may be taking place—but, in fact, what the stat shows is the attackers are in an abundance of homes and communities. Schurman-Kauflin writes, "In those instances, the illegal immigrants typically gained access to the victims after having worked as a day laborer at or near the victims' homes." The illegal alien doing yard work and tinkering with household chores gains access to more than the women in the homes; they have a direct path to our children. "Victims ranged in age from 1 year old to 13 years old, with the average age being 6."

After molesting or raping children of their own race, 47 percent, they go after 36 percent Caucasian, 8 percent Asian, 6 percent black, and 3 percent other. The research continues to show that illegal alien criminals "gradually commit worse crimes and are continually released back into society or deported. Those who were deported simply returned illegally again." Indeed, the study noted that "Nearly 63% of the offenders had been deported on another offense prior to the sex crime." Schurman-Kauflin continues:

> Only 2% of the offenders in this study have no history of criminal behavior, beyond crossing the border illegally. There is a clear pattern of criminal escalation. From misdemeanors such as assault or DUI, to drug offenses, illegal immigrants who commit sex crimes break U.S. laws repeatedly. They are highly mobile, work in low skilled jobs with their hands, use drugs and alcohol, are generally promiscuous, have little family stability, and choose victims who are easy to attack. Their attacks are particularly brutal, and they use a hands-on method of controlling and/or killing their victims.

If only 2 percent of the attackers in Dr. Schurman-Kauflin's research had no prior arrests and convictions, then every time a "sanctuary city" police officer, whose hands are tied, stops an illegal immigrant for speeding, driving without a license, having no registration, or any of the many minor infractions that lets him walk away, there is a good chance he is either an abuser or knows of one.

The illegal alien sex offenders covered most, if not all, possible crimes found in this category, including incest, rape, statutory rape, indecent exposure, serial rapes, serial murders, child molestation, and sexual homicides.

One of the most common sex crimes happens when children, or young ladies, are kidnapped, abused, and trafficked as sex slaves. Dr. Schurman-Kauflin explained her findings in "Profiling Sex Trafficking: Illegal Immigrants at Risk":

Women and girls are trafficked from many countries in Europe, Asia, Africa, Latin America, and the Middle East. Mexico is the number one source for young female sex slaves in North America. Tlaxcala, in Central Mexico serves as a hotbed for slave traders. Young women and girls are abducted, tricked, and sometimes sold by poor families into a caged life. Highly prized are 12-year-old girls sneaking across the border into the United States. The girls are grabbed by Los Lenones, aka pimps, and dragged to unfamiliar areas where they are "broken in." It is well known that this often occurs in Mexico. The initiation process entails 20–30 men per day having brutal sex with the girls and women. Victims are beaten, drugged, and repeatedly raped until their wills are broken. It is then that the sale is possible.[10]

Besides the brutality inflicted on innocent children, the other factor to consider is the byproduct the U.S. society will have to address as the child grows into a woman and her childhood demons grow within her.

———✹———

A full frontal assault of a nation's laws, crime fighters, and systems that were developed to ensure civility can erode citizens' perspective on right versus wrong or good versus evil. To remain vibrant, sovereign and autonomous, civilized people must act, well, civilized. America is still esteemed as one of the most benevolent nations in the history of the world, but we're struggling right now. We want to be the people with arms stretched wide but can't afford to lose the very things that have set us apart from all others. We have faced seemingly insurmountable obstacles over the years, but this assault impacts all avenues of our existence. A mistake or miscalculation now, while we all struggle to find our footing, could easily lead to a downward shift from which we may never recover.

DIECISIETE

TERRORISM'S ATTACK ON SOVEREIGNTY

Y ou can bet that I am deeply troubled by the number of people blending in as though they belong here, but of even greater concern are the hundreds of thousands of bona fide criminals and terrorists integrated into the figures we hear about. If there is a bigger crime in this mess, it is the way these details are suppressed by leaders in the federal government.

The House Committee on Homeland Security stated in the well-documented report "A Line in the Sand" that during 2005 our Border Patrol apprehended approximately 1.2 million illegal aliens;[1] of those, 165,000 were from countries other than Mexico. In April 2006 the Department of Homeland Security released a fifty-two-page report highlighting that approximately 45,000 of those aliens were from countries that sponsored terrorism. [2] Congress was in the middle of selling us its amnesty lies, so what was done with this information? Well, somehow the report sat quietly on a D.C. desk where it could do little damage.

When it was finally released, after Congress attempted to guide us over a cliff with new immigration laws, Homeland Security director Michael Chertoff highlighted that 85 percent of these detainees would merely disappear into the population once released (which they did), leaving us to guess where one or two rogue leaders from Syria, Lebanon, Egypt, Iran, Iraq, Pakistan, Saudi Arabia, and similar countries might be hiding selected well-trained and well-placed killers. Am I the only one, or is anyone else concerned that 45,000 potential terrorists are loose on U.S. soil?

At the same time as that Assets Report, Representative John Culberson, while testifying at a House International Relations subcommittee on terrorism, established the foundation for concerns that terrorists may already be in America. He stated that he and FBI director Robert Mueller had discovered that "a number of individuals from countries with al Qaeda connections are changing their identities. They're changing their Islamic surnames for Hispanic surnames, adopting false Hispanic identities . . . and hiding among the flood of illegals coming over our border and disappearing into the country."[3] When I walked the streets of Mexico, waiting for my chance to cross back into the U.S.A., I identified many people of Middle Eastern descent who were blending with the people in the community, but Congressman Culberson supported my worst fears—they are already here.

In late November 2007, *The Washington Times* newspaper ran with a story based on confidential law enforcement documents that told of a plan by Islamist terrorists to attack Fort Huachuca in southern Arizona—the nation's largest intelligence training center. "A portion of the operatives were in the United States, with the remainder not yet in the United States."[4] The *Times* information was based on an FBI advisory that was disbursed to the Defense Intelligence Agency, the CIA, Customs and Border Protection, and the Department of Justice, among numerous other law enforcement agencies throughout the nation. "The Afghanis and Iraqis shaved their beards so as not to appear to be Middle Easterners." Intel suggested that Mexican drug lords traded access to their tunnels for terrorists and assorted weapons in exchange for some of the weapons and about twenty thousand dollars per crosser.

Lt. Col. Matthew Garner, spokesman for Fort Huachuca, said, "We are always taking precautions to ensure that soldiers, family members, and civilians that work and live on Fort Huachuca are safe." He added, "With this specific threat we did change some aspects of our security that we did have in place."[5] The FBI report also stated that some of the weapons had already made it into America via Arizona and New Mexico, and some of the terrorists were in safe houses in Texas.

Within a few days of the reports, the FBI distanced itself from the details but admitted they were aware of instances where terrorists and weapons had punctured the less-than-secure U.S. border—like the six foreign-born Muslim men arrested in early 2007 and charged with plotting an attack on Fort Dix Army Base in New Jersey. Just like the Fort Huachuca details, the terrorists were planning on killing as many soldiers as possible in an armed assault with high-powered weapons.

While I was broadcasting my show from the Arizona desert, I fielded a variety of calls, including one from Hamid, who had called me a few times in previous months from his home in Saudi Arabia, where he listened via the live streaming on our company's Web site. I had been talking about seeing Arab-looking men during my adventure, and I received this warning:

HAMID: My insight is you better get out of there as soon as you can.

Because there are many—you said that you saw Arabs in the desert out where you are. They are probably from my clan or from members of my tribe, and they are terrorists that are trying to get into America. And so, what is happening is that you are in a zone that is—we have come to Mexico now. I am a Christian. I am not a terrorist. I don't want that stuff. I don't think that's right. But—but— that is where—that is where you are. Get out of there; get back to Phoenix, as quickly as you can.

ANKARLO: What do you know that I need to know?

HAMID: I am from the north of Saudi Arabia. I'm in what's called Halil, which is a region called "Nafoud. Al Nafoud." Arabs are teaching the illegal Mexicans how to cross the desert, because our entire country here is desert, and if Mexicans know how to operate in desert, we will be able to help them even more, and they will allow us to come up with them, and I say "up" because I have family members that are there right now. You may have seen my uncle, my dad, my nephew is out there, I mean—I'm isolated here in Halil . . .

ANKARLO: What do these terrorists, these relatives of yours want?

HAMID: They want to die for Allah. They want martyrdom. They want to jihad. They want to do jihad. They want to do terrorism. And they want to be able to say, "Ha, ha, ha, ha, ha. Look, you stupid American." You know, "Look at how much better I came to your country; I did terrorist acts there. They want 9/11—you know, they say that 9/11 is good. It really kills me every day when I hear you."

When a foreigner is detained for immigration violations, he is tracked in multiple categories, including Mexican and Other Than Mexican (OTM). From 2001 through early 2005, the inspector general reported that more than six hundred thousand OTMs had been arrested in this country, but roughly 51 percent were released back into the U.S. population to return to see a designated judge at a later date. It may be a wild guess, but something tells me all those people probably didn't make it back to court. Instead, they disappeared with little or no trace as our less-than-perfect bureaucratic system seems to beg for another September 11 attack.

Since we're looking at crimes and criminals, it is only wise to look at the courts where some of the subversive element actually appears. As our courts change by outside forces, the way we handle potential terrorists and criminals will as well.

Supreme Court justice Antonin Scalia said, "Acknowledgment of foreign approval has no place in the legal opinion of this court," and then added, "this Court's Eighth Amendment jurisprudence should not impose any foreign moods, fads or fashions on Americans." Justice Clarence Thomas said it was a sign of weakness, and the late chief justice William Rehnquist labeled it "meaningless and dangerous dicta."[6]

The issue they were addressing is the newfound love affair that U.S. judges, courts, and even the U.S. Supreme Court has in citing international law or another country's laws when ruling on a U.S. matter of law. Former U.S. attorney general Alberto Gonzales echoed it "anti-democratic." He said in a speech at George Mason University Law School, "Foreign judges and legislators are not accountable to the American people. If our courts rely on a foreign judge's opinion or a foreign legislature's enactment, then that foreign judge or legislature binds us on key constitutional issues."[7]

It is true that through the years U.S. courts and justices have reviewed the laws of other nations, but it is a recent phenomenon that has judges like Ruth Bader Ginsburg, Stephen G. Breyer, and former justice Sandra Day O'Connor heading abroad for their perspectives. Immigration lawyers in Illinois and other states routinely cite decisions of the International Court of Justice as our judicial system becomes so complicated that regular Joe Citizen no longer understands how it operates. Criminal defense lawyers in Michigan have used decisions of the Constitutional Court of South Africa to make their cases. And plaintiffs run to a federal statute called the Alien Tort Claims Act (ATCA) that allows foreigners to bring complaints of violations of the "laws of nations" to U.S. courts for adjudication. The record is clear; many in the U.S. want the world's approval.

With each ruling or opinion that relies on other countries' laws, America loses a little of her sovereignty and autonomy.

DIECIOCHO

HOW MUCH BLAME DOES AMERICA DESERVE?

H i, Lima. Welcome to *Ankarlo Mornings*," I said to the listener on line 4.

Lima: "I thought NAFTA was supposed to have taken care of a lot of the problems down there. You know, they're talking about how they're helping us in our country and they're keeping costs down and stuff. But that's not true. If you go to a produce section today—you know, you used to get eight avocados for a dollar. Now you're lucky if you can get one for a dollar, so it's not helping our economy. You know, a head of lettuce—two dollars? Give me a break."

Lima speaks for millions of Americans who wonder what went haywire with the government godsend called the North American Free Trade Agreement (NAFTA) and what it may lead us to in the future. The free trade concept has been controversial since the first U.S. secretary of the treasury, Alexander Hamilton, called for tariffs to ensure that American products would have a fighting chance. For decades leading up to NAFTA, politicians paraded their beliefs that if goods and services could flow freely, minus undue taxes and tariffs, between the power-base countries of North America, then the competition would yield quality products and low prices. On its surface, the concept makes sense, especially for the world's capitalist monster that we are.

No doubt, if I wanted to, it would be very easy to place all the blame for Mexico's ills at 1600 Pennsylvania Avenue. Even though a fair amount should be aimed there, let's not forget that despite our best efforts, we haven't exactly had willing or able colaborers in the illegal immigration invasion.

Very few humans can see the poverty, reports of sexual assaults, murder, and other horrendous conditions associated with illegal immigration and not have the compassionate side of their hearts break just a little. I have been a staunch opponent of people breaking through our borders, but I was deeply touched by the humanity I saw on the other side of the border.

The humanity issues notwithstanding, it is healthy to look for the causes as well as the players on both sides of illegal immigration so that we may find solutions and recognize the signs when the issues, or their by-products, appear before us again.

Since NAFTA's inception, citizens from both the Republican and Democrat parties blame the other for the unintended impact created by NAFTA. It should be noted that leaders like Ronald Reagan, Bill Clinton, and the two presidents Bush all played major roles in its development. The disturbing and seldom-discussed issue is that the leading political figure who steered Mexico into the deal was President Carlos Salinas de Gortari of the Institutional Revolutionary Party (PRI), the dominating and extremely corrupt party that plagued Mexico's people for most of the twentieth century. America, in essence, hooked up with a political ideology directly rooted in the Socialist International organization and thought that somehow there would be no graft, corruption, deception, or painful hits on citizens. I know—when we look at it this way, it was a terribly stupid idea. To expect a failed leader and his corrupt party to change stripes is not just bad policy; it is ignorant leadership—by both U.S. political organizations.

NAFTA went into effect in January 1994 with excessive bureaucratic red tape and so many moving parts that it is almost impossible to track its complete success or failure. When billionaire businessman Ross Perot ran against Bill Clinton for the U.S. presidency in the early 1990s, he tried to warn our citizens about the consequences of the plan. He lambasted NAFTA with the now-famous quote, "The giant sucking sound are jobs leaving the United States." Another presidential contender, Ralph Nader, echoed the sentiment, but for every naysayer who read and hated the original nine-hundred-plus-page document, or the tens of thousands of additional pages added later, I can give you someone just as fervent on the other side, because the by-products of trade, business development, and bankruptcy are so far-reaching.

Truth be told, NAFTA *has* worked very well in a variety of areas. The concept removes investment barriers and tariffs and creates friendly working relationships between the three member countries: Canada, Mexico, and the U.S.A. According to the United States Department of Agriculture, Canada has become our number one export market, Mexico is number two, and the U.S. is the number one export market for both countries.[1] According to the International Trade Administration within the U.S. Department of Commerce, U.S. exports increased 88 percent from 1993 to 2004. Isn't this exactly the relationship every country hopes to have with its neighbors? The logic is simple: as exports increase, companies have to expand their infrastructures and work forces to keep up with the demand, thus ensuring a healthy and growing economy. Again, this is a *good* thing, and since it is shared by the three power countries in North America, it is supposed to strengthen the parts as well as the whole of the continent.

While so many good things are happening via the agreement, a fallout of monumental proportions has also been growing, one that has the ability to wrap itself around an economy and strangle it. The short version: the small businessman fell victim to the power of super-rich and ultrapotent mega companies.

For instance, early in the NAFTA deal, more than a million Mexican farms disappeared, in part because U.S. crops flooded the markets there. Corn, a perennial favorite of the diet in Mexico for centuries, is now a dirty word. American farmers who are chiefly connected to the jumbo-conglomerate machines of Wall Street hedge their bets through powerful U.S. subsidies that were originally created to save the poor U.S. farmer in the Great Depression but were never rescinded. The big boys were able to get more than 51 billion tax dollars from 1995 to 2005 in corn subsidies alone, so the decision to load up cargo containers with their harvest and point them south has been a no-brainer. This is not indicative of all American farmers—the backbone of our country—but enough to cause grave consequences for the small guy trying to compete.

On another front, under deals developed in the 1960s between the two countries, U.S. companies routinely send pieces of their products to Mexico to be turned, snapped, glued, and fitted in every conceivable manner and then wait for them to come back to the U.S. for final assembly or inspection. Though other nations have jumped on the U.S. outsourcing gravy train, it is still a key issue south of the border. After NAFTA, employment in the *maquiladoras*, as the assembly plants are called, increased by more than 86 percent.[2] Although most business authorities can easily draw the link between NAFTA and the marked increase, our federal government refuses to link one with the other.

NAFTA created jobs, but some would argue that it also created conditions for slavelike labor too. Then, around 2004, as China became a stronger trading partner, many of the Mexican people who migrated from the south and central parts of the country found it easier to leave their maquiladoras, intentionally built within seventy-five miles of the border, and come into the U.S. than to migrate back to their hometowns and villages. It's almost as though the U.S. government goes out of its way to screw up even the simplest of deals.

The first assumption is that America is coming to the rescue of the impoverished Mexican workers by creating jobs in connection to the maquiladoras. No doubt there is some truth to this, but with the average Mexican wage set at five dollars a day, and many daily goods and services set at prices similar to those found in the United States, a Latino family can never grow strong; it is forced to merely exist. Ninety percent of maquila employers in Mexico have direct links to American companies, so two things come into play: (1) workers in America watch as their wages subtly diminish, and (2) workers in Mexico look for ways to find a better life.

One year after NAFTA hit the books, 1,850,000 jobs disappeared in Mexico. With millions of their friends and neighbors writing from El Norte boasting of the beautiful lives they were creating, where would many of those newly displaced workers head but the good ol' U.S.A.? Where would a million farmers with no land left to plow look for sustenance but the U.S.A.? Extreme poverty (defined in Mexico as a family of four bringing in $1.60 per person per day) and poverty ($4.00 per person per day)[3] represents more than 60 percent of Mexico's population. If you can't feed your family, where do you go? The U.S.A.!

In the first few years of the trade relationship, several reports put the number of middle-class Mexicans swept into poverty at approximately eight or ten million. For a correction to this devastating slide, multiple generations would have to be born and die before a correction might take place. While commenting on the illegal immigration problem, the *New York Times* pointed a finger at NAFTA, too, when it wrote, "A major factor lies in the assumptions made in drafting the trade agreement."[4] The *Times* linked countries, citizens, businesses, and markets with expert forecasts to draw a parallel to some of the immigration nightmares.

One of the most alarming statistics calculated from the relationship between Mexico and the U.S. is the dollars flowing over the border and into the Mexican economy. In 2006, our southern neighbor exported almost $249 billion worth of goods; oil topped the list. But it can be argued that their number two export is the illegal immigrant population herded here by Mexico's policies who, in turn, send $50 billion back into their economy.[5] If this figure is accurate, it represents one in five Mexican export dollars being removed from the U.S. economy to prop up another country. This $50 billion won't pay down debt, help with infrastructure projects, fund a military, or earn interest.

What does the U.S. federal government plan to do as a follow-up to the "successful" NAFTA program? The current plans feature a hush-hush ubertrade deal called the Security and Prosperity Partnership, which will make the fifteen years of NAFTA look like a pony ride at a fifth grader's birthday party. SPP (www.spp.gov) will have the potential to create a system where the laws, economies, money, and workers of Canada, Mexico, and the U.S.A. are shared. I'll devote a complete chapter to this brewing horror movie, courtesy of politicians who aren't thinking through the sovereignty ramifications.

DIECINUEVE

U.S. CITIZENS REALLY *DO* WANT TO WORK

I can't count the number of times some sophisticated accessory to the illegal alien assault has told me, "Americans just won't do the jobs" or "We just don't have enough workers." In fact, in October 2007 I had an on-the-air argument with Tom Donohue, president of the U.S. Chamber of Commerce, over this stupid concept. I explained that when business leaders call with this excuse, I routinely give the company's phone number out so people can apply for the "jobs Americans won't do," and the positions are filled. Mr. Donohue wanted to debate further, but was trapped by the ridiculousness of his argument and the statistics I used to take it apart. Allow me to re-create my position:

If I said I would pay you eight dollars an hour to shuck corn, would you do it? What if I upped the price to twenty-five dollars an hour? If you were unemployed, or even if you had a decent job, you would certainly pull back the husks from a few ears for that kind of cash; at least most people I know would. Senator John McCain, in a 2007 presidential stump appearance in Mason City, Iowa, propagated the same big business line when he, too, told the small crowd that "there are jobs Americans simply will not do" and followed it up with a challenge for them to go work in the fields in Yuma, Arizona.[1] His misleading argument is made daily by corporate America, educators, and many other politicians, either because they don't have a true grasp of the issue or because enough lobbying money helps them choose their words for them. Either way, it is a disservice to the psyche of the U.S. worker, because it creates an aura of elitism that says, "I'm American; I'm too good to do that kind of work"—which can be construed as racist in its very foundation.

Rather, their statement should be "jobs Americans won't do for limited wages" because, depending on a person's location or motivation, the right money will get the right reaction. I traveled the Iowa presidential campaign trail with key candidates and found it strange that the people driving the taxis, making up my hotel room, and working in the restaurants were U.S. citizens—all with a perfect command of the English language. In Arizona, where I live, we are routinely propagandized with a "the state will shut down" message if the illegal immigrants go home. How, then, do states like Iowa, Illinois, or Montana thrive? When I was a kid, my father took us kids to the local farm to pick up the leftover corn remnants. We were given fifty cents for every full burlap bag we tugged to the barn. We were poor, and this was the chance Dad gave us to earn some spending money. Later, as an early teen, I shoveled horse manure to earn my three bucks an hour. Last time I checked, my birth certificate lists my home country as U.S.A. Odd, isn't it?!

Christine e-mailed these words:

> This person called me because she was tired of not being able to communicate with her housekeeper. I gave her a price quote over the

phone and she said that that was fine and she would look forward to me cleaning her house. Well about a day later she sent me another email telling me that she had discussed it with her husband and they decided to keep their NON English speaking housekeeper because she was cheaper. Needless to say my price was double what the Illegal is charging.

Christine knows what her bottom line is, so all her competition has to do is hire a few slaves, and guess who wins the business? As in all things, let me have an unfair advantage over you and I will usually come out victorious—Barry Bonds and alleged steroid abuse, the New England Patriots and their illegal videotaping of the opponents' playbook in their 2007 super season, or Enron's excess. They all share the same ideology.

To blame are the very leaders who cry that illegal immigrants are required for us to function because they know if we buy their story, they can continue to bring in cheap labor to ensure lower expenses, which guarantees more money for their big bank accounts and their favorite politicians. It's a mad cycle that must be broken. I have had thousands of listeners call in to my radio show over the years to tell me how they are losing their standards of living because they have to take a pay cut if they want to maintain their jobs.

"Pete" called one day in early 2007 to say that his boss was letting him go from a bricklaying job he had had for sixteen years. He was making nineteen dollars per hour, and "some new guys were coming in at twelve dollars." When Pete said that he would match the fee, his boss put his arm around his shoulder and said, "I would do it, Pete, but I know I can get them or their Spanish-speaking friends down to about seven or eight dollars an hour." So is bricklaying a job Americans won't do?

Sally called. She is a forty-something business owner in Phoenix who does auto body painting and airbrush art. "I have lost over 50 percent of my business in the last two years to companies who have only illegals working for them, companies that pay their employees less than I can." Sally was obviously a little hacked off, and who can blame her? How is she supposed to compete against an unscrupulous, cheating U.S. business owner who undercuts the competition by breaking the law? Is this one of those Americans-won't-do-it scenarios? If I wanted this book to be five or ten thousand pages, I could fill every paragraph with similar stories, but by now we have all heard our share. The outrageous part is that U.S. citizens have been bombarded with the "Americans won't do it" message for so long that many believe and parrot it, thus giving it credence as some sort of fact.

In economics the principle of supply and demand dictates the cost of a product. If I glut the market with ample supplies, then the price plummets, but if the item is hard to get, the price soars. The same principle applies to illegal immigration. By allowing so many to come into the country, the workforce is oversaturated, which allows businesses to pay the least money permissible. If you don't like it, too bad—there are a thousand marching through the desert right now to take your place.

An interesting historical parallel to today's "won't do the jobs" argument dates back to the 1860s, when more than a third of the South was comprised of black slaves. Plantation owners and businessmen argued against abolition with a doomsday message that the South would go bankrupt and the rest of the country would crumble along with it. The "leaders" were wrong then, and they are wrong now; the argument is nothing more than a fear tactic.

The list of prominent business leaders and publications who are trying to warn us no longer grows by the week; now it increases daily and hourly. Frosty Wooldridge, noted author and lecturer on America's immigration problem, writes, "Illegal immigration hurts America's poor. In a recent account in the *New York Times*, Black children suffered 50% greater poverty in the past 10 years due to immigration."[2]

Harvard Professor George Borjas has reported that illegal aliens displaced American workers at a cost in excess of $133 billion in 2005.[3]

The Wall Street investment firm Bear Stearns published a report in 2005 that underscores what so many have been saying for so long: The government is not telling us the full story about the number of illegal aliens! In part, their findings included:

1. The number of illegal immigrants in the United States may be as high as 20 million people, more than double the official 9 million people estimated by the Census Bureau.

2. The total number of legalized immigrants entering the United States since 1990 has averaged 962,000 per year. Several credible studies indicate that the number of illegal entries has recently crept up to 3 million per year, triple the authorized figure.

3. Undocumented immigrants are gaining a larger share of the job market, and hold approximately 12 to 15 million jobs in the United States (8 percent of the employed).

4. Four to six million jobs have shifted to the underground market, as small businesses take advantage of the vulnerability of illegal residents.

5. On the revenue side, the United States may be foregoing $35 billion a year in income tax collections because of the number of jobs that are now off the books.

6. There are approximately 5 million illegal workers who are collecting wages on a cash basis and are avoiding both income and FICA taxes. [4]

Big government and big business have been working hand in hand for decades to keep the real numbers away from the citizens, because the end result would be revolt. Now one wonders if it is too late to fight back because of the monster that roams so freely in cities large and small throughout the nation.

Let's go through some numbers from a survey by the Pew Hispanic Center. Illegal immigrants account for: food production—12 percent; cleaning—17 percent; agriculture—24 percent; construction—14 percent; service jobs—21 percent; and manufacturing jobs—23 percent.[5] The backbone-of-society jobs that we've been told are now beneath Americans are still dominated by Americans (and legal immigrants). The percentages of U.S. citizens in these low-wage jobs have fallen in the past few years due to a readily available black-market labor force, but these numbers shoot holes in the long-touted propaganda campaign that citizens refuse to do the work.

On another job front, recent surveys show that illegals with better or specialized educations are landing spots in accounting, administration, management, research, tax analysis, teaching, sports instruction, nursing, dental assisting, and other middle-class positions. And we can be assured that soon, government and business leaders will tell us that Americans don't want these jobs either.

The Financial Times, in its May 10, 2005, edition hit us with this headline: "U.S. Real Wages Fall at Fastest Rate in 14 Years."[6] To ensure the number wasn't a fluke, I checked the following year, and *BusinessWeek* hit the story again, "Real Wages Still Falling."[7] In fact, the *New York Times*, Harvard, and *Business Times* all echoed the same story. No doubt inflation plays a role in the real wage earnings, but so do things like unemployment, less pay in job categories, employee pay reduction, and no hikes in personal wages. Think about it, could millions of uninvited guests willing to work in harsh conditions and at lower wages impact this number? The answer is a resounding yes.

In July 2007 the U.S. Department of Labor (DOL) set the number of unemployed Americans at 54,277,000;[8] more than one-sixth of our population. America, like any nation, has its share of lazy sit-in-a-lounge-chair-eating-Twinkies citizens, and the DOL figure includes these people and many other types, but it also represents hardworking Americans who have worked at jobs for fifteen or twenty years, who lost their positions to cheaper laborers from other countries. These U.S. citizens are on the sidelines, drawing unemployment, welfare, food stamps, government retraining money, and an assortment of other taxpayer-supported programs. Don't get me wrong; I believe society should have a safety net for its citizens, but I also believe it is immoral to displace an employable worker by paying an illegal entrant to do the job. We can all buy knock-off Rolex watches and Coach purses for pennies, but it doesn't make it right, or does it?

In January 2008, Harvard's Borjas released some of the most telling labor cost details available to date. Called the "pre-eminent scholar in his field" by the *New York Times*, Borjas's extensive research project examined the effects of illegal immigration on labor in Arizona, where he noted that illegals cost Arizonans at least $1.4 billion in lower wages in 2005.

But something else is happening, and I'm amazed that it is not making headlines too. According to the Center for Immigration Studies, the number of immigrants with a high school degree or less in the labor force increased by 1.6 million in early 2007.[9]

Consider what this means: if legal immigrants are not getting an education, statistics show their ability to earn strong wages is diminished. Statistics also show that they end up using taxpayer-supported programs as a result. In 2006 there were 17 million less-educated adult citizens and legal immigrants working in occupations with a high con-centration of immigrants. Think strategically for a moment. Those 17 million will eventually get squeezed out of positions and be replaced by those who make less money and even less trouble for the employer.

More than 40 percent of all illegals entering this country did so since 2001. But with a million more coming each year, some track-ing statistics are lagging behind by a few years. When they hit, it will become evident that the undereducated American doesn't have a fighting chance. I predict when he joins the more than 25 million less-educated, currently unemployed people, our system will struggle as never before, as the American economy, welfare system, and taxpayers pick up the check.

From 2000 to 2006, America's national unemployment rate aver-aged 5.085 percent,[10] and most pro-illegal voices point to that number to explain that illegal laborers are our lifeblood because we have too many jobs and not enough workers. But a closer examination shreds the argument. The jobs most illegals do, like dishwashing, meat pro-cessing, janitorial, maid service, and similar types represent low-skilled jobs. According to the Bureau of Labor Statistics, the unemployment average in this category is more than 10 percent—twice the national unemployment average we see on the evening news. And without swift action and strong resolve it may get worse. Employed U.S. citi-zens lacking a high school degree jumped from 4.8 to 5.3 percent between 2001 and 2006 as they appear to be losing out to equally uneducated illegals.

According to Numbers USA, an organization tracking the influ-ence the illegal has on our society, almost half of America's children depend on a less-educated worker, while 71 percent of children of working poor citizens rely on a worker with a high school degree or less.[11] In a short generation or two, our society will feel the effects of the undereducated raising undereducated children. And if you are a less-educated black American male, you are really in trouble. A September 2006 National Bureau of Economic Research paper showed a one-third decline in employment among black males,[12] thanks to the men and women infiltrating our borders. It is difficult enough for a country to provide opportunities for its own citizens, let alone the extra two million legal and illegal immigrants arriving yearly.

The same element that tells us "Americans won't do the jobs" also sells the theory that we would not be able to afford anything in this country if illegals were not involved in the process, because they keep prices low. University of California economist Phillip Martin thoroughly dismantled the argument in one of the categories most often affected: agriculture. He states that due to technological advancements, only about 20 percent of the farming industry relies on workers. Manpower is usually required in the vegetables and fresh fruit sectors. Author Rich Lowry detailed Martin's findings in a 2006 column:

> The average "consumer unit" in the U.S. spends $7 a week on fresh fruit and vegetables, less than is spent on alcohol, according to Martin. On a $1 head of lettuce, the farm worker gets about 6 or 7 cents, roughly 1/15th of the retail price. Even a big run-up in the cost of labor can't hit the consumer very hard. Martin recalls that the end of the bracero guest-worker program in the mid-1960s caused a one-year 40-percent wage increase for the United Farm Workers Union. A similar wage increase for legal farm workers today would work out to about a 10-dollar-a-year increase in the average family's bill for fruit and vegetables. Another thing happened with the end of the bracero program: The processed-tomato industry, which was heavily dependent on guest workers and was supposed to be devastated by their absence, learned how to mechanize and became more productive.[13]

Don, an Arizona farmer, nervously laughed when I told him of the professor's calculations. "He's really broken this down, hasn't he!?" Don had been trying to persuade me that he has to have these employees or he can't make a living, and besides, people would not be able to afford his produce. This American farmer, like so many others, is getting the squeeze and can't figure out what he should be doing. He will be demonized by many as the enemy for his hiring practices, but what if he is just a pawn—like most of us—in the hands of politicians and industry leaders who are purposely creating a system to lure illegals into our country?

Let's look at another example that makes one wonder if someone might be engaged in sinister activities: The Immigration & Nationality Act, section 101(a)(15)(H), gave us the H-1B visa, which is a device that allows U.S. employers to temporarily hire skilled foreigners to help with a "specialty occupation" like software and technology. But according to a Center for Immigration Studies April 2007 report entitled "Wages and Skill Levels for H-1B Computer Workers, 2005" only 40 percent of the visas are held by persons working in IT fields.[14] Closer examination shows they averaged $12,000 to $16,000 less than the median income for their contemporaries. At the same time, 51 percent were in the bottom 25th percentile of U.S. wages.

If a business can save considerable money by hiring from abroad, using this visa makes perfect sense. Since the cap for the H-1B is set at 65,000 people a year, it can be limiting, so many businesses discover ways to circumvent that number by using readily available loopholes created by friendly politicians. As a result, two-thirds of companies get around the cap, thus displacing more American workers.

In March 2003, the American Engineering Association reported 560,000 jobs were lost in our high tech industry in January 2001 and December 2002.[15] Big business will say two words, "Dot-com bust" to account for it, and they would be truthful. But will they explain why, during the same period, companies sponsored more H1B and other "temporary" visas than the numbers of jobs lost? Probably not. Nor will they speak to a 2002 number that shows the INS issued 312,000 visas—more than five times the original cap.

In the 1990s the northern corridor in Dallas was known as Little Silicon Valley with places like Plano and Allen, Texas, doubling as boom towns. Then, technology companies in the sector discovered ways to hire professionals with the visa program. Soon, IT top dogs watched home after home foreclosed upon as salaries plummeted.

How is Congress reacting to this abuse of the system? They plan to raise the cap by 77 percent. And the new system guarantees never to go lower and provides for mechanisms to increase the cap whenever it hits its max. The end result could yield almost 350,000 visa holders per year by 2014—which will allow companies ample time to figure out new ways to cheat. Yet again, corporate America and their handy politicians have figured out a way to look outside the nation for employment solutions, showing little, if any, confidence in the American worker.

And while illegal immigration is breaking our bank on one front, H-1B visa abuses cost us more on the other. Edwin S. Rubenstein, an economist and director of research for the Hudson Institute, documented the drain in a 2002 research project:

> An estimated 500,000 foreigners are in the U.S. on temporary H-1B visas under the 50-year-old program designed to fill employer needs unmet by U.S. residents for professionals and specialists with a bachelor's or higher degree, including architects, engineers, accountants, doctors, college professors and even fashion models. Nearly 54% are involved in computer-related fields, according to a recent federal study. Their median income is about $50,000, and half are expected to earn between $40,000 and $60,000.[16]

These "guest workers" use our roads, parks, clinics, schools, and countless other citizen-funded programs, and if they paid into Social Security, they could put almost $2 billion a year into the system, or enough to help with the benefits for almost 100,000 retirees. What's worse is that after six years the visa holder can apply for a green card to receive Social Security benefits he never paid for.

While wandering through an industrial area of Nogales I saw what appeared to be fifteen or twenty U.S. citizens, but I was a little confused why they would be in this part of town. So, microphone in hand, I approached them. "What are y'all doing here?"

The group was a little taken aback at first, which is usually the case when I just walk up, but that faded quickly as soon as the people realized I was trying to track the immigration issue. A forty-something woman with golden hair and the smell of cigarettes on her breath agreed to respond. "Why are we here?" she said. "We're training new people down here in Mexico since we lost our jobs in the U.S."

"All of you people have lost your jobs in America?"

"Yes."

"What kind of work?"

"Medical."

"Are you training the Mexican people to take the jobs that you lost in the States?"

"Exactly." As the lady spoke, some of the others moved a little closer to hear the questioning.

I looked at the man who moved closer from the crowd, "How many people lost jobs in this go-round?"

"Five hundred, roughly."

"Five hundred. In, like, one fell swoop, over the course of a year, or how long?"

"Over a year."

"Don't tell me how much money you made, but give me a ball-park [of] what kind of money you guys were making in the States and what they're going to be making here in Mexico."

"I don't know. To start up there, it's probably $10.50 an hour and down here it's $2.00, $2.50."

"So, once you guys are done training them, are you out of a job too, or do you shift your jobs down here?"

"No," the man answered. "They're unemployed. After their training is over with, they're done, but I will continue the training. I think it stinks."

"And why do you think it is?" I asked.

"I know we can't compete with the labor."

"Is it America's fault or Mexico's fault?"

"I think it's the government's fault." His face grew stern, and most of the group now surrounded us. They were nodding with each answer.

"Our government? Are you blaming our government?"

"You bet. But they're taking our jobs, which we have mastered up there in a very, very intricate product. They're bringing it down here. They're losing quality. We've lost our jobs, and these products are not going to be near as good when they get back over there. They've got to get the government to get their noses on straight and keep our jobs in America instead of us down here training people to take our jobs."

"So what are you guys going to do when you get back to the States after you're done with the training?"

"Unemployment."

"You have any hopes? Anything in the hopper?" I made eye contact with each one of them, but saw the lost look that accompanied my question. "None of you have jobs yet, do you?"

The answer was obvious. I felt sorry for them.

The power that has led this country to world domination is the "find a solution" mentality, epitomized by every generation back to Plymouth Rock. Bifocals, sewing machines, oil wells, telephones, cameras, the Internet, and an almost endless list of other inventions are fine examples of an America that can find a reasonable solution to the immigration morass—legally. Instead of looking to take product development offshore and inviting lawbreakers to destroy regular citizens' dreams, employers and politicians should be presenting the problem directly to the people.

It was the American worker who was told about a foreign satellite and reacted by putting men on the moon. After the American worker created the automobile industry, he laid down the best highway system in the world to make sure his cars traveled well. The success stories are legend around the world because of the spirit that indwells us.

What happened to the days when leaders told us what we were up against so we could shoulder some of the burden? In World War II, the teen who would later become my mother went to work in a bullet factory in Alton, Illinois, to do her part. Wouldn't it be nice if leaders would tell us how difficult it is to compete with slave labor in China, French health care systems, and a Russian resurgence, and then let us help with an answer?

We are a cocky, independent, and wildly fanatical bunch of folk who love to hear that we are too rich, too fat, and too incompetent to compete on the world's stage, because then we get the fire back in our bellies and look for ways to win—just because we want the victory. Stop telling us that "Americans won't do the work," because, eventually, we'll start to believe it. And when a nation relies on outside resources for her sustenance, her sovereignty is at great risk.

VEINTE

ANCHOR BABIES HELP TO SINK AMERICA

A merica had only thirty-seven states when the Fourteenth Amendment was ratified in July 1868. Since immigration laws were nonexistent, the concept of "illegal alien" wasn't an issue with anyone, especially our legislature. Yet, it is still the first of the five-part Amendment that lawyers, judges, business owners, and pro-illegal immigrant forces use when they explain why a complete stranger to the country has the "right" to call her child a U.S. citizen if she can just make it onto our soil before giving birth.

Section 1 of Amendment 14 reads:

> All persons born or naturalized in the United States, and subject to the jurisdiction thereof, are citizens of the United States and of the State wherein they reside. No State shall make or enforce any law which shall abridge the privileges or immunities of citizens of the United States; nor shall any State deprive any person of life, liberty, or property, without due process of law; nor deny to any person within its jurisdiction the equal protection of the laws.

"Tom" called in to my radio show, and his questions and attitudes are the same ones boiling to the surface nationwide:

TOM: I've been informed by somebody who has studied a little more in-depth on the subject that, uh, regarding the Fourteenth Amendment—get here, pop out a baby, you've got the golden ticket—well, I've been told that it takes at least one American parent to make that baby a legal U.S. citizen. The Fourteenth Amendment is being abused wholesale and I want every last one of those people rounded up and shipped back.

ANKARLO: When you say it requires one U.S. citizen in—

TOM: At least one U.S. parent, one American parent for that baby to be a legal U.S. citizen.

ANKARLO: No. No. Uh-uh. No. Wrong. I don't know where you heard it, but all any foreigner from anywhere around the world has to do is have that baby on our soil and the child is a U.S. citizen. As it stands in the U.S., the Fourteenth Amendment is constantly abused to the tune of 380,000 "anchor babies" a year according to the Census Bureau. That's almost four hundred thousand noncitizens gaining every single right and benefit that members of this greatest land get, and there are zero repercussions—other than a system buckling under its own weight.

The following conversation really struck home as "John," a physician in Phoenix, called.

JOHN: We are spending millions and millions, if not billions, of dollars each year on health care for illegal immigrants. For example, if a pregnant woman comes across the border—I don't know if they get a visiting pass or how they get across—I've never gone to that point—but they come over by the hundreds, and they come to my hospital, and, of course, they go to the ER, and we can't turn them away. They're shipped up to the OB and, if they've had a prior C-section, they automatically get another surgery, which, you know, is thousands of thousands of dollars, and then they eventually deliver their baby free of cost and then return back to Mexico. I see this kind of thing every single day; they come often, so this could be their fourth or fifth kid that they've delivered in the U.S., and before they leave, each kid will get a birth certificate, so they are now a U.S. citizen because they delivered their baby on U.S. soil.

ANKARLO: They are coming here and timing it hoping they don't just drop the baby in Mexico, and I have been told that some hospitals intentionally induce labor so the trip was not in vain. What do you know about that?

JOHN: I've seen it all. Some of them take medicine to cause their uterus to contract. Others come and hang out until they go into labor. Or they come at just the right time. They know when they're going to deliver. They start contracting, so they come over. And on top of everything, it takes away from my ability to give you the care you deserve—you're sitting in the ER, you're sitting in the OB and not getting the proper care because I have to take a nurse or a medical assistant to be able to go translate for, you know, hundreds of these patients that are coming in daily. And then patients get mad at us because the wait is so incredibly long—and it is. But it's not my fault. I'll tell you this: if I knew this was waiting for me when I was going through med school—I would have chosen a business profession.

As a sample of the overall problem, demographers look to California's troubled times. According to Congressman Lamar Smith, 20 percent of all children born there are to illegal mothers, which costs the taxpayers more than a billion dollars a year in health care-related expenses.[1] Additionally, each illegal immigrant with less than a high school education costs taxpayers $89,000.[2] The two calls I just referenced represent thousands I have fielded on the subject of "anchor babies," so named because once the child turns twenty-one, he can use his citizen rights to sponsor immediate and extended family members to come and stay, including the illegal mother who ran for the goal line that is America just so the child could one day provide a reciprocal salvation. Many say this is the morally right thing to do. To this point I ask, how many mouths could be fed or poor U.S. families housed with the dollars spent on health care for illegal aliens in California alone? Now multiply the answer by 50 and the morality question is easily answered.

Anchor babies became a part of the U.S. vocabulary because Congress failed to clearly explain the first segment of the Fourteenth Amendment, though individual members fought hard to avoid any miscommunications. Now, 140 years later, citizens are stuck under legal precedents created after parsing adequate words and phrases that reflected the spirit and mood of the time but that have taken on new meanings over the years. This ultimately led to the concept of "Birthright Citizenship," or, if you are born here, you belong here. The glaring problem: legal historians see the process through the totality of the main issues leading up to the need for the Fourteenth Amendment: slavery and state's rights.

The Civil War had been fought, and the North was declared the victors. Part of their winnings included an end to slavery. To ensure the newly freed would not be forever relegated to a "lesser human" status, politicians created Constitutional protections. The intent, when viewed under the microscope of history, was always aimed at citizens already living here. But lawyers pointed to Section One's wording, "All persons born or naturalized in the United States, and subject to the jurisdiction thereof, are citizens of the United States and of the state wherein they reside" and dumbed down the good to include anyone making their way here.

During the debates on the amendment, Senator Jacob Howard, one of the authors, wanted the language to be very clear when he read into the record, "This will not, of course, include persons born in the United States who are foreigners, aliens, who belong to the families of ambassadors or foreign ministers accredited to the Government of the United States, but will include every other class of persons." When other senators argued about the inclusionary language of "all persons," Senator Lyman Trumbull objected, "The provision is that 'All persons born or naturalized in the United States, and subject to the jurisdiction thereof, are citizens.' That means 'Subject to the complete jurisdiction thereof' . . . Not owing allegiance to anybody else. That is what it means." To this day, persons born into ambassadors' families and the like are not covered as U.S. citizens, but those hiding in trunks, trucks, or plane cargo, or jumping the border are. How does this make sense?

Author Robert Locke stated what should be obvious in a 2002 article:[3]

The key to undoing the current misinterpretation of the Fourteenth Amendment is this odd phrase "and subject to the jurisdiction thereof." The whole problem is caused by the fact that the meaning of this phrase, which was clear to anyone versed in legal language in 1868, has slipped with changes in usage. Fortunately, there is a large group of court precedents that make clear what the phrase actually means:

1. The Fourteenth Amendment excludes the children of aliens. (The Slaughterhouse Cases, 83 U.S. 36 (1873))
2. The Fourteenth Amendment draws a distinction between the children of aliens and children of citizens. (Minor v. Happersett, 88 U.S. 162 (1874))
3. The phrase "subject to the jurisdiction" requires "direct and immediate allegiance" to the United States, not just physical presence. (Elk v. Wilkins, 112 U.S. 94 (1884))
4. There is no automatic birthright citizenship in a particular case. (Wong Kim Ark Case, 169 U.S. 649 (1898))
5. The Supreme Court has never confirmed birthright citizenship for the children of illegal aliens, temporary workers, and tourists. (Plyler v. Doe, 457 U.S. 202, 211 n.10 (1982))[3]

One must remember that the Civil War was not simply a fight over slavery, though it was a big part of the contentious spirit in the country; rather, the war was about "states' rights" as citizens grew tired of federal demands and directions. This is important to remember in light of the constitutional debates of the day, because several in Congress wanted it understood that states should continue to dictate futures, and citizens' status, for themselves. And their words were purposeful and unambiguous—the California Government Code Section 240–245 of the law states:

240. The people, as a political body, consist of: (a) Citizens who are electors. (b) Citizens not electors. 241. The citizens of the State are: (a) All persons born in the State and residing within it, except the

children of transient aliens and of alien public ministers and consuls. (b) All persons born out of the State who are citizens of the United States and residing within the State. 242. Persons in the State not its citizens are either: (a) Citizens of other States; or (b) Aliens.[4]

California, South Dakota, Montana, and others states adopted their definition of "citizen" from New York State. Once again, it appears the federal government and, later, the U.S. Supreme Court needed to call upon U.S. states before botching the citizenship issue since we now see what the human and economic toll is to the rest of the country.

Early naturalization rules of the United States required an applicant for citizenship to renounce his former government no less than two years before the final application process. The certainty of the vast number of laws, political commentary, citizenship applications, and the like is that our government deliberately wanted it to be a decision made only after much time and thought—not via an intentional act of border jumping. Numerous polls tell us that the majority of illegal aliens would like and/or have plans to one day return to their home countries. These people and their children failed one of the initial tests of citizenship in their failure to renounce—reject, abandon, forsake, disown, and give up—their allegiances elsewhere. This alone is enough to demonstrate the obscenity of the "Birthright Citizen" argument that is helping to destroy a once strong and invincible country.

VEINTIUNO

THERE IS A RIGHT WAY

ANKARLO: On line three is a longtime listener who calls in occasionally, Terri the Brit. How long have you lived in America?

TERRY THE BRIT: Seventeen.

ANKARLO: Seventeen years. You're a U.S. citizen now. How difficult was it to get that status?

TERRY THE BRIT: I am as mad as you times two, man. Because I was sponsored by a major, major company here to come over back in 1990, and I not only had to jump through hoops; I had to jump through fire hoops here. They made me prove all of my education. I had to go back into England and get the offices of the companies I'd worked for to verify I was at those positions and I had the experience I said I had. At year three I applied for a green card, sponsored again by my company. After that, I had to wait another five years to be in the country, so I ended up waiting about nine years. During that time I was bringing experience, taxes, and all the good stuff. And when I heard three hundred illegals had come over in under an hour—it really got to me.

Terry the Brit provides a snapshot of millions of Americans who came to this land, or are in the process of doing so, and feel completely ripped off by the system. They fill out their forms, wait in line, pay their fees, wait some more, and try to remain on their best behavior since they are visitors. But all around them are line jumpers, forgers, identity thieves, and people who believe that America's laws are unfair so they are going to do it their way. If U.S. citizens are angry at the injustice (and we are), an angrier group is the one full of immigrants trying to do it the right way—like so many of our ancestors did before them.

From 1882 to 1954 almost 12 million people landed at the little piece of land in the Hudson River proudly remembered in family artifacts, pictures, and diaries as Ellis Island. I can only imagine the emotions the people aboard the ships must have felt when they first saw land, then the lights and skyscrapers of Manhattan, and finally the Statue of Liberty (after 1886). Excitement, wonderment, and fear must have collided as they tried on their new title: "American." To this day, many who made the trip still weep when asked to describe the experience, it was just that powerful.

The immigrants ran from famine, massacres, foreclosures, wars, and devastation of all sorts because word of this vast frontier was the talk of people around the world. "If I could just get to America," they would say, "I'll have a chance." When they arrived at Ellis or Angel Island in San Francisco, or any of the other twenty-eight immigration centers nationwide, they immediately went through a program that typically lasted several hours as they passed through hearing and detention rooms, hospitals, cafeterias, administrative offices, and railroad ticket offices. If the immigrant failed his physical, he was moved to the clinic for further processing, which led to one of three things: (1) the immigrant was treated and allowed entry; (2) 2 percent were returned to their home countries; or (3) more than three thousand died on Ellis due to illness. Rules were rules, and all new entrants followed them.

U.S. citizens wanted people to help grow their vast, wide, open territories, but by the late 1800s they clamored for restrictions due to problems brought by the immigrants: cut-rate workers, cheap labor, a downturn in the economy, and disease. The difference between then and now is found in the way Congress and the courts react and the volume of participants.

After the Civil War several states created their own immigration laws, which stayed in effect until the U.S. Supreme Court determined that immigration should be a federal issue. To ensure the U.S. did not become lopsided with too many persons from any single heritage, the federal Immigration Act of 1924 was passed, setting the limit on the number of immigrants who could be admitted from any country to 2 percent of the number of people from that country who were already living here.

In recent history, those same safeguards have been severely tested as many lawmakers have played dumb about jurisdictions and resources. In the last several years, instead of focusing our full attention on the problem, we have allowed as many illegal immigrants offering cheap labor, disease, and lawlessness as the sum total of all legal immigrants allowed into America at the turn of the last century.

In fact, from 2000 to 2007 more immigrants (legal and illegal) entered the U.S. than in any other seven-year period in the history of the nation. People who came over on crowded, oceangoing vessels must look at the current process in wonderment. "Did America scrap its immigration program?" State statistics make it appear this way. Of all immigrants in Florida, 30 percent are illegal. It gets worse—look at some of these numbers: illegal Texas immigrants are right at 50 percent; North Carolina, 58 percent; Georgia, 53 percent; and the border state of Arizona tops the list at 65 percent.[1]

Few question that one of this nation's proudest heritages is our open arms and broad shoulders; we have been there when people needed a fresh start or a do-over. But as in most areas of life, there is a right and wrong way to do things. Sadly, the modern-day immigration story is littered with the kinds of stories that won't be fondly or proudly recalled by anyone. Years ago our rigidity sent 2 percent of the wannabe Americans back home even after they sailed halfway around the world because they didn't pass muster. Now our ultratolerant

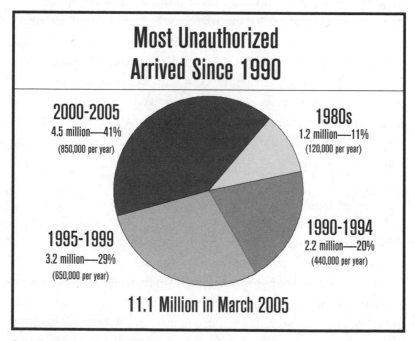

Most Unauthorized Arrived Since 1990

2000-2005
4.5 million—41%
(850,000 per year)

1980s
1.2 million—11%
(120,000 per year)

1995-1999
3.2 million—29%
(650,000 per year)

1990-1994
2.2 million—20%
(440,000 per year)

11.1 Million in March 2005

© 2006 Pew Hispanic Center, a Pew Research Center project, www.pewhispanic.org. Used by permission.

disposition lets any and all come, have babies, and send for relatives. The math can't work forever.

The illegal immigration explosion is a phenomenon unique to the past quarter of a century; the Pew Hispanic Center breaks it down by time period:

In addition, many believe a direct correlation exists between the millions who burden the system and the thousands who patiently fill out the forms, answer questions, and stand in line—for years. The system wants to respond, but it doesn't know how.

BECOMING A CITIZEN

A person becomes a United States citizen in two ways: by birth or through naturalization. If the person was born in the U.S. or its territories, then he is one of us. Otherwise, as a visitor eighteen years or older, he fills out a Form N-400 to become naturalized. But the U.S. government won't even consider a person unless he has been a permanent resident for at least five years, a lawful permanent resident for three years and married to a U.S. citizen, a lawful permanent resident child of U.S. parents, or he has qualified military experience.

THE VISA PROCESS

A visa allows a person to come to a U.S. port or inspection point and to apply to be admitted based on the language detailed in it. Once inside our borders, the person can legally reside while working toward citizenship. The U.S. consul provides the person with either an "immigrant" or "nonimmigrant" visa, depending on the person's plans. If he hopes to stay, he will need to qualify for permanent residence and will then be granted a green card. Applications vary depending on family relations, employment, or refugee status. As a nonimmigrant visa holder, the person promises to stay for a specified period for education, work, or business activities and then go home. Forty percent of all illegal aliens in the U.S. received this type of visa and simply stayed past the deadline. At this point, America has no workable solution to keep track of these dates or the offenders.

Besides gaining visa or green card status and becoming a permanent resident, most people expect to invest another two to four years minimum to get through the requirements. Most gladly do it. America has wide-open arms, which has given us access to great dreamers, inventors, and persons who want only to make their new home become even better. Sadly, many people are using our system against us to gain access to all we have to offer, with little intent of giving anything back to this nation.

Who pays when our immigration departments get slammed by the millions of uninvited guests, if not the honest, law-abiding folks who struggle to do it right, even when it now means that a few years can turn into twelve, fifteen, and, in some cases, almost twenty? Consider the message we are sending to the world: come to America the right way and invest at least a decade, or sneak into America and enjoy her benefits tomorrow. If I am a forger, thief, con artist, or another unscrupulous type, I've just watched the welcome mat roll in my direction.

NumbersUSA2 is a committed citizens group that is attempting to put a spotlight on our broken immigration program. In the dramatic presentation on the next few pages, they show just how out of control things have become:

COMPARISONS OF 20TH CENTURY
U.S. POPULATION GROWTH BY DECADE

DECADES OF THE GREAT WAVE OF IMMIGRATION

1900–1910 👤👤👤👤👤👤👤👤👤👤👤👤👤👤👤👤 16.3 million

1900–1910: The Great Wave of Immigration began in 1880 but exploded into peak numbers during the first decade of the twentieth century. The massive numbers of immigrants reached a cumulative total that began to substantially change the character of the entire country from one primarily of towns and farms into one of densely packed urban centers. This decade saw more growth than any previous decade in U.S. history. The rapid population growth was destroying huge sections of the country's once bountiful natural resources, leading to the establishment of federal systems of parks and other preservation programs.

1910–1920 👤👤👤👤👤👤👤👤👤👤👤👤👤👤 14.1 million

1910–1920: World War I slowed immigration considerably during the middle of the decade. But high immigration at the beginning and end, and high immigrant and native fertility, kept total population growth high.

1920–1930 👤👤👤👤👤👤👤👤👤👤👤👤👤👤👤👤👤 16.6 million

1920–1930: Americans of nearly every station in life rose up in revulsion at the incredible pace of change and congestion caused by the previous two decades of immigration-driven population growth. By 1925, Congress had reduced immigration numbers toward more traditional levels. The annual population growth rate at the end of the decade had been cut almost in half from the beginning. But very high immigration of the first half of the decade, and the momentum caused by the high fertility of the greatly enlarged population, helped the 1920s to set yet another record for highest population growth.

THE GREAT DEPRESSION DECADE

1930–1940 ♟♟♟♟♟♟♟♟♟ 9.0 million

1930–1940: The 1924 immigration law and the Great Depression kept immigration below traditional levels. And Americans greatly reduced their fertility to respond to the dire economic times, cutting total population growth for the decade nearly in half from each of the previous three decades.

THE BABY BOOM DECADES

1940–1950 ♟♟♟♟♟♟♟♟♟♟♟♟♟♟♟♟♟♟♟♟ 20.1 million

1940–1950: After the end of World War II in 1945, immigration grew back toward traditional levels and Americans began to create very large families. The giant spike in fertility came to be known as the Baby Boom, a demographic phenomenon that changed every aspect of American society and that continues to drive a lot of the social and political agenda to this day.

👤👤👤👤👤👤👤👤👤👤👤👤👤👤👤👤👤👤👤👤👤👤👤👤👤👤👤👤

1950–1960   28.4 million

1950–1960: This was the peak of the Baby Boom, adding nearly the equivalent of the entire U.S. population at the time of the Civil War. Combined with other factors, this led to an enormous conversion of farmland and natural habitats into sprawling suburbs. This new record for the biggest population boom ever was widely thought to be a special phenomenon reflecting pent-up pressures from the Depression and the war, and one that would never be repeated or exceeded.

1960–1970 👤👤👤👤👤👤👤👤👤👤👤👤👤👤👤👤👤👤👤👤👤👤👤👤 24.2 million

1960–1970: Exhausted from years of frantic efforts to expand the nation's infrastructure to handle its large families and burgeoning population, Americans rapidly reduced their fertility through the last decade of the Baby Boom. The growth rate at the end of the decade was a third lower than at the beginning. A vigorous social and political movement emerged calling for Americans to keep their fertility to a replacement level rate to enable the country to eventually stabilize its population.

LOW-FERTILITY/IMMIGRATION TIDAL WAVE DECADES

1970–1980 👤👤👤👤👤👤👤👤👤👤👤👤👤👤👤👤👤👤👤👤👤👤 22.2 million

1970–1980: The American fertility rate fell to replacement level in 1972, making it possible for the nation to eventually reach a widely held dream for a stable population. A national government commission recommended that the nation would be best served in reaching its environmental, economic, and social goals by a stabilizing population. Numerous experts and commentators predicted that each decade would see lower and lower population growth, and until early in the twenty-first century there would be no growth at all.

1980–1990 ♟♟♟♟♟♟♟♟♟♟♟♟♟♟♟♟♟♟♟♟♟♟ 22.2 million

1980–1990: Despite continuing below-replacement-level fertility, population growth continued at the level of the previous decade. The reason was that Congress had created a system of chain migration that snowballed and doubled annual legal immigration over traditional levels. Further adding to the population, Congress for the first time ever rewarded illegal aliens—about three million of them—with a path to citizenship. Federal immigration policy was negating the results of Americans choosing to have smaller families.

1990–2000   32.7 million

1990–2000: The dream of a stabilized—or even a stabilizing—population was proven to be nothing but a fairy tale as U.S. population exploded with its biggest growth ever. The Baby Boom peak was exceeded—not by a big increase in Americans' babies but because Congress further increased immigration to a level almost quadruple the traditional level. And federal decisions to stop enforcing most laws against illegal immigration in the interior of the country led to additional higher levels of illegal aliens in the country. Yet another cause of the boom was immigrant fertility. Although American natives maintained a below-replacement-level fertility rate, immigrant fertility was at a similar rate to the U.S. Baby Boom fertility of the 1950s.

PROSPECTS FOR THE FUTURE

The immigration tidal wave of the last three decades has made it impossible for Baby Boomers ever to enjoy the 1970s dream of a stabilized country—even if all immigration were stopped tomorrow. The Census Bureau states that if immigration were reduced to replacement level, the United States population would still be growing at the end of the century because of the momentum created by the last three decades of immigration.

Used with permission. NumbersUSA Education & Research Foundation (www.NumbersUSA.com)

According to a variety of statistics, America's first two hundred years saw an average of approximately 250,000 (legal) immigrants per year, followed by a figure that more than doubled in the following eighty years to 507,000 annually. But when Congress changed earlier immigration standards by passing the Hart-Celler Act of 1965, they opened the floodgates to more than 1.5 million immigrants per year—in fewer than twenty-four years. Our systems were never built for this kind of influx.

The Hart-Celler Act is the heart of today's debacle of an immigration system, because it rests on a concept of family reunification instead of the earlier national origins quota system that maintained a checks and balances protocol. The bottom fell out even as President

Lyndon Johnson made promises to the contrary: "This bill we sign today is not a revolutionary bill. It does not affect the lives of millions. It will not restructure the shape of our daily lives." As the number of legal and illegal immigrants has increased, so has the exponential growth of the family ties that open the U.S. to the record numbers. If Congress doesn't overhaul the failed system it created, how can immigration figures do anything other than increase—every year?

Writer Louis Adamic moved to America from southeastern Europe in the early 1900s and described his blanketless night at Ellis Island with this phrase: "I shivered, sleepless, all night, listening to snores."

Today in America, the shivering, sleepless, and snore-filled experiences are still the same—except now they happen in truck beds, desert sands, and drop houses.

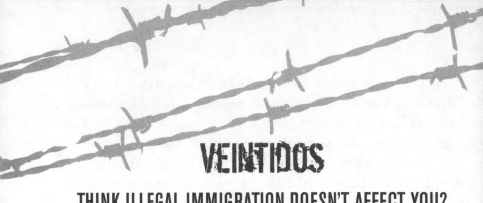

VEINTIDOS
THINK ILLEGAL IMMIGRATION DOESN'T AFFECT YOU?
THINK AGAIN!

I am reminded all the time that a free market system will ultimately take care of itself. Though I embrace such a system, what we are experiencing within the illegal immigration industry is not a pure free-market model. While big business and their politicians tell us the market will adjust, they fail to explain that by propping up illegal immigrants with welfare, services, education, and other benefits created for citizens, we give an unfair advantage to the people who break the law to be here. For a fairer assessment, the cost of the benefits consumed must be factored in.

On May 10, 2007, Heritage Foundation researcher Robert Rector appeared before the House Judiciary Committee as it met in one of a set of hearings devoted to illegal immigration. Convening at the Marine Corps Recruit Depot in San Diego, legislators said they wanted to hear the future. Using the government's own data, Mr. Rector painted a bleak picture for the United States unless something is done to deter the influx of humanity. His testimony described approximately

9 million illegal immigrants. (Most reliable figures easily double this number; thus the figures he supplied should increase accordingly.)

Mr. Rector's statistics should make even the most supportive fan of illegal immigration pause for reconsideration. The researcher methodically pointed out that half of the immigrants (legal and otherwise) have no degree, while a third dropped out of school (compared to 9 percent of our citizens). The results will soon be unmanageable. His findings include the following:

- Each illegal immigrant receives approximately $30,000 in benefits per year from local, state, and federal sources like 60 means-tested welfare programs, education, police and fire, and Medicare.
- Though each illegal immigrant pays approximately $10,000 in taxes from sales, Social Security, or consumption taxes, immigrants pay little or nothing in income taxes. As a direct result, they see net or actual benefits of about $19,500 more than any taxes paid. This group costs U.S. taxpayers $89 billion a year, net.
- Over a lifetime, the net cost to U.S. citizens is $1.2 million for an illegal who has a family here.
- When an illegal reaches retirement age, he/she will receive approximately ten dollars for every dollar paid in taxes.
- The cost to U.S. taxpayers will be dramatic as illegals reach retirement age in large numbers in about twenty years. They will use Social Security, Supplement Security Income (SSI), Medicare, and Medicaid while having paid little or nothing into the system under any proposed amnesty or earned citizenship program, with an approximate cost of $2.5 trillion just as the Social Security program goes bankrupt.
- A guest worker program will be even more expensive.

In the same hearing, further cost details emerged when Representative James Sensenbrenner (R-Wis.) outlined how hospitals in the southwestern United States are losing $190 million annually to care for uncompensated health care for illegal immigrants and that almost one in five federal inmates are noncitizens, adding another almost $2 billion annually to the mushrooming expense layer.

By bringing diseases that are indigenous to their homeland or not properly treated there or elsewhere, the illegal immigrant is waging a private, quiet, and unintentional attack of a different sort. Though it's improbable to believe a nation's sovereignty might be at risk due to sickness, the right combination of diseases could burden a nation's law enforcement, military, and health care systems to such an extent that numerous systems could fail.

Some of the vilest diseases to invade the human body, many of which were long ago eradicated in the U.S., are once again proliferating on our shores.

From 1962 through 2002 there were a little more than nine hundred cases of Hansen's disease (leprosy) in America. From 2002 to 2005 more than nine thousand cases were reported—mostly in the illegal immigrant community. Dr. William Levis, who heads up New York's Hansen's Disease Clinic has been quoted as saying, "This is a real phenomenon. It's a public health threat. New York is endemic now, and nobody's noticed." The majority of Levis's patients are immigrants.

Malaria disappeared here in the mid-1940s, but Texas, New York, California, and New Jersey have all seen return engagements.

Hepatitis A–E is out of control worldwide, with as many as one-third[1] of all humans infected with one level or another as it silently attacks the liver and kills about a million people annually. Third-world nations have been hit hardest, but America is feeling the impact at higher levels than in previous years because people from those countries move here so freely without medical treatment.

In late 2007 Alabama health officials moved into one of America's top poultry plants to test 765 workers for tuberculosis (TB). After the batteries of tests were completed, no fewer than 28 percent were identified as infected. The majority of those infected were "foreign born" according to Scott Jones, interim director of the Tuberculosis Control Division. TB kills more than two million people a year around the world and could increase to 36 million by 2020 because, according to many health care providers, as many as ten persons will be infected by each carrier. Meanwhile, a drug-resistant TB has recently emerged, which can cost from $250,000 to $1.2 million and more than two years to treat—per person. In America, this strain increased by more than 13 percent from 2003 to 2004. Popular Web site WorldNet Daily reported that three-quarters of the 2,903 cases in California in 2005 were among foreign natives.[2]

Other diseases, like cysticercosis, HIV, worm infection, Chagas' disease, schistosomiasis, guinea worm, whooping cough, Morgellon's, and more are turning up in various parts of the nation, popular with foreign-born nationals and illegal immigrants. U.S. immigration procedures have strict guidelines for visitors and visa holders. Most eyes must look to the illegal immigrant community for the resurrection or establishment of so many old and cured diseases gaining new strangleholds, since most of these people duck under our health care radar.

Other sources from public and private sectors have also been tracking the outgo. The National Academy of Sciences estimated an annual cost to taxpayers of approximately $100,000 per immigrant.[3] Los

Angeles County supervisor Mike Antonovich went on record with a figure showing 30 percent of public health patients in Los Angeles County are illegal immigrants.[4] Harvard professor George Borjas estimates that in a single year, illegal aliens displaced American workers to the tune of more than $133 billion dollars, and that figure is growing.[5] Author Frosty Wooldridge noted that U.S. citizens "paid $27 billion to provide forms, ballots, interpreters and brochures for languages other than English in 2003."[6]

In 2005 in my home state of Arizona, we spent nearly $1.3 billion to cover our unwanted guests with health care, education, welfare, and incarceration fees,[7] and another $1.4 billion in lower wages.[8] For 2004 and 2005, the Federation for American Immigration Reform (FAIR) issued fiscal cost studies for California, Arizona, Texas, and Florida looking at the same cost factors studied by the Urban Institute ten years earlier, i.e., education, emergency medical care, and incarceration. Findings of the annual net fiscal costs were:

California	$8.8 billion	($1,183 per native household)
Arizona	$1.03 billion	($717 per native household)
Texas	$3.73 billion	($725 per native household)
Florida	$9.1 billion	($315 per native household)

FAIR further estimates the local annual costs of illegal immigration from those same categories at about $36 billion, and that "by 2010 our estimate is that the annual fiscal costs in 2010 would increase by nearly 70 percent to $61.5 billion for just these same three program areas. The amount would swell by an additional nearly 73 percent to $106.3 billion by 2020."[9]

What should be just as troubling are the ramifications from these costs: if one out of three immigrants needs and uses public health care because they have none of their own, is it any wonder that presidential candidates push for universal health care? One-third of the burden is imported. If we legalize the millions of illegals, and they cost us $2.5 trillion a year, as Heritage Foundation researcher Dr. Robert Rector says, then we watch a Social Security program we all have funded go bankrupt. If they use our education, police, fire, and welfare programs, for which we have to pay more than $19,500 per illegal immigrant, who pays for it? Taxes go up. Social Security gets changed. Health care is scrapped and overhauled, and much of the burden comes from border jumpers. Why is everyone afraid to point their fingers at the real dollar drain?

These figures are representative of the grave and growing financial burden facing the American taxpayer with each new year that comes along. They are offered as a snapshot only, as complete volumes have been written to outline the costs associated with illegal immigration in America.

America's sovereignty has been hard fought and hard earned, and there is too much history of its importance to the balance of power in the world for it to be destroyed overnight. It won't—no, it *can't*—happen that simply. For our borders, language, laws, and bank accounts to be stripped to the bone, two formidable foes must be faced: (1) time, which has already been ticking away on this issue, and (2) a perfect storm of many grinding and circling elements—a storm that is brewing and growing by the hour.

Will we weather it?

VEINTITRES

THE PRICE WE PAY: AN INTERVIEW WITH
STEVE CAMAROTA, CENTER FOR IMMIGRATION STUDIES

I have tried to provide a balanced snapshot of the immigration, especially the illegal immigration, picture in the U.S.A., with numerous stories and statistics so together we may be able to find balanced solutions. It's easy for most of us to get lost in the numbers, so let's see how dearly we pay for our failed immigration system by reviewing the basics. For years the Center for Immigrations Studies (CIS) has researched the fallout, so I invited Steve Camarota, director of research for CIS, to explain how education, taxes, health care, and even the environment are negatively influenced by this country's border policies.

ANKARLO: You have been researching immigration issues for over twelve years. What are the numbers telling you?

CAMAROTA: The trend has been up, up, up, up. Both legal and illegal immigration have been rising pretty fast. Immigrants or foreign-born population of the United States, legal and illegal, has been growing pretty rapidly by about a million a year. Maybe 1.5, 1.6 million new people are coming, legally and illegally, settling in the country each year, but some die and some go home each year, so the net increase is about a million a year. It's growing faster than it has at any time in our history, and we are now to the point where one out of every eight people residing in the United States is either a legal or an illegal immigrant. That's really one of the highest totals in American history, and certainly the highest since 1920.

ANKARLO: From 2000 to 2007 was the greatest influx of immigration or immigrants into this country than at any other seven-year period of time in the history of the country. Correct?

CAMAROTA: Yes, over 10 million people came and settled in the United States during that time period, and probably more than half, almost certainly more than half, came in illegally.

ANKARLO: I've always wondered how the research is done, and how do we know they are right. Where do you get your stats?

CAMAROTA: Well, believe it or not, the Census Bureau does an excellent job of collecting some really good data. We think about 90 percent of illegal aliens actually respond to the census survey, and we think that more than 95 percent of legal immigrants do, so we get a sample of over twenty-five thousand legal and illegal immigrants, and then we can begin to look at the foreign-born overall, or we could try to pick out the illegals based on their socioeconomic characteristics and get a profile of just illegals.

ANKARLO: Steven, that's the part that has always confounded me, though. If I'm in a country illegally, and somebody knocks on my door and says, "Hey, I want to ask some questions," I am not answering you, and if I do, I'm lying because I think you're from the government and you're going to take me away.

CAMAROTA: Yeah, except that illegals are smarter than that. They recognize that there is really no fear of enforcement, and so they do respond. The Census Bureau does a good job of reassuring them; they have Spanish-speaking interviewers, and roughly 80 percent of illegals speak Spanish. Here's one way to think about it: The surveys showed over 37 million foreign-born people in the United States. There should be only about 26 million legal immigrants. So, it showed 37 but there should be only 26. So, who are the other 11 million?

ANKARLO: Right. Let's look at Arizona's illegal population as example—since the state is ground zero on the immigration issue. Paint that picture.

CAMAROTA: Right, though that's a somewhat more recent phenomenon. Arizona's immigrant population wasn't quite as big in the not-too-distant past. Just to give you an example: in Arizona as recently as 1995, the immigrant population of the state was only about 500,000. Now, in the state it is more like 900,000 and, of that 900,000, roughly about 65 percent, or two-thirds are here illegally, which really makes Arizona stand out. And that is that the share of Arizona's immigrants that are illegal immigrants is higher than anywhere else in the country, though, believe it or not, in places like North Carolina and in Georgia, it's almost as high.

ANKARLO: Well, yeah, when I saw those stats, like, I think Georgia was 58 percent or something like that? North Carolina within a point or two of that. What the heck's going on in this country, Steven?

CAMAROTA: Well, those places have gotten enormous influx—I mean, there are as many immigrants in Georgia now as there are in Arizona, and Georgia is not a border state, you know; it's hundreds of miles from the border, so that's important to note. These are states that have seen their immigrant populations in Georgia and North Carolina roughly triple in twelve years.

ANKARLO: Walk us through education for just a minute. Of the immigrants who are here legally, what kind of education level do they have, and are you able to break down the illegal part of that as well?

CAMAROTA: We looked at the total foreign-born, legal and illegal. About 31 percent of immigrants who arrive as adults do not have a high school education, and for illegal immigrants, it's higher. We estimated it at 57 percent. Now, what's important about that is that, as you know, education is the single best predictor of whether you're going to live in poverty, whether you're going to use welfare, whether you're going to lack health insurance. It determines your income, your likely tax contributions, and so, the comparison, instead of the 31 percent and the 57 percent, about 8 percent of natives haven't graduated high school, and that is one of the key sources, one of the reasons immigration has become so problematic. In the past immigrants were roughly as educated as natives. I mean, everyone was less educated than we are now, but everyone was about the same. Now this enormous gap has opened up between immigrants and natives, and as a result—let me just give you one statistic—we estimated that 19 percent of native-headed households use at least one major welfare program. For immigrants it was about a third. So, immigrant households are using a fair amount of welfare, but not because they're not working; most of them are. It's just that the people in those households, many of them have little education and so they make very little money.

ANKARLO: Go back to the number. When you say "about a third," is that 32 percent, 33 percent, 34 percent? What is it?

CAMAROTA: Oh, the share of immigrants?

ANKARLO: Yep.

CAMAROTA: About 32 percent of immigrant households use at least one major welfare program.

ANKARLO: On your Web site, www.cis.org, you list all your research. In the documents you provide several tables. One is called "Poverty and Near-Poverty Among Illegal Aliens." I reviewed your numbers and actually shared them with former presidential candidate Pat Buchanan yesterday, and he was surprised, so I thought, *Well, maybe I misinterpreted it*. So, set me straight if need be—according to your stats, Colorado leads the nation in poverty or near poverty at 75 percent, and an illegal alien who has a U.S.-born child under the age of eighteen, otherwise—an "anchor baby"—75 percent of all of the illegals in that category in Colorado are on or near the poverty level. Is that accurate?

CAMAROTA: In Colorado, yes.

ANKARLO: That's huge.

CAMAROTA: And in Arizona it's 73 percent. It is very similar.

ANKARLO: So, 73 percent in Arizona, 75 percent in Colorado, Texas is 68 percent, and I can go through the list—these persons, if they've had the anchor baby, it's turning around and costing them dearly, and they're sitting in poverty or near poverty. These are monstrous numbers, aren't they?

CAMAROTA: Right. People sort of get confused about a lot of things, and maybe you're right to focus on this table. If you have a group that mostly works, but 73 percent of them live in or near poverty, the impact, say, on public services is going to be a lot. Yes, they're going to pay some taxes, but given their low income and large numbers of dependents, the taxes are going to be relatively modest. And they cannot access all services on their own behalf, but very often their U.S.-born children qualify, and so, yes, you're right. You're right to focus on that, because that's why we estimate in a state like Arizona that 32 percent of households headed by immigrants in the state use at least one major welfare program, and that's a lot higher than it is for natives in the state.

ANKARLO: Follow my thought process for a minute: The impact is significant enough that many citizens pause to wonder what we should do, which brings the politicians out of the woodwork to demand more services and higher taxes to pay for them. For instance, health care is out of control, so our elected leaders drag out universal health care. Our schools are strapped for cash, and teachers can't keep up with the extra steps to teach other languages, so now we need more money for education. Crime is up dramatically in areas with large concentrations of illegal immigrants, so mayors ask for property or sales tax increases to put more officers on the streets. I have attended presidential campaign rallies where superstar politicians promise more and more services because the people deserve them, but if the pressure from illegals was not in the system, many of these areas would be manageable.

CAMAROTA: You're right. One out of three people without health insurance in the United States is either an immigrant—legal or illegal—or the U.S.-born young child of an immigrant. So, you know, these are enormous numbers. If we look at the growth over the last seventeen years, about three-fourths of that increase is accounted for by immigrants who entered in the last seventeen years. And so, immigration is not—it is correct to say that to a significant extent, the nation's health insurance crisis, including Arizona, is being driven by our immigration policy. And this is not happening because the immigrants are all lazy, don't work, and came to get welfare. It happens because so many have very little education. In effect, you're importing folks who have a tough time in the modern American economy. That fact, coupled with the existence of a modern welfare state, and I mean broadly speaking, I don't mean just cash welfare. I mean everything from free school lunch for kids to—

ANKARLO: Well, yeah, I think—What are there? Like, sixty means test to welfare programs that these people can attach to.

CAMAROTA: That's right. Most people don't know that. So, those things is what drives these numbers. It's not that people are lazy and it's not that they came to get welfare. In effect, what's happening is you're transferring the poverty of rural Latin America to a large— to the United States.

ANKARLO: And go back to it, Steven, because you used the word *import*, and I'm sure our big businesses are doing that, but I also use the word *export*. I think that there has been a move afoot in Mexico for the last few years—several, perhaps—that said, "Get rid of the riff-raff, get rid of the nonproductive people, let them go to the land of plenty, and that way they're off our backs." And as a result, you know, that country is still destabilized, [and] our country is becoming destabilized.

CAMAROTA: Actually, if you look at the education level of Mexican immigrants in the United States, they are about as educated as people in Mexico. Surveys show that most people who come illegally to the United States had a job back in Mexico; it just wasn't as good as the one they can get here, so what's happening is—but I think your basic analysis, unfortunately, tragically, is probably right. It forestalls or at least slows down the pace of reform that they would have to otherwise implement. And so, yeah, in effect, they're getting rid of a large share of the population—people who might otherwise demand reforms. Better they go to America. And then it's even better because the Mexican government and elitists can claim to speak for their illegals, particularly in the United States. So, not only do they shed this problem on the United States, but then they can say to [their] own citizens, here or there, "Hey, look, we are a good government. Look how we're pressuring the United States government to respect the rights and so forth of immigrants in the United States." So it's really a win-win situation for the Mexican elite, though Mexico itself may not benefit.

ANKARLO: As a numbers guy, anything else just leap out of your research?

CAMAROTA: Well, [in] our latest study and one we put out in the summer of 2007, we just looked at the current level of immigration and projected it forward: assuming it doesn't change, illegal and legal immigration is going to add 105 million people to the U.S. population by 2060. That's people who haven't yet come but will start to come tomorrow, plus the children that they have. The U.S. population will be over 100 million people larger. In Arizona it's going to add several million people too. The total impact is the equivalent of thirteen New York Cities. And that is something that politicians who claim to want better environment or claim to want to reign in global warming, and so forth, are completely unwilling to talk about—how [the] U.S. population is going to grow dramatically.

ANKARLO: But we're told America is aging and needs this influx.

CAMAROTA: Even with all that population growth, it has almost no effect on making the country younger. Some nondemographers think immigration makes us a much more youthful society but actually, the immigrants, not surprisingly, grow old over time and, yes, they have larger families but not that much larger, so even with that extra 100 million, about 90 percent of the aging that would have occurred had we had no immigration will still occur. So, in other words, we'll be just about as old, but just a much more densely settled country.

ANKARLO: Folks, discount tickets for Prozac—just go to my Web site and you can buy as much as you need, because God knows we're going to need it. You scare me, but your stats should scare us all.

VEINTICUATRO

SENATOR JOHN McCAIN—AN INTERVIEW

John McCain is a war hero, former POW, and well-established senator from Arizona. Oh, and if you ask him questions he doesn't like, he has the ability to behave like a spoiled brat. I should know—I've seen his long-rumored bad behavior firsthand. There is really no reason for me to include details about his temper in this book except that he is a multiterm legislator who has made a couple runs at the White House and considers himself to be an expert on the issue of illegal immigration.

In November 2007 I made a trip to Iowa to assess the mood of the people a year prior to the national elections of '08. Among the politicians I watched perform at stump speeches was the seventy-year-old legislator.

For almost a year the senator and his office dodged every question I had about illegal immigration in his home state. More than any other state in the Union, Arizona is on the front lines. Although I have liked Senator McCain from afar, I was troubled by some of his comments regarding illegal immigration and was deeply disturbed that he and fellow Arizona senator John Kyl would lend their names and support to a failed piece of legislation regarded by most as an amnesty deal for illegals. In fact, the pages, nearly a thousand of them, crafted by the likes of Teddy Kennedy, were lovingly referred to as the "Shamnesty" bill. I was one of the first broadcasters in the country to read and share the contents with my audience and was gratified when U.S. senators and representatives agreed with my position. During that time, I tried daily, sometimes up to five or six times a day, to get Senator McCain to explain his position, but to no avail.

No doubt, immigration is a *huge* issue, and on this chilly autumn night the last thing a presidential wannabe could afford was unexpected questions. This was McCain's night, and I never intended for our conversation to turn ugly—I just wanted him to be clearer on a point or two.

My team had jumped through all the required hoops all night in hopes that we would have a chance for a private interview with the senator, but the most they were willing to offer was "two or three quick questions after the press gaggle." We said yes, of course.

Just the day before, McCain was quoted in various newspaper reports as adjusting his immigration position. He said, "I understand why you would call it a, quote, shift."[1] He added, "I say it is a lesson learned about what the American people's priorities are. And their priority is to secure the borders." McCain was now saying what most of us had been saying for a while—seal the borders.

I was learning that, like most politicians, he was capable of taking a variety of positions on the monumental problem that is illegal immigration, and now I had a chance to lock him in. As a broadcaster, it is always great to get the story, but on this night I was coming to him as a citizen hoping to speak with a very evasive elected leader. I wanted to hear the details of his "shift." From his earlier speeches and positions[2] he listed opposition to the funding of projects such as a detainee facility in Prescott, Arizona; a border guard service processing center; border stations in Yuma and Douglas; and more. He actually criticized the $25 million U.S. Border Patrol station in Tucson,[3] even though it would become the most used center in the battle against illegal immigration anywhere in the nation. He also complained about the $500,000 used to erect a very effective border fence on the Nogales border. Immigration policy should be cut-and-dried, but this man and many of his pals in D.C. confuse me—do they want to stop this mess or not?

It should be noted that I have nothing but admiration for Senator McCain as a war hero, and actually approached him carefully and with honest respect. After all, I am the father of a Fallujah, Iraq, war veteran myself.

Instead of finding a serious thinker on the subject, I would witness, within a few brief seconds of my first question, a hotheaded approach to a very serious issue. At first I thought that it might be an "age" thing since he was already in his early seventies, but I later learned that numerous U.S. congressmen and senators have letters of apology from Senator McCain, sent after he went off on them too. Later, all I could consider was how a misunderstood question or terse word from a foreign leader and this man's anger might create an international incident. He made up my mind—this candidate would *not* be getting my vote. If more Americans get serious in holding our elected officials accountable, we might still have a fighting chance.

So, the "gaggle" was gaggling, and my producer, Rob Hunter, was running a video recorder so we could post questions to the blog for my radio show. In Arizona, we have passed some of the most comprehensive immigration laws in the country, led by the Employer Sanction Bill, a law that punishes employers for knowingly hiring illegal immigrants.

It has been the talk of the state, served as fodder for countless national radio and television talk shows, and considered for national possibilities. Even the snowbirds, older adults coming back to Arizona for the warm winter weather, know about the sanctions bill—though they've been gone half the year. Looking through his viewfinder, Rob asked McCain what I thought was an easy question. We had hoped Senator McCain would share a few strategies. That was not going to happen!

HUNTER: What do you think of the Employer Sanctions Bill here in Arizona?

SENATOR MCCAIN: I haven't examined it. I-I-I really haven't examined it. So I do know that because we failed at the federal level—because we failed, it is a federal issue and we should have addressed it, and we failed to do so because there is no trust or confidence in Washington. Then you see a patchwork of different kind of laws enacted in different cities, states, and counties, and that's clearly not the way it should be done. We should act from the federal level.

I was shocked by his answer. Here is a man running for the White House from Arizona—a state with the worst illegal immigration problem in the nation, who has lent his name to more than a couple pieces of legislation dealing with immigration—and he doesn't know what's going on in his home state on an issue this important? I know that to win the presidency one must say things they have been prepped for, but to claim ignorance on a subject like this could bury a candidate. I thought I would give the senator a chance to elaborate in order to change the upcoming headlines.

ANKARLO: Take that message all the way back to Arizona, you're going to get hit as a flip-flopper. Kerry got hit with it. You have changed your position on the border a little bit, haven't you?

SENATOR McCAIN: No.

ANKARLO: Not at all?

SENATOR McCAIN: No.

ANKARLO: So, the original idea was amnesty, or that's how it was presented as we all got together about five or six months ago. Now, it's "let's seal the borders"?

The senator's face lost its usual ashen look and was turning red. His body went noticeably rigid, and his jaw clenched.

SENATOR McCAIN: No, I was never for an amnesty, and I'm sorry that you are so terribly misinformed. Most people that have questioned me are better informed than you are.

His answer was either a blatant lie or the direct result of a failing memory, because the senator had used the term countless times, including this quote from a May 28, 2003, press conference in Tucson, Arizona: "I think we can set up a program where amnesty is extended to a certain number of people," McCain said. "Amnesty has to be an important part, because there are people who have lived in this country for 20, 30 or 40 years, who have raised children here and pay taxes here and are not citizens."[4]

I was obviously more than a little surprised by his refusal to take ownership of his own failed perceptions and legislation on such an enormously important issue, so I tried again to get Senator McCain to respond.

ANKARLO: Let's walk through that for a minute, Senator. I'm coming from Arizona and have been down on the border and gone into Mexico and come back trying to see what it's like for these folks—

SENATOR MCCAIN: You think I haven't done that?

ANKARLO: I'm sure you have.

SENATOR MCCAIN: You think I haven't done that—that somehow you think that I haven't been on the border and down into Mexico for many, many years. I've been a senator from that state for now nearly twenty-one years, so I understand the conditions on the border. Umm, I don't know what your credentials are, but if you have a question for me, I'll answer it.

ANKARLO: That's where I was going earlier.

SENATOR MCCAIN: Then just ask the question.

ANKARLO: The question I asked was, are you going to be seen as a flip-flopper as a result of the statements you've made in the last couple of days?

SENATOR MCCAIN: Of course not.

He snapped his head in a different direction, clearly dismissing me, and a few words later, the senator and his staff made a retreat for the exit door. I tried to hand him my press card—just in case he wanted to chat later—but he would have none of that. His staff intercepted me long enough for Mr. McCain to disappear. I wondered why the senator chose to be so rude and condescending, and why he was afraid to answer the questions. It was bizarre behavior to say the least. I was embarrassed. Not for myself—for him. When asked a question that is deemed too tough, politicians are schooled to do a couple of things, and yes, they go to classes for this: (1) answer the question without really answering it—we see this in debates all the time; just talk, and (2) put the questioner on the defensive. Some passed the classes with flying colors.

Several weeks later, Senator John McCain became the last Republican standing in the race for the White House. Shortly after that he was asked about the "Shamnesty" bill again, this time McCain said he wasn't sure it had the legs to pass into law but would still support it if it did—if he were the President of the United States!

At the point of our exchange, Senator McCain had been walking around the Buckeye State with about 6 percent of the vote, dangerously close to the bottom of the Republican ladder, and he needed to change strategies if he was to move up the rungs. The changed direction would need to include an extreme makeover on the immigration issue—in other words, he needed to put his amnesty support pretty far back in the rearview mirror, and he didn't need me to stir the pot.

He wanted my questions to disappear, but I promised myself I wouldn't allow that to happen. Catch a politician playing politics with my country's well-being and future existence, and it is my responsibility to keep the issue in the forefront. We all share this same requirement!

I watched with great interest in the weeks between that November evening and the Iowa Caucus in January 2008 as the senator notched up his rhetoric about border protection, immigration enforcement, and other laundry list items strategists said he needed to "own" in order to move up in the polls. And, sure enough, the Arizona senator ratcheted the language and pointed at the camera with a firmness that made him appear to be an authority. He finished Iowa tied for third place, and his first win in New Hampshire's primary a week later gave him the shot in the arm that led to winning a nod of approval from his party.

In six months this man changed his tune, and We the People started to flock to him—just like we always do when politicians say what we want them to. Wouldn't it be a nice change of pace if they actually started *doing* what we wanted them to?

VEINTICINCO

SENATOR JOHN KYL—AN INTERVIEW

O n Thursday, June 28, 2007, the American people put the fear of God in the hearts and minds of Congress—on both sides of the aisle—when they applied mass pressure as few times before. When finished, the Comprehensive Immigration Reform Act of 2007—which was heralded as the cure-all for America's immigration woes—was dead. It was crafted by a dozen Democratic and Republican congressmen, along with Homeland Security Secretary Michael Chertoff and commerce secretary Carlos Gutierrez, all of whom worked on the deal over a six-month period. And though many of its architects regularly appeared in the media to support it, it was bound for defeat due to the extraordinary number of loopholes intentionally and unintentionally added to placate opposing politicians.

Labor Unions, the ACLU, radio and television talk show hosts (myself included), illegal immigrants, and just about everyone who hasn't been named here lent their time to participate in phone, mail, protest, and e-mail campaigns to stop it. U.S. Representative Jeff Sessions went so far as to publish a list of the loopholes that he said would give gangs and illegal aliens the upper hand while failing to make immigrants learn English for up to twelve years. It was a nasty, painful fight.

One of the bill's creators, Senator Edward Kennedy (D-Mass.), suggested the fight was similar to the civil rights battles of the 1960s and beyond. In response, Senator David Vitter (R-La.) looked for the closest news reporter and said, "To suggest this was about racism is the height of ugliness and arrogance." Even Senator John Kyl (R-Ariz.), one of the bill's sponsors, jumped into the quote matches when he said, "The American people don't have faith in their government's ability to win a war, enforce border security, or even process passport requests."

The bill was, in some ways, a looser version of the failed Kennedy-McCain immigration legislation from a year earlier, the same one that was chastised for rewarding people sneaking into the country with fines and a path to citizenship. Both pieces of legislation failed to address a key obstacle: Americans consider the right of citizenship to be one of the greatest honors a person can ever receive, and believe it should not be diminished by politicians hoping to easily solve a problem they, and their predecessors, allowed to happen in the first place. On top of that, legal immigrants and naturalized citizens were not pleased to think they had waited, legally, for years to get their chance, and border jumpers would get there too—usually sooner.

Senator Kyl agreed to answer a few questions about the state of the immigration problem in America.

ANKARLO: We have an illegal immigration issue in this country. You and I both know that. Senator, if I've got to put blame on one group, who would that be?

SENATOR JOHN KYL: Well, it's pretty hard to pick out one, because there are so many different folks to blame. Frankly, both administrations in the last sixteen years could have done a lot more to deal with the problem, but that is by no means to suggest that Congress is free of blame or states or localities or businesses or immigration groups or any number of other folks that you could say are at least partially to blame for the problem that we've allowed to develop.

ANKARLO: When we talk about the blame, there are so many people that are involved in the process. Let's look at some of the solutions. One is to protect the borders. You and I have discussed this numerous times—we've got a major issue in the United States of America. Would you, as a senator, be in favor of more border patrol? Would there be weaponized border control? How far do you go?

SENATOR JOHN KYL: Well, my record of what I favor doing is very clear. I have hundreds of pages of legislation that I have authored or supported that is a mosaic for all of the different solutions to the problem. And there isn't just one. They are many. They start with control of the border through a variety of means, which includes more personnel, more technology, more fencing. It includes the associated components of that, which include more detention spaces so that you can affect policies that detain people and, therefore, provide more deterrent to crossing. It extends to the personnel for prosecution throughout the criminal justice system, all the way from the lawyers through the judges, and so on. And, then the elements that deal with internal enforcement of the law: more ICE agents and ability to cooperate more closely—state, federal, and local authorities—to detail people when that's appropriate; the ability to enforce the visa laws that we have. Over 40 percent of the people who are here illegally have simply overstayed a visa. We need to be able to track that and to provide that information immediately into state and local databases as well, so that when

those people are stopped, they can be referenced to the appropriate authorities and removed, if that is appropriate. And perhaps,
most important of all, are the employee verification systems for
work and the employer sanctions that must accompany that. We
have a system right now that doesn't work well in terms of verify-
ing employee ability to work, and that needs to be put into place.
So, there is a very large, overlapping mosaic of policies, and that
doesn't even begin to talk about the temporary worker programs
that would help remove some of the pressure for illegal employment and some of the other things that need to be done.

ANKARLO: Talk to me for a minute as a senator. With all the things that
you deal with, can you rank the place illegal immigration should
hold? Is it number one on the list, or lower down—say, number
five? Where does it fall?

SENATOR JOHN KYL: National security, the work that we do in trying to
stop the terrorists and deal with the other national security issues,
is probably the most important thing. There is a component of that
that relates to the broken borders, but it is not by any means the
biggest part of the illegal immigration problem. Keeping our economy strong through low taxes is another very important part of
what I try to do. But in terms of issues that are most important to
Arizonans, after the terrorist and Iraq war issues, immigration is by
far and away the most important on their mind. And because it is
unique to Arizona— over half the illegal immigrants come through
our state—I think Senator McCain and I view this as probably the
most important domestic issue that we have to deal with.

ANKARLO: Here are some stats that I have, and again, yours may be
different: 1.6 million legal immigrants who went through the proper

channels have a high school equivalency or less; 1.5 million illegals came into America last year, give or take a few. Most are, you know, very low educated, and there are 25 million undereducated U.S. citizens. When you put all those together, you have a class of people who don't have the education; (a) they are not the future of the United States of America unless they can grow to the next level, and (b) they represent what is bringing down real wages, and some would say the economy, because of the supply and demand from these groups. How frightened are you by this?

SENATOR JOHN KYL: Well, I don't know the exact numbers either, but whatever the precise numbers are, the phenomenon that you're discussing is a very serious one, and it does challenge our future way of life in the United States. Forget the elements of illegality and the current costs to society from this phenomenon; because of the low skill and lower education that you talk about, it will put enormous pressures on our country as we go by, unless we can solve the problem.

ANKARLO: Go through the numbers again, though. So, according to statistics that I have found, Senator, 43 percent of all illegals from Mexico—43 percent—use some system of the United States welfare system—and it goes up to 75 percent in some states when the illegal has a U.S.-born child. Colombia, Cuba, Dominican Republic—and I have a dozen more, but I won't go on to them—all use some kind of resource within our "welfare system" in the state or in the country. When you have the number of uneducated and low-paid people using the system like this, eventually we won't be able to support the costs.

SENATOR JOHN KYL: There are those who say that it is a great economic benefit for the United States to be able to take advantage of all of this low-cost labor. While that is true in some areas for some people, the overwhelming cost that it imposes on American tax-payers in the long run will far exceed any benefits that are temporarily available to us. Studies reveal that the two groups that benefit the most from illegal employment are the illegals themselves and their immediate employer. The rest of us end up paying the tab, and I concur with you that the long-term threat to our economic well-being is significant. If, on the other hand, you had a way to create a temporary worker program that is limited to the needs for those specific industries that cannot get Americans to do the jobs, then you can both enhance our economy and not cause any harm to anybody else, because those legal temporary workers wouldn't be taking advantage of our welfare system. But, to the extent that we have the illegal problem that we have today, you're absolutely right. There will be costs, and you haven't even mentioned all of the law enforcement costs—which are huge.

ANKARLO: We had another Phoenix police officer shot, and luckily he lived because of his bulletproof vest. Yet again, it was an illegal alien who did the shooting. Instead of stopping for his ticket at the red light, he put two bullets in our officer's chest. If all of these businessmen want to hire illegals, perhaps we should make them responsible for them by providing housing, health care, and an accountability program. If the alien gets in trouble, we call the business. If you want to hire illegal immigrants to pick your lettuce for you, then you are responsible for them. Does this idea have any merit?

SENATOR JOHN KYL: Well, as a matter of law, it's not good law that you're proposing, but the answer, I think, is to ensure that we don't have illegals coming into the country and impose on the employers the kind of sanctions that will prevent them from hiring illegals in the first place. I think that is a better way to solve the problem than what you are proposing.

ANKARLO: Let me go back to it for a second, because I want to hear the good law/bad law. I have a Canadian lady I work with who is just now becoming a U.S. citizen. In order to come here, her mother had to be her sponsor. So, anything that happens to this lady, her mother is called, and mom has to guarantee that she would be there to support her in every way, shape, or form.

SENATOR JOHN KYL: And that's our immigration law to date. You vouch for—every legal immigrant has to have someone who is a sponsor, and that sponsor has to vouch for and ensure that the individual does not become an economic charge.

ANKARLO: Why not do that with employers who say they cannot operate without illegal immigrants since it is, as you just described, the employer who is making the most gains off of the problem?

SENATOR JOHN KYL: Well, there's a big difference between being an economic charge on the one hand and being responsible for somebody killing a cop on the other. That's why I say you can't hold somebody criminally responsible for the act of another when they didn't have the knowledge—

ANKARLO: So take the criminality out of it. How about the economics of it? Could we go that far with some sort of an economic program aimed at the employer making them responsible?

SENATOR JOHN KYL: Sure. No problem with that except that it's very, very difficult to enforce because you don't know. Look, if you knew in the first instance that the person was illegal, they couldn't be employed there to begin with. So, it all is premised on the knowledge that you know that the person is illegal. The employer—

ANKARLO: 40 percent of all illegals are people who are here, overstayed a visa, and never went home. In light of all the crime that we have in Arizona, people popping the borders, stealing, carjacking, shooting cops, et cetera, would you be in favor or ever be in favor of some sort of a tracking device, an implant; if somebody is caught here for the first time, they're implanted, and then sent home. Would you ever see a scenario for that?

SENATOR JOHN KYL: Well, I think there is a less intrusive way to resolve the problem, and that's an effective entry-exit system. It's just taken us a long time to get it going. But it essentially provides that when you enter the country legally, you must report when you leave the country, and if you haven't reported in within forty-eight hours, your name is put out on a bulletin that goes to all federal, state, and local law enforcement as someone who should be reported to federal immigration authorities. If they're picked up, then appropriate action could be taken for their removal. So I think that's a less intrusive means of—and that system could be implemented—again, that was part of the legislation that failed.

ANKARLO: As a matter of fact, what you just described has been on the books as a requirement from the federal—

SENATOR JOHN KYL: No. The creation of an entry-exit system has been on the books, but it hasn't been implemented except at the airport land ports of entry.

ANKARLO: Right. I thought it became legislation; it just has not been implemented.

SENATOR JOHN KYL: Correct.

ANKARLO: I thought eleven years ago it was legislation.

SENATOR JOHN KYL: No. You're correct. But we have not adequately implemented it, and there is a contention that we could never adequately implement it at the land ports of entry. We can do it where airplanes land, but not where you've got, literally, millions of people going across our southern border—maybe not millions, but certainly tens of thousands—every day. I don't think that's too much to ask. I think we could implement it if we really put our mind to it.

ANKARLO: English as a federal law. English only? English first?

SENATOR JOHN KYL: Well, first of all, we did pass, and it was part of our legislation, an explicit statement that English is the national language of the United States of America, and there were specific provisions within that as to what was permissible and what wasn't permissible in terms of conducting government business. I mean, obviously, you can put signs in Spanish at the border, nobody objects to that, but you should be conducting your governmental business in English unless you cannot reach people any other way, and if we're going to have a legal program, by definition folks are going to learn English before they can become U.S. citizens. So, I think with the vast majority of Americans, well over 80 percent believing that this is still a country in which the business of the country should be conducted in English, that we should do that.

ANKARLO: Final question, since you've been on the front line on the illegal immigration problem: What one thing do you wish we knew about this illegal immigration issue?

SENATOR JOHN KYL: Well, I wish there were a little better understanding of how difficult it is to get any meaningful legislation passed through a very partisan Congress. It is very difficult to do. People are angry, they're frustrated, they want the federal government to enforce the law, but some of the law needs to be changed before it can be adequately enforced. We don't have a good employee verification system, for example. But to get one, we're going to have to pass a law and that's very, very hard to do, given the partisanship that exists in the Congress today.

VEINTISEIS

SOME SOLUTIONS

It goes without saying that immigration is on the lips of almost every person living in the border states, and the topic routinely makes it to my radio show because people are both fed up and searching for answers. This is a good thing. The best ideas ever born have fathers named Insurmountable, Impossible, Obstacle, and Can't. Luckily, those guys were married to ladies with names like Yes We Can, Roll Up Our Sleeves, Believe, and Join Forces. Contrary to the way illegal immigrant supporters try to paint us, most U.S. citizens do not hate immigrants; we just want a workable system to be followed. We do not hate Mexicans—we just want them to be included in the immigration process the same way everyone else in the world is when they come to this nation. To fast-track them above all others is blatant discrimination. One thing is for certain—we must keep asking questions *and* searching for answers, because the solution is out there.

ANKARLO: Hi, it's Ankarlo—you're on the air.

STARLA: What's an everyday citizen like me, a stay-at-home mom in Maricopa, Arizona, [to] do about this immigration problem?

ANKARLO: *Ankarlo Mornings*—you're on.

PATRICK: We all need to go on July Fourth to the capitols of every state in our country and especially the capitol of our country.

ANKARLO: KTAR FM—what's going on?

LESLIE: I used to work for a company that builds perimeter security systems, and the ones they do are at prisons, nuclear power plants— and they have security systems around entire countries.

ANKARLO: And?

LESLIE: They have just developed a new buried cable system, and in between, say, two fences, they would put a buried cable that can track any kind of running, walking, crawling, rolling on the ground, and it can pinpoint up to a few meters where somebody is. This company does stuff for the president, for Secret Service, CIA—and why they haven't considered using them for this problem, you know, makes me kind of wonder, because it's available, and they can do it.

Over the years, I have fielded thousands of calls on this issue, but the escalation I am seeing in the past few years tells me citizens are at a breaking point; we want solutions. We want our kids to have access to the same America we had, and we know that right now it is not possible. So, Starla—get engaged. Call, write, and demand action from your elected officials from local to national. With the easy access of libraries and the Internet, no American citizen can honestly say he or she doesn't know how to do it. In this chapter, I'll give you a few ideas.

Patrick—millions of illegals marched, but whenever U.S. citizens have tried to, the results have been abysmal—for many reasons. Pro-illegal forces paint marchers as racists, which is enough to shut down even the most ardent citizen. The marchers in 2006 and 2007 were predominately Latino, Latina, and Hispanic, so they were able to take to the streets with a false sense that they were supporting their race as much as their cause. Meanwhile, Americans may be upset enough to rally, but we represent so many races, creeds, and cultures that it is difficult to bring a group of mobile strangers together. And many U.S. citizens may complain about their places in life, but, at the end of the day, they are earning far more than five dollars a day or a few more under the table. We are getting motivated by the things our children will endure, but we're not there yet. Besides, we are busy paying for three-car garages, satellite TV, DVRs, IPODs, Iphones, and big-screen televisions. To win this battle, we need to reach critical mass so elected reps and other countries realize we mean business. We're getting there.

Leslie—this is the kind of thinking we need. Cutting-edge technology is needed to fully execute a winning strategy, and it sounds as though you have access to a company that could make something happen. It's worth a call to them, isn't it?

We all have brains, and now is the time to combine for the greatest effectiveness and good of the nation. Most polls in 2006 and 2007 gave Congress a failing grade—a *failing* grade, with Republicans and Democrats residing in the teens—on our perception of their effectiveness. This is an abomination! We are a representative republic—which means the masses hire a few to represent their will—and I don't want to change it, but I do think citizens are using the system as a crutch. We don't have to engage ourselves in the process, because it is easier to cry about someone else's failures than to jump in and work by their sides. Remember, *they work for us.* If you owned a company and the employees were struggling to the point where you could lose everything, wouldn't you do whatever you could to save it?

Immigration policies in every country in the history of the world have always been developed to benefit the host nation's citizens, but by allowing more than a million and a half foreigners to come to the U.S. legally and illegally annually, our politicians and bureaucrats have been setting the stage for a variety of converging events that may easily wipe out our most esteemed way of life. Language, lower wages, laws, and rules based on another's system, crime and city and traffic congestion, are just a few of the areas negatively impacted. Failed policies must be corrected.

We are in the season of change, and if we fail, our grandchildren will be raised in an America starkly different from what has made us the country most others have tried to catch or copy over the years. The choice is ours.

These suggested solutions are just that: suggestions. They are placed on paper with the hope that every person reading them will add to, delete from, and think about each one until we, as single citizens and a society on the whole, will develop a few that will work.

THE ANKARLO IMMIGRATION TOP 30

1. A temporary moratorium on new immigration to the U.S. for five years. Three hundred million people call this country home, and there should be zero doubt that from even the simplest of mathematical perspectives, we have access to persons who can fill available jobs from the mundane to the most complicated. While the doors are closed, we get our own house and our own rules and regulations in order for new guests.

---

2. An accurate and immediate employee identification program is mandated. To suggest that we can't do this is another example of stonewalling by politicians who have pockets lined with special-interest cash.

3. Employers who hire illegals will be fined and ultimately lose their business licenses for repeat offenses. However, since some business owners claim they "need" the illegal immigrants to function—which is not true—and so many of these persons are in America already, a special option could be available: Persons legally immigrating to the U.S. need a sponsor to vouch for them, and businesses could follow a similar model. The owner will: (a) provide an equal wage to U.S. citizens, (b) provide housing and health care, (c) help the illegal employee learn English and apply for citizenship, and (d) be available to post bail and help with legal fees if their employee gets into trouble. Obviously, the owner will have to cover these new expenses without passing the costs on to consumers, and in annual audits they will face heavy fines and jail time if they are discovered to be abusing the rules or their employees. The illegal immigrant will be granted a special U.S. ID card showing his or her relationship with and responsibility of the business owner. This ID card would not grant citizenship or citizenship rights; it would serve only as an ID card showing the relationship and contact information for the sponsoring business.

4. All local, state, and federal governments shall print official documents in English and use only the English language in recitations, renderings, and communications. If a translator is required

for any business or court purposes, the person or persons requiring the translator shall pay for or reimburse the government for such use. President Bill Clinton signed Executive Order 13166 into law, which promises to "improve access to federally conducted or federally assisted programs for persons who, as a result of national origin, are limited in their English proficiency." The order suggests that it is discrimination and a violation of Title VI of the 1964 Civil Rights Law if government entities receiving federal funds do not communicate in the language the person receiving the benefits chooses. Scholars rightly argue the 1964 law was never meant to be applied to something as broad as language, yet American politicians catering to special-interest groups have unnecessarily splintered the nation again. The 1965 Voting Act should be amended to repeal all foreign language provisions.

5. Non-English-speaking students will spend a year in full-immersion language classes that will be held apart from regular public school classes. The classes are mandatory before the non-English speaker is allowed to proceed with mainstream classes, and at least one parent, grandparent, or legal guardian is required to attend. If, after the first year, the student is not ready for mainstream classes, he will be required to continue with English immersion classes paid for by the non-English speaker's home country, family, or via age-appropriate work opportunities in the community.

6. Repeal of the Fourteenth Amendment, which has been abused to the point that, annually, more than 300,000 children become automatic citizens. The most educated scholars on Constitutional

Law agree that the Fourteenth was created for U.S. citizens, but since so many people continue to debate the issue, the simplest answer is to put an immediate stop to the nonsense of anchor babies by repealing it altogether.

7. Persons doing work at the homes of private citizens will be required to register with their county and provide proof of citizenship; a small fee will be assessed. Private citizens will be required to call a hotline or visit a Web site to verify the worker's identification. The registration fee will be used to offset the costs. Citizens hiring illegals will be fined.

8. State governments *must* stop passing the buck! Almost every border-state governor has refused to step up to the challenge by blaming Washington. Then, as illegal aliens pillage the various states, the governors see little political fallout because they can say Washington failed us. This is lazy thinking and must end. No doubt, the federal government's main objective is to provide its citizens with security, but states also have a mandate to protect their borders and livelihoods. This is as much a states' rights issue as were those that led to the U.S. Civil War.

9. Local leaders and law enforcement personnel are the first line of defense to a variety of issues. They should start acting like the leaders they claim to be by working to guarantee the safety of the local citizens. By mid-2007, local areas in America had created more than 171 new regulations in an attempt to slow the flow of illegal aliens. Sadly, many are being challenged by aliens who have joined forces with lawyers from the ACLU.

Some cities, like Farmer's Branch, Texas, penalize landlords who rent to illegal immigrants, and in Arizona, Maricopa County sheriff Joe Arpaio arrests illegals congregating at day labor facilities. The localities fighting the fight are minimal, but with opportunities for special funding and recognition, perhaps more will join the fight. The old adage "All politics is local" also applies to the fight against a group that is destroying the country.

10. Current visa holders are required to abide by all U.S. laws. Violators of minor laws will receive the same punishment as U.S. citizens, provided their visa is current. If a visa is expired or the person has no proof of permission to be in the country, he will be deported immediately and may return only after resolving any issues. Major violators will appear before a U.S. judge, where evidence and testimony will be reviewed. The violator and the package of evidence will be returned to his home country, where he will be adjudicated and imprisoned if found guilty. If the host country refuses to cooperate with the program, then immigrants from that country will not be allowed access to the U.S. The U.S. will reserve the right to try, convict, and imprison in our country if circumstances warrant. Once created, if the host country violates the relationship, then economic and diplomatic sanctions will be used. This solves a few problems: (1) U.S. prisons will stop being overwhelmed by crimes committed by noncitizens, (2) guests go to greater lengths to abide by rules, and (3) respect returns where it is presently missing.

11. No less than 30,000 additional border agents are dispatched to the two borders, where they remain stationed at the same post

for no more than three months before being reassigned into a new border area. The current policy calls for too few agents and leaves the ones we do have in the same area long enough to be marked for death, attack, or pay-off. In addition to the agents, the U.S. should create several new military bases on both borders. Instead of closing other bases that insure safety and workforces for those areas, we take ten to fifteen percent of the military from several of them to populate the new ones. Now, especially in problematic border crossing areas we have trained military who do routine patrols, exercises, and shows of strengths.

12. Stiffer penalties for those who illegally enter. Fingerprints, retina scans, and other identifying characteristics are gathered and saved before the illegal alien is returned to his home country, and that nation is required to repay all of the associated expenses. The home country can choose to retrieve the expenses from the illegal immigrant by fines, garnished wages, or jail. The second offense carries a U.S. fine of no less than one thousand dollars and deportation. If the person cannot pay, he will work for the county where he was arrested until the fine is paid. Number three requires twelve months in jail and a five-hundred-dollar fine. The jail time shall be served in the alien's home country. If the person is housed in American jails, the host country will repay all costs. At the fourth arrest the person is jailed for no less than three years, required to work to repay the costs, fined no less than one thousand dollars, and banned from all entry to the U.S. If caught on U.S. soil he will serve a minimum of five years in prison. Non-compliance by the host countries will be met with economic sanctions.

13. Illegal immigrants cost the U.S. tens of billions of dollars per year in addition to all the societal attacks. To get ahead of a problem decades in the making, taxpayers agree to fund the latest in technology, aircraft, and lethal and nonlethal weapons to guarantee a secure border. Towers mounted with heat, motion, infrared, and other available cameras will send images back to centralized patrol areas at distances that ensure every single mile is covered. With the extra agents it should be easier to round up and deport.

14. Federal funds with strict time limits need to be earmarked and applied to this national disaster immediately. To properly move forward, multibillions in tax dollars will be required, but as the door closes on the handouts, entitlements, and welfare, the money saved will return to the general funds. Any politicians caught spending this money (or not returning incoming fees to the general fund) will be impeached.

15. A majority of illegal aliens come from Mexico. It is in America's best interest to see our southern neighbor become strong and stable. We can help the process along by applying serious diplomatic pressure to our friends and allies to create businesses, industry, and jobs there. Since the current minimum wage there is approximately five dollars per day, the incoming plant would need to triple or quadruple the daily wage in order to help citizens of Mexico make the choice to remain. Some countries are already moving in this direction by placing television and technology plants there, but this plan would attempt to move the process along.

16. In areas of America where it is difficult to fill positions, notice of the employment opening and salary would be posted in the town squares, town halls, and via the Internet for a specified time period. If the positions are left vacant, able-bodied U.S. citizens who receive any kind of public assistance within the county where the jobs are available will be given an option: do the work or give up the assistance. If the positions continue to remain open, then prisoners from minimum security facilities will be given the opportunity to do the work. They will be paid a wage less than a regular citizen but can apply for a reduced sentence.

17. Illegal aliens who currently reside in the U.S. will be allowed to return to their home countries without penalty and will be considered for legal reentry based on current law. If the illegal alien owns any property in the U.S. it will be sold and the profits split between the U.S. and the individual. If the illegal immigrant disregards this grace period and is later arrested, he will be deported and barred from ever returning. All property remaining in the U.S. will be sold, and all proceeds will be deposited into operating funds for the U.S. Border Patrol.

18. All visitors to the U.S. will be required to use tamper-proof IDs that use fingerprints, biometrics, or similar. I will never be in favor of planting tracking chips in humans, but it may be time to consider some sort of similar technology to any person illegally found in the U.S.A. After all, they have already proven they can't be trusted by crossing and using an innocent person's ID or Social Security card.

19. U.S. banks and lending institutions that cater to illegal immigrants sending money back to their home countries will be fined and lose the opportunity to bid on any government projects.

20. A promise to fight illegal immigration, with specific language, will be added to the oath of office all elected officials must take. The elected official will be impeached if evidence is provided that proves that he or she has not fulfilled the oath. Annual reviews will be mandatory.

21. Schools, hospitals, and other publicly supported entities shall not provide free services to illegal aliens. If a person needs emergency treatment, he will be required to pay no less than 50 percent of his costs before leaving a treatment facility. Remember, illegal aliens pay more than two thousand dollars to come to the U.S. and send $50 billion back to their home countries, so the poverty excuse is an overused one.

22. Corrupt border agents or other entities charged with not protecting our borders will be prosecuted to the fullest extent of the law, with no pleas for reductions available.

23. Imprison any and all persons convicted of engaging in any part of the identity-theft and document-counterfeiting puzzle, using the same criteria established for illegal criminals from other nations. If the participant is a U.S. citizen, the full extent of the law shall apply.

24. Improve the infrastructure at all border crossing stations for

better identification and quality customer service—which can lead to more persons helping identify and catch violators.

25. In order to vote, a photo ID will be required. Though this is common sense, some U.S. congressmen and women and senators say this is discrimination because the poor, elderly, and persons not wanting to take a picture would be less likely to vote. When smart politicians say stupid things like this: impeach 'em.

26. If foreigners want to become U.S. citizens, once they have been identified, investigated for security reasons, and have made application, they may join an appropriate arm of the United States military for no less than three years, at which point they will be granted fast track citizenship.

27. Non-U.S. citizens may not receive in-state tuition at any school, college, or higher-learning institution. Schools that create "shield" categories or scholarship programs for the sole purpose of bypassing this law will be fined, may lose accreditation, and funding may be removed.

28. Any noncitizen living in the U.S. without a valid and proper visa will not be allowed to file for any tax return even if taxes have been withheld.

29. Any U.S. citizen or citizens group that assists, shields, hides, or shelters an illegal immigrant will be charged with a crime and will pay a fine. After three convictions on the same charges of

helping illegal immigrants, the crime will become a felony with mandatory jail time.

30. All government programs and voting district reapportionments that rely on population counts to arrive at a decision shall use only U.S. citizens in their calculations.

31. Bonus solution: Lease the entire nation of Mexico (because this country is the driving force behind illegal immigration) for 150 years. We will have access to any and all resources she has, and in return, we will help build programs, roads, schools, and develop infrastructures. We keep everything we cultivate, earn, and develop but agree to create a strong wage base for the people there. After the lease expires, the country would be returned to the citizens—hopefully, healthier than before. Does this sound like a crazy idea? It probably is, but at least it is out-of-the-box thinking. U.S. companies have successfully used this concept for years, and America moved a similar concept along when it relinquished control of the Panama Canal.

32. Bonus solution: Annex Mexico.

A few of these ideas are hybrids of legislation passed or pending. Many of the thoughts are building-block oriented; they will work only after we seal the borders, stop the employment opportunities, and give law enforcement the permission and support it needs to stop the flow at the local level. Local + State + Federal on the same page always equals success.

FINALLY

I called several mayor friends of mine, checked with a few pals at city halls, and asked them to assess the illegal immigration issue from their perspectives. They said it was the most important issue facing their offices because of its divisiveness and the chipping-away effect at their once-solid infrastructures. I expected as much. What surprised me was the additional commentary.

This is an actual exchange I had with a top U.S. mayor, and it represents the other conversations.

"Darrell, my office gets one complaint more than any other, and we get it ten times more often than any other. What do you think it is?"

"Crime, I guess," I said.

"The overwhelming calls are from angry citizens who want us to send illegal immigrants back. They're tired of twenty people in a house in their neighborhoods, the sounds of chickens getting slaughtered in backyards, and the way their communities are disintegrating."

"Mayor, pardon me; is this supposed to surprise me?"

"Who do you think is making the call?"

"Okay, you've got me. Who?"

"My phones are swamped daily by Latinos who want the illegals removed. Latinos are the ones outraged."

In hindsight it makes sense. The U.S. citizens of Mexican or Hispanic heritage are tired of being lumped in with the lawbreakers. I mentioned this theory to my mayor friend, and the response was, "They want the illegals gone because they are eroding the American Dream for everyone born here or who came the right way. They want them gone—now!"

At the same time, it is in the best interest of U.S. citizens to apply as much pressure as we can to create positive and revolutionary change in Mexico. Her culture is inviting. Her people are mostly kind and peaceful and share a faith similar to those of us in the U.S.

How does faith factor in? While terrorists worldwide, the majority of whom are Islamic extremists, want to bring us to our knees, we need nations to our south and north who share common beliefs. We need Mexico to be a strong and vibrant trading and security ally, but until this illegal immigration issue is resolved, the U.S. remains at greater risk.

You've read the stories and reviewed the stats and can see just how much trouble this nation is in. This is not a race issue; it is an American issue—it is a *you* issue. America has become a nation of LetSomebodyElses. You have read my ideas; perhaps you have one that is better. Great! Go for it! It's time to stand again.

All great men and women of change and honor achieve their status not by hearing but by doing. They have no understanding or tolerance for excuses. Get involved before it is too late.

America has treated us well.

Now it is time to repay her.

She deserves it.

She will die if we sit idly by, doing nothing.

THE ANKARLO TOP 15 CONGRESSIONAL AND IMMIGRATION TRACKING SITES

Not sure where to start or how to get involved? Here is a starting place:

1. http://www.fairus.org – Track illegal immigration policies and link up with fellow citizens who want to make a difference. Nongovernment site.

2. http://www.cis.org/ – Center for Immigration Studies. One of the best sites available. Nongovernment site.

3. http://www.grassfire.org/42/petition.asp – One of the most popular sites aimed at stopping illegal immigration. Sign the online petition so your voice will be heard. Nongovernment site.

4. http://www.ilw.com/ – The Immigration Portal is run by immigration lawyers. An excellent resource if you want to dig deeply into this issue. Nongovernment site.

5. http://numbersusa.com/index – Perhaps the most detailed sites dedicated to only the immigration issue. This is a one stop site if you want an overview of the issues. Nongovernment site.

6. http://www.usillegalaliens.com/ – This is clearing house of the chief ideas and perspectives on illegal immigration. Nongovernment site.

7. http://www.uscis.gov/portal/site/uscis – U.S. Citizenship and Immigration Services. Government site.

8. http://www.cbp.gov/ – The official site for the U.S. Border and Customs department. Apply for a job if you're up to being one of our first defenders! Government site.

9. http://www.ice.gov/ – Immigration and Customs Enforcement (ICE) Web site. Turn in an illegal! Government site.

10. http://www.congress.org – Very easy interface for tracking and contacting Congress. Nongovernment site.

11. http://thomas.loc.gov/ – An excellent resource for tracking all U.S. legislation. Government site.

12. http://www.loc.gov/index.html – The official Library of Congress Web site that makes it easy to find your politician. Government site.

13. http://www.usa.gov/ – Sponsored by the U.S. government. Very useful to citizens wanting to know what's going on in the government. Government site.

14. http://www.conservativeusa.org/mega-cong.htm – Phone numbers and Web addresses for all members of Congress. Nongovernment site.

15. http://immigration.findlaw.com/ – A popular site that makes it easy to track laws, find attorneys, and review immigration laws. Nongovernment site.

NOTES

INTRODUCTION

1. Center for Immigration Studies, March 2007. In or near-poverty defined as income under 200 percent of the poverty threshold. http://www.cis.org/articles/2007/back1007.html.
2. Center for Immigration Studies, March 2007, Current Population Survey. Figures for use of any welfare include use of public/rent-subsidized housing in addition to cash assistance, food assistance, and Medicaid. http://www.cis.org/articles/2007/back1007.html.

UNO: THE TRIFECTA: COYOTES, ILLEGALS, CORRUPT MEXICAN LEADERS

1. "Border Crossings Rarely Prosecuted," Associated Press, as quoted by Michelle Malkin in her column "Six, Seven, Eight Strikes, You're Out," 23 March 2007.
2. Alfredo Corchado, "Smuggling Game Gets Deadlier," 15 May 2006, *Dallas Morning News*.
3. "Human Smuggling/Trafficking: The Trade in People," CBC News Online, 13 April 2006.

CUATRO: NOT YOUR TYPICAL MEXICAN TOURIST TRAP

1. Gaiutra Bahadur, "Workers Step from Shadows," *Philadelphia Inquirer*, 15 February 2006, A1.

CATORCE: WHY THE FEDERAL GOVERNMENT WANTS ILLEGAL IMMIGRATION

1. Judicial Watch Releases Pentagon Records from "North American Forum" Meetings, 29 January 2007, http://www.judicialwatch.org/6123.shtml.
2. Security and Prosperity Partnership Meeting with U.S. Secretary of Commerce Carlos Gutierrez, Washington, D.C., 15 March 2006, information paper, p. 3 (Judicial Watch Freedom of Information Act request, 25 September 2006).
3. Frank Gaffney, "Assault of the 'Transies,'" 2 April 2007, http://www.military.com/opinion/0,15202,130863,00.html.
4. William F. Jasper, "Continental Merger," *The New American*, 15 October 2007, 10–11.

5. Ibid.
6. *Index of Economic Freedom,* The Heritage Foundation, 2008 Ed.
7. "Greenspan: Let More Skilled Immigrants In," *Bloomberg News,* 14 March 2007.
8. *Index of Economic Freedom*, 2008. Online at: http://www.heritage.org/index/country.cfm?id=Mexico.
9. "David Frum's Diary," National Review Online, 10 November 2002.

QUINCE: THE POWER OF A LANGUAGE

1. Theodore Roosevelt, *Works,* vol. XXIV (New York: Charles Scribner's Sons, 1926), 554.
2. House Speaker Newt Gingrich (R-Ga.): *Congressional Record,* 1 August 1996, H9768.
3. *Congressional Record,* 21 March 1994, H1716.
4. Population Reference Bureau, September 2007, http://www.prb.org/Articles/2006/IntheNewsSpeakingEnglishintheUnitedStates.aspx.
5. June Kronholz, "Tab for Teaching English Put at $3 Billion," *Wall Street Journal,* 1 August 2007, http://blogs.wsj.com/washwire/2007/08/01/tab-for-teaching-english-put-at-3-billion/.
6. Susan Headden, "One Nation, One Language?" *U.S. News & World Report,* 25 September 1995, 38ff.
7. Jurist Legal News and Research, March 2006, http://jurist.law.pitt.edu/paperchase/2006/03/up-to-12-million-illegal-aliens-now-in.php.
8. "Californians for Population Stabilization," October 2007, http://www.cap-s.org/facts/immigration.html.
9. The Linguistic Society of America. Presented and approved at the LSA Business Meeting in New York City, December 1986. Submitted to and passed by membership in a mail ballot, March 1987.

DIECISÉIS: IMPORTED CRIMINALS

1. Sam Roberts, "Minorities Now Form Majority in One-Third of Most-Populous Counties," 9 August 2007, *New York Times* online edition.
2. Heather MacDonald, "The Illegal-Alien Crime Wave," The Manhattan Institute, 2004. http://www.city-journal.org/html/14_1_the_illegal_alien.html.
3. Edwin S. Rubenstein, "Criminal Alien Nation," *National Data,* 30 June 2005. Online at: http://www.vdare.com/rubenstein/050630_nd.htm.
4. "Information on Criminal Aliens Incarcerated in Federal and State Prisons and Local Jails," General Account Office Report # GAO-05-337R, http://www.gao.gov/htext/d05337r.html.
5. David A. Anderson, "The Aggregate Burden of Crime," Centre College Danville, 1999.
6. Joseph Farah, "Illegal Aliens Murder 12 Americans Daily," 28 November 2006, © 2008 WorldNetDaily.com.
7. "A Line in the Sand: Confronting the Threat at the Southwest Border," 3. Prepared by

the Majority Staff of the House Committee on Homeland Security Subcommittee on Investigations, Michael T. McCaul, Chairman.

8. Ibid.

9. Deborah Schurman-Kauflin, "Profiling Sex Trafficking: Illegal Immigrants At Risk," Violent Crimes Institute, 2006.

10. Ibid.

DIECISIETE: TERRORISM'S ATTACK ON SOVEREIGNTY

1. "A Line in the Sand." Prepared by the Majority Staff of the House Committee on Homeland Security, Subcommittee on Investigations. Michael T. McCaul Chairman. http://www.house.gov/mccaul/pdf/Investigaions-Border-Report.pdf.

2. "Detention and Removal of Illegal Aliens." Department of Homeland Security Office of the Inspector General. April 2006, http://www.dhs.gov/xoig/assets/mgmtrpts/OIG_06-33_Apr06.pdf

3. Sara A. Carter, *The Washington Times*, 25 November 2007, http://www.washingtontimes.com/apps/pbcs.dll/article?AID=/20071125/NATION/71125002/-1/RSS_FP.

4. Sara A. Carter, "Terrorists Target Army Base—in Arizona," *the Washington Times* 26 November 2007, http://www.washingtontimes.com/apps/pbcs.dll/article?AID=/20071126/NATION/111260034/1001.

5. Yitzchok Segal, "The Death Penalty and the Debate over the U.S. Supreme Court's Citation of Foreign and International Law," *Fordham Urban Law Journal*, 1 November 2006, http://goliath.ecnext.com/coms2/summary_0199-6199410_ITM.

6. Address to students at George Mason University Law School in Arlington, Virginia, http://www.law.com/jsp/article.jsp?id=1129626313552

DIECIOCHO: HOW MUCH BLAME DOES AMERICA DESERVE?

1. http://www.fas.usda.gov/itp/Policy/NAFTA/NAFTA_Overview_2006_files/frame.htm.

2. Environmental Working Group's Farm Subsidy Database, 12 June 2007, www.ewg.org.

3. William C. Gruben and Sherry L. Kiser, "NAFTA and Maquiladoras: Is the Growth Connected?" Federal Reserve Bank of Dallas, June 2001, http://www.dallasfed.org/research/border/tbe_gruben.html.

4. Kevin P. Gallagher, "FDI as a Sustainable Development Strategy: Evidence from Mexican Manufacturing," Center for Latin American Studies CLAS Working Papers (University of California, Berkeley), Year 2005, Paper 14.

5. Louis Uchitelle, "Nafta Should Have Stopped Illegal Immigration, Right?" *New York Times*, 18 February 2007.

6. Senator Hillary Clinton (D-NY) in a presidential campaign speech to Wartburg College Students in Waverly, Iowa, 5 November 2007.

NOTES

DIECINUEVE: U.S. CITIZENS REALLY *DO* WANT TO WORK

1. Senator John McCain (R-AZ) in a presidential campaign speech to citizens of Mason City, Iowa, 4 November 2007.
2. Frosty Wooldridge, "Our Country Coming Undone," 2 November 2004, NewsWithViews.com.
3. "'Illegal Aliens' Impact on American Jobs—Part II," Family Security Matters, http://www.familysecuritymatters.org/index.php?id=1265436.
4. Robert Justich and Betty Ng, "The Underground Labor Force Is Rising to the Surface," CFA, 3 January 2005.
5. "The Labor Force Status of Short-Term Unauthorized Workers," 13 April 2006, http://pewhispanic.org/files/factsheets/16.pdf.
6. Christopher Swann, "U.S. Real Wages Fall at Fastest Rate in 14 Years," *Financial Times*, 10 May 2005.
7. Michael Mandel, "Real Wages Still Falling," 16 August 2006, http://www.businessweek.com/the_thread/economicsunbound/archives/2006/08/real_wages_stil.html.
8. Americans, ages 16–64, U.S. Department of Labor, Bureau of Labor Statistics (BLS). Labor Force Statistics from the Current Population Survey, July 2007.
9. Steven A. Camarota, "Immigration Is Hurting the U.S. Worker: Low Paid American Workers Have Borne the Heaviest Impact of Immigration,"*America's Quarterly*, Spring 2007.
10. U.S. Department of Labor Bureau of Labor Statistics, http://www.bls.gov/cps/prev_yrs.htm.
11. Immigrant Entry and Native Exit from the Labor Market, 2000–2005, Numbers USA, http://numbersusa.com/interests/jobless.html.
12. "Immigration Is Hurting the U.S. Worker."
13. Rich Lowry, "Jobs Americans Won't Do," King Features Syndicate, 14 March 2006.
14. John Miano, "Low Salaries for Low Skills Wages and Skill Levels for H-1B Computer Workers, 2005," Center for Immigrations Studies, April 2007.
15. James Hertzel, "Offshore IT Outsourcing Hurts Us All," *Denver Business Journal*, 6 June 2003.
16. Edwin S. Rubenstein, "Can Immigrants Save Social Security?" http://www.zazona .com/ShameH1B/Library/Archives/SaveSS.htm.

VEINTE: ANCHOR BABIES HELP TO SINK AMERICA

1. Lamar Smith, "Immigration: Many Questions, A Few Answers," No. 1046, 30 July 2007.
2. Center for Immigration Studies "Findings: The High Cost of Cheap Labor, Illegal Immigration, and the Federal Budget," http://www.cis.org/articles/2004/fiscalfindings.html.
3. Robert Locke, "The Fourteenth Amendment Mess," FrontPageMagazine.com, 9 September 2002.

4. In the California Government Code Section 240 245 as documented by FindLaw.com, http://caselaw.lp.findlaw.com/cacodes/gov/240-245.html.

VEINTIUNO: THERE IS A RIGHT WAY

1. Center for Immigration Studies *Backgrounder*. Steven A. Camarota, "Immigrants in the United States: 2007 Profile of America's Foreign-Born Population," November 2007. http://www.cis.org/articles/2007/back1007.html

2. "Decades of the Great Wave of Immigration," Copyright 2007, NumbersUSA Online, http://www.numbersusa.com.

VEINTIDOS: THINK ILLEGAL IMMIGRATION DOESN'T AFFECT YOU?

1. World Health Organization, http://www.who.int/whr/1996/media_centre/50facts/en/index.html.

2. "Chicken-plant Workers Test 'Positive' for TB," Published Online, 4 November 2007, http://www.worldnetdaily.com/news/article.asp?ARTICLE_ID=58501.

3. Report: "Illegal Immigration Could Cost Taxpayers Trillions," Congressional Hearing on Immigration Held in San Diego, 2 August 2006. Online at http://www.10news.com/news/9620142/detail.html.

4. "How Does Illegal Immigration Impact American Taxpayers and Will the Reid-Kennedy Amnesty Worsen the Blow?" Hearing Before the Committee on the Judiciary House of Representatives, 109th Congress, Second Session, 2 August 2006, Serial No. 109–135.

5. Frosty Wooldridge, "Chilling Costs of Illegal Alien Migration," 9 November 2004, NewsWithViews.com.

6. Ibid.

7. "Opinion by State Rep. John Kavanagh: Illegal Immigration Has High Cost, Tucson, Arizona," *Arizona Daily Star*, 31 December 2007.

8. Ronald J. Hansen, "Report: Illegal Immigrants Cost Arizona $1.4 Billion to Lower Wages," *Arizona Republic*. January 9, 2008.

9. Federation for American Immigration Reform (FAIR). Executive Summary: The Costs to Local Taxpayers for Illegal or "Guest" Workers. http://www.fairus.org/site/PageServer?pagename=research_localcosts.

VEINTICUATRO: SENATOR JOHN MCCAIN—AN INTERVIEW

1. Associated Press, 5 November 2007.

2. McCain Release, 13 September 2001; 2001 and 2002 Congressional Pig Book.

3. Gannett, 10 April 2003; 2003 and 2005 Congressional Pig Book.

4. "McCain Called Plan 'Amnesty' in 2003: GOP Hopeful Now Claims He 'Never Supported' Reprieve for Illegals," WorldNetDaily.com, 7 January 2008.

ABOUT THE AUTHOR

DARRELL ANKARLO is a gifted radio talk show host who has won many awards, including seven *Talker's* magazine Heavy Hundred Awards (the top 100 talk hosts in America out of more than 3,500); two Dallas Press Club Katie Awards; a *Billboard* magazine Air Personality of the Year Award; and the Scripps Howard Excellence in Journalism Award. The White House honored him with the President's Volunteer Service Award for his efforts to raise money, support, and awareness for America's military. On the television side, Ankarlo picked up an Emmy for a syndicated show he created and hosted and was nominated for a second program that he also created/hosted/wrote. He has appeared on the *O'Reilly Factor*, *Hannity and Colmes*, *Glenn Beck*, *Anderson Cooper 360*, NBC's *Today Show*, Fox, CNN, MSNBC, NBC, the BBC, and other radio and television outlets around the world. Darrell's first book is called *What Went Wrong with America and How to Fix it*. Darrell has been married to Laurie for thirty years, and they have four children.

THANKS—

To my wife, Laurie, for putting up with my trips to the border and months of follow-up research. To Kris, Adam, Ben, and Katie for being good kids and fine citizens. To my brothers and sister, especially Orv and Jeanne, who saved my life more than once. To Erik Hellum and Russ Hill from KTAR-FM for believing in the mission and providing the resources to get the job done. They are first class and represent the Good Guys in my industry. To Rob Hunter, who is becoming a world-class producer. To the Minutemen for showing me border areas few see. To the U.S. Border Patrol—Tucson Sector. To Adam, Gary, and Alonzo for helping to create the stories and expose this story. To Deanna Hollifield for transcribing hours of audio, making it possible for me to create several of the stories told in this book. To Thomas Nelson for wanting this book to happen, and David Howell for setting everything in motion. To my fellow Americans, who still have hope.

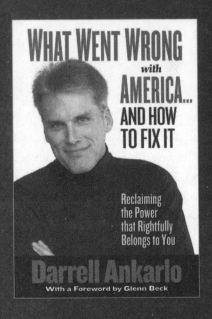